מסורה

ArtScroll® Series

Rabbi Nosson Scherman / Rabbi Meir Zlotowitz
General Editors

*Enlightening stories
that boost your spirit
and enhance
your emunah*

Published by

**ArtScroll
Mesorah Publications, ltd**

Touched
by Their
Faith

RABBI YECHIEL SPERO

FIRST EDITION
First Impression … March 2014

Published and Distributed by
MESORAH PUBLICATIONS, LTD.
4401 Second Avenue / Brooklyn, N.Y 11232

Distributed in Europe by
LEHMANNS
Unit E, Viking Business Park
Rolling Mill Road
Jarow, Tyne & Wear, NE32 3DP
England

Distributed in Australia and New Zealand
by **GOLDS WORLDS OF JUDAICA**
3-13 William Street
Balaclava, Melbourne 3183
Victoria, Australia

Distributed in Israel by
SIFRIATI / A. GITLER — BOOKS
Moshav Magshimim
Israel

Distributed in South Africa by
KOLLEL BOOKSHOP
Northfield Centre, 17 Northfield Avenue
Glenhazel 2192, Johannesburg, South Africa

ARTSCROLL® SERIES
TOUCHED BY THEIR FAITH
© Copyright 2014, by MESORAH PUBLICATIONS, Ltd.
4401 Second Avenue / Brooklyn, N.Y. 11232 / (718) 921-9000 / www.artscroll.com

---

To contact the author with comments or stories, he can be reached via e-mail
at chiely1@gmail.com

ISBN 10: 1-4226-1478-6 / ISBN 13: 978-1-4226-1478-5

Typography by CompuScribe at ArtScroll Studios, Ltd.
Bound by Sefercraft, Quality Bookbinders, Ltd., Brooklyn N.Y. 11232

מכתב ברכה מאת הרב דוד קוויאט זצ"ל
ר"מ בישיבת מיר
ורב דאגודת ישראל סניף חפץ חיים

ב"ה

י"ג מנחם אב תשס"ג

מכתב ברכה

לכבוד ידידי הרב יחיאל ספירא שליט"א, רבי בישיבת הק'
חפץ חיים בבלטימור,

הנה בא לפני עלים מספרך אשר כתבת ושמו "נתרגש פון א
מעשה" הנה כשמו כן הוא כולו ספורים יקרים המביא
רגשות קודש להקוראים בו, מה שנחוץ זה למאוד לחזק
האמונה וללמוד איך להתנהג באמונה ובמדות טובות כמו
שעולה מהספורים. ולכן אברכהו שיצליח בספרו ושיהנו
הקוראים בו,והשם יתב' יברכהו להרבות תורה ומוסר
ויגדיל תורה ויאדיר.

ממני ידידו המברכו בכל לב

דוד קוויאט

Michtav Berachah written for *Touched by a Story*

INTRODUCTION
The Treasure Inside of Us

WHEN RAV CHATZKEL ABRAMSKY WAS INCARCER-
ated in a prison camp in Siberia, he was given menial
jobs, including chopping wood in the forest. He was
fortunate, though, that his work was overseen by a decent gentile.
One day, Rav Chatzkel sat down on a tree stump, deep in thought.
The overseer, instead of getting angry at him, approached and
asked what he was thinking about. Rav Chatzkel answered that he
was thinking about the prayer he recites every morning, *Modeh
Ani,* and he proceeded to explain the prayer.

But then he added his dilemma. "I began to wonder: What
exactly am I thanking the Al-mighty for? I don't have the opportunity to learn every day; I can't perform His commandments; I
can't don *tefillin.* But then I realized that I am thanking Him for the
two final words of the prayer: *rabbah emunasecha* — abundant is
Your faithfulness. He gives us the ability to continually have faith
in Him. And that is indeed valuable, perhaps more than anything
else."

When Rav Chatzkel related this story to the Rayatz, Rav Yosef
Yitzchak Schneerson, he responded, "Rav Chatzkel, it was *kedai*
[worthwhile] to have endured the difficulties of the slave labor
camps of Siberia to come up with that *derher* [insight]."

Over the past 2,000 years, we have faced many challenges and endured much pain. We have witnessed the destruction of our beloved *Beis HaMikdash* and experienced torment under Roman rule, followed years later by unspeakable suffering at the hands of the Crusaders, the Inquisitors of Torquemada, and the Cossacks led by Bogdan Chmielnicki. Less than 70 years ago, the Jewish people experienced the most horrific atrocities known to man. But none of these broke us. Throughout, we held onto the one constant that can never be taken from us: our faith.

And today, as we live peacefully among the nations of the world and we are treated well, we face other dangers. Social media, Internet, and other vicissitudes that have arisen over the past 10 or so years threaten our families, our youth, and our fear of Heaven as never before. The solution to these threats, as well, is a strengthening of our faith.

You see, faith strengthens us and solidifies our beliefs. It is one of the greatest resources we have.

The Purim *seudah* led by the Beis Avraham, Rav Avraham of Slonim, lasted 12 hours. While some of those in attendance were inebriated, many were inspired by his words, which caused them to pause and reflect. At one point, the singing and dancing had reached a frenzied pitch, when he said the following, which brought many of his followers to tears.

Rav Avraham cited a *pasuk* from *Megillas Esther* (4:7), "*lishkol al ginzei hamelech baYehudim le'abdam* — to pay to the royal treasuries for the annihilation of the Jews." Using the word *melech* to refer to the ultimate *Melech,* Hashem, he focused on the phrase, "*ginzei haMelech baYehudim* — the treasuries of the King for the Jews," and remarked, "The *Ribbono Shel Olam* has a treasure house hidden inside the *neshamah* of every Yid. Even the *pachos she'bepechusim,* the most inferior individuals, need to be aware of its presence inside them."

This treasure is a gift from the Al-mighty. The storage house of jewels that He hides inside of us is the spark that connects us to

Him. It is an unbreakable bond that can weather even the fiercest of storms and the most terrifying conflagrations; waves of persecution and mountains of self-doubt cannot sever the tie that we have with the Al-mighty. It is a connection so deep and strong that we have been able to traverse the globe, scale insurmountable heights, and overcome impenetrable obstacles with our faith intact.

My Bubby Moses, about whom I have written in earlier books, survived three concentration camps. Throughout her ordeal, she never prayed for life or health. She asked for one thing: *"Mir zohl nahr blieben bie di emunah."* She just wanted to hold onto the one thing that was most dear to her: her faith.

This was my bubby's challenge. And I am certain that your bubby and zeidy had theirs, as well. Whether one's ancestors survived persecution and anti-Semitism in Europe, or the hardships of growing up in America, only one thing allowed them to survive: their faith.

When Rav Mottel Pogromansky, a great Torah personality from pre-war Lita, came to Versailles, France, after World War II, he walked into the *beis midrash* one day and stood before a group of young men, who ranged in age from 15 to 30; many of them were refugees from Russia, who were on their way to the United States or Israel. Yet, he did not notice them at all, for his mind was in the Heavens.

As he spoke to the Al-mighty, they listened in. *"Oy, Tatte in Himmel. Es iz nit dah kein ghetto, nit dah kein tatte, nit dah kein mamma, nit dah kein shtoob, nit dah kein mishpachah. Nahr ein zach is gebliben. Es iz nahr Du un ich. Du un ich — Oy*, Father in Heaven. There is no ghetto, no father, no mother, no home, no family. Only one thing remains. It is just You and I. You and I." He repeated these words over and over, yearning, longing... and coming ever closer.

After he finished, he closed his eyes and was completely lost in thought. The *bachurim* stood around him first for 5 minutes, and then 10 minutes. Finally, after 15 minutes had passed, they realized that he was in a completely different place. A place where only Hashem and Rav Mottel existed.

You and I. *Du un ich*.

That is all we have. It is all we have ever had. For nothing else matters in this world. Everything else, all materialistic entities, will come and go. But our faith, and thereby our connection with the Al-mighty, lasts forever.

Du un ich.

In a speech to the Sisterhood of K'hal Adath Jeshurun in 1989, Rav Shimon Schwab stated, "If somebody would ask, 'Because of what *zechus* do the Jewish people today deserve the Mashiach?' I would answer, 'Because of our *emunah* in *bi'as haMashiach* [the coming of Mashiach] and our continued *bitachon* despite constant disappointments.' Normally, a person who is disappointed over and over again would give up. Consider a woman who hears that her husband is coming home after not having heard from him for many years. Every day, for a full year, she goes to the airport to await his arrival. But he does not come. That is when she finally gives up.

"Mashiach has not come yet; he has not given any signs of life. Imagine what that means. My father and yours, my mother and yours, and our grandparents and great-grandparents, year after year at the Seder, all said, '*Leshanah haba'ah bi'Yerushalayim* [Next year in Yerushalayim].' Then came another year, and another Seder, and he still did not come. Nevertheless, they did not stop singing, '*Bnei beischa be'karov be'yameinu* — Build Your home speedily, in our days.' And if he does not materialize, we still do not give up.

"This requires *bitachon* and *emunah*. And if we ask what our generation can say for itself, why it deserves the coming of Mashiach, we reply that we deserve it for only one reason: We didn't give up."

We live in meaningful times. The world is changing at a dizzy-ing pace, and it is hard for us to continue to hold on. The *chevlei*

Mashiach, the birth pangs of Mashiach, can be unbearably painful. But the Baal Shem Tov explained that the phrase *chevlei Mashiach* also means the ropes of Mashiach. Imagine, if you will, a rope dangling down from Heaven, which we must hold onto. Yet sometimes, the rope is shaken so vigorously that we feel our grip loosening. But if we hold on, and continue to dig into our reservoir of faith, the Al-mighty will pull the rope for us, ushering in the Final Redemption.

In *Tzidkas HaTzaddik* (154), Rav Tzaddok HaKohen says, "*Ke'sheim she'tzarich adam le'haamin baShem Yisbarach, kach tzarich achar kach le'haamin be'atzmo* — Just like a person must believe in Hashem, he must also believe in himself." Rav Shmuel Dishon says that this means that Hashem doesn't give a person a *nisayon* he cannot withstand. But he can pass the test only if he believes that he can!

The treasure inside of us is what helps us believe in the *Ribbono Shel Olam,* believe in ourselves, and believe in each other. We must learn to treasure it and cherish it and admire it in others. For each of us possesses something very special: **A Touch of Faith.**

We are holding on, *Ribbono Shel Olam,* and we don't ever want to let go.

Acknowledgments

FIRST AND FOREMOST, I AM HUMBLED BY THE GOODNESS the Al-mighty has bestowed upon my family and me. *Ein anachnu maspikim lehodos lecha, Hashem* — We cannot thank You sufficiently, Hashem!

My connection with **Rabbi Meir Zlotowitz** and **Rabbi Nosson Scherman** began 12 years ago, in the form of an employer/employee relationship. Since then, they have graciously guided and mentored me in many areas, as our relationship has metamorphosed into a family connection. I am eternally grateful for their warmth and know-how.

My heartfelt thanks to the **ArtScroll staff:**

Gedaliah Zlotowitz — Thank you for your treasured *yedidus.*

Avrohom Biderman — Thank you for your friendship and for going beyond the call of duty.

Mendy Herzberg — Thank you for your smile and calm in the face of the storm.

Eli Kroen — A cover is worth a thousand words, or in this case, even more. Your cover is magnificent.

A special note of thanks to: **Mrs. Mindy Stern** for spending time perfecting the stories with her unique mastery of language; **Mrs. Faygie Weinbaum,** for her meticulous proofreading; **Mrs. Estie Dicker,** for creating a beautiful piece of work.

I would like to thank my parents, **Dr. and Mrs. Abba and Sarah Spero,** for their constant support and love. My parents are my biggest fans, but never fail to remind me how important it is to keep striving to be a better person. I have never had a problem accepting their gifts. I'm still working on accepting the gentle *mussar*.

Living right near us, **Rabbi and Mrs. Yehuda and Nusy Lefkovitz** dispel the in-law myth. As they shower us with encouragement at every juncture and decision of our lives, their unfailing support is greatly appreciated.

Mrs. Tova Salb takes my words and makes them sound so much better. She knows my work better than I do. Her expertise in the written word camouflages my shortcomings. For that, I am most thankful.

To the hundreds of people who have shared their stories with me: Thank you! Although I am not able to use them all, I don't take them for granted. I appreciate that you had me in mind, and I hope to use them in some way in the future.

A special note of gratitude to the many institutions around the world that have invited me to speak on behalf of their organizations. Thank you for thinking of me.

I would like to express *hakaras hatov* to a master author and storyteller, **Rabbi Hillel Goldberg,** who taught me a tremendous lesson about doing a job right. He recently shared with me that sometimes, he rewrites a story 100 times; in addition, some stories take him 30 or 40 years to write! His stories are all so meaningful and so powerful — and now I know why.

My children, **Tzvi, Avromi, Efraim, Miri, Shmueli, Chana Leah, Henni,** and **Chayala,** have given us more *nachas* than we ever hoped for. May it just continue.

And finally, to my wife, **Chumi,** who brightens every room she enters.

May the Al-mighty continue to bless us with limitless *siyata d'Shmaya.*

Yechiel Spero

Adar Sheni 5774

Table of Contents

Emunah BaShem

Hashgachah Pratis

Faith in the Strength of Torah

Believing in Ourselves

Returning to Their Faith

Keepers of the Faith

Emunah
BaShem

Not Our Hope

R EB MOSHE FRIEDMAN, A RESIDENT OF RECHASIM, A city near Haifa, stood in line at London's Heathrow Airport, waiting to board his plane to Israel. He could not figure out what was taking so long. He had come to the airport with plenty of time to spare, but something was holding up the line. He walked to the front to see what was causing the delay. He noticed a very short Jewish man, barely tall enough to see over the ticket counter, having some sort of problem with the ticket agent. He offered his help, hoping that would make the line begin to move again.

The agent explained to Reb Moshe that she could not give the man a boarding pass because his ticket was not valid for a flight to Israel. Reb Moshe realized that, for some reason, the ticket was for a flight *to* Heathrow and not *from* Heathrow. He bent down to explain the situation to the fellow, but the man stubbornly replied, "I am a *sheliach mitzvah*, and I need to get to Eretz Yisrael. This woman is not going to stop me."

Had this statement come from anyone else, Reb Moshe would have put him in his place. But Reb Moshe recognized the short fellow; he was the famed *maggid*, Rav Yankel Galinsky, and he had a way of making things happen. Reb Moshe stepped back to his place in the line and waited to see what would happen.

He was not surprised when, as he boarded the flight, he noticed that Rav Yankel was already on the plane, seated comfortably and smiling broadly. As fate would have it, Reb Moshe was assigned the seat right next to Rav Yankel's.

Reb Moshe placed his luggage in the overhead bin and sat down next to Rav Yankel, who explained to him that a Yid can never give up hope. Just because we are turned away once, twice, or three times, this does not mean we should give up hope. We must continue to try time and time again.

After giving Reb Moshe this quick lesson in *bitachon*, Rav Yankel explained how he had come to this point of faith: Unfortunately, and to my great sorrow, my wife and child died at the hands of the Nazis; only I made it out of Europe alive. After the war, I was so depressed that I was ready to give up hope on everything. I had no interest in starting a new family. I just wanted to live out my life the way I was. But when I went to pour out my heart to Rav Avraham Yeshayah Karelitz, the Chazon Ish, he told me a story that changed my perspective on everything:

> There was once a fellow who would travel to the Leipzig fair
> every year. He would come to the city with a great deal of
> money and spend a few days looking for the best deals. Once
> he found them, he bought lots of merchandise and then located
> buyers for the items he had just purchased. In this manner, he
> was able to make a fortune in just a few days, and he didn't
> even have to transport any of the merchandise to his hometown.
> It took him a lot of wheeling and dealing, but each year he made
> enough money to support his family for the coming year.
>
> One year, however, the fellow got sick right before the
> fair. Although his wife was timid and not much of a business-
> woman, he had no choice but to ask her to take his place at the
> yearly fair. She was completely overwhelmed and balked at the
> idea. But what other option did she have? A year's parnassah
> was dependent on this fair.
>
> So her husband taught her everything she had to know to

be successful at the fair. By the end of the lesson, her head was spinning just trying to remember all of her contact information. Sure enough, by the time she got there, she had no idea where to go or what to do.

She had a great deal of money with her to buy lots of valuable merchandise. But as the day progressed, the marketplace became more and more chaotic. She tried to make some deals, but everything fell through. She was terribly dejected. She knew she could not go home; the family's livelihood for the entire year depended on her. So at the end of the first day, she resolved to keep trying her best with the hope that it would all work out in the end.

As she made her way to the inn at the end of the day, she discovered that her purse was missing! She ran back to the fair and retraced her steps. With each passing moment, she became more and more hysterical. What could she do? What would her husband say?

Suddenly, she noticed a man standing in the center of the town's square holding a wad of money and counting the bills. She ran over to the man, who had a big smile on his face, and asked him if he had just found that bundle of money. The man admitted that he had, and a huge feeling of relief swept over her.

But then he informed her that he was going to keep the money. "Let's face it," he said, referring to a halachah regarding finding lost objects (*Bava Metzia 21*). "You gave up hope. Therefore, the money is mine."

She didn't know what to do. Moments earlier, she had been swept up in the euphoria and relief of finding her money and now, just like that, it was gone again. In truth, she had to admit that the man was right; she had given up hope. Still, she tried to convince him to return the money. Eventually, since there was a large sum of money at stake, and people had gathered to see what was happening, he agreed to go with her to *the rav, confident that the rav would rule in his favor.*

The two of them headed to the rav and presented their cases. The man explained that he had found the money in a place filled with non-Jews, and the woman most certainly had already given up hope of finding the money.

The woman told the rav that her husband was generally the one who conducted all the business. But because he was sick, she was the one who had to come this year. She went on to say that since she had been nervous about her lack of business skills, she had lost all the money her husband had given her.

Listening carefully to her words, the rav noted an important point and asked her to repeat her last sentence: "What did you say?"

"I said that I lost all of my husband's money."

The finder interjected vehemently, "But she gave up hope!"

The rav looked at the two of them. The man was quite confident, the woman completely beside herself.

The rav exclaimed, "It is not her money that she gave up hope of finding! It doesn't belong to her!"

Based on that point, the rav decided that the woman would get to keep the money.

"When the Chazon Ish finished sharing this story," continued Rav Yankel, "he looked me in the eye and said, 'The *Ribbono Shel Olam* placed you on this world for a purpose. He wants you to build a life for yourself, a family. I know things have been difficult for you and you want to give up hope, but it is not yours to give up.'

"When I heard the story and the Chazon Ish's explanation," concluded Rav Yankel, "I realized that even when things don't appear to be going our way, the *Ribbono Shel Olam* placed us here for a purpose. Even if we want to give up hope, it is not ours to give up."

This beautiful story was told over in Eretz Yisrael by a fellow who had waited over ten years to have a baby. He had wanted to give up hope countless times, until he realized that it is not his to give up.

One year after relating this story, the fellow and his wife were the proud parents of a baby girl.

It Could Be Better...
And It Could Be Worse

In many homes, a meaningful scene transpires each Friday night, as the father lovingly places his hands on each child and gives him a special berachah, using the words: "Yesimcha Elokim ke'Ephraim ve'chi'Menasheh — May Hashem make you like Ephraim and like Menasheh" (Bereishis 48:20).

When he brought his sons to Yaakov to receive these blessings, Yosef placed Menasheh, his older son, opposite his father's right hand. Ephraim, the younger child, was then placed opposite his father's left hand. But Yaakov insisted on switching the order. Rav Moshe Sheinfeld gives a very enlightening reason.

When Yosef was in Egypt, he endured much suffering and pain. He was separated from his father for many years. He was persecuted and jailed, although he was innocent. To remember the times of difficulty, he named his eldest child Menasheh, "Ki nashani Elokim — For Hashem has made me forget" (Bereishis 41:51). He lamented the fact that because of all his suffering in Egypt, he had forgotten his glorious past.

Yet, while he was in Egypt in that very situation, he also took note of the success and prosperity he enjoyed. He became viceroy of Egypt and supplied food for the entire region. He was respected and beloved. To commemorate that, he named his second child Ephraim: "Ki hifrani Elokim be'eretz anyi — for the Al-mighty has made me fruitful in the land of my suffering" (ibid. v. 52). Even in the midst of this very challenging time in his life, Yosef had positive experiences, as well. In fact, his wife bore him a second son, something not to be taken for granted.

There are two ways to view our lives. We can say things could be better, and we can look at life and say things could be worse.

In giving his grandchildren the blessing that will endure until the end of time, Yaakov insisted that when one has suffered, he must first thank the Al-mighty that things could have been worse. Therefore, he wanted Ephraim, who was given this name because Hashem made his father fruitful, to be by his right hand.

First remember that things could have been worse, and only then contemplate how things could be better.

RAV CHAIM VOLOZHINER'S SON RAV ITZELE WAS A *TZAD-dik* in his own right, and he was blessed with a beautiful family. Rav Itzele and his wife suffered a terrible tragedy when their young child was taken from them. Throughout the days of *shivah*, many tried to find the proper words of comfort, but no one succeeded; Rav Itzele was inconsolable. As *shivah* concluded, Rav Chaim approached his son and gave him a sharply worded message of comfort. "Don't you think Rav Eliyahu Strashun would have hoped for such a *nisayon*?"

Rav Eliyahu, a rav in the neighboring village, had been childless for many years. Rav Chaim was hinting to his son that even though this tragedy was unbearably painful, things could have been much worse. Up until this point, nothing anyone had said had given Rav

Itzele the comfort and perspective he needed. But his father's penetrating *mussar* was exactly what Rav Itzele needed to hear.

As a fascinating postscript to the story, a year later, Rav Eliyahu and his wife were blessed with a child, a baby boy, whom they named Yosef. One year later, this child was stricken with typhus. With the child's life hanging in the balance, his father cried out to the Al-mighty, "This is not what Rav Chaim meant! Please don't take away my Yosef. . ."

His desperate pleas were heard by the Al-mighty and the child survived the ordeal. He grew up to become a fine, *ehrliche* Yid and a *talmid chacham*. His son, Shmuel, became the *gaon* and *tzaddik*, Rav Shmuel Strashun, the famed Rashash.

> *It should be noted how sensitive one must be when trying to comfort those who have suffered a devastating loss. Yet, great people somehow find the right words.*
>
> *Rav Chaim Volozhiner found the right words — the words most appropriate for his son.*
>
> *Sometimes, initially there are no words to convey, since the pain is too overwhelming. But eventually, even people who are suffering are ready to be comforted with the words of Rav Chaim — that things could be worse.*
>
> *Parents with sick children could have no children at all. Childless couples could be single. Older singles could be sick and incapacitated. All people can find the blessing in their lives. For the Al-mighty loves us and has given us so much goodness and love.*
>
> *As Rav Sheinfeld explains, Yaakov Avinu conveyed that message to Yosef (Bereishis 48:19): "Yadati ve'ni yadati — I know, my son, I know; I know that Menasheh is the elder son. And I also know of all the pain that is alluded to by his name. I do not minimize your pain in any way, for I, too, have endured much suffering in my life."*
>
> *Yaakov understood that this is the message Klal Yisrael*

must hear: "My dear children, there will be times of Menasheh and times of Ephraim, times of difficulty and times of blessing. But before you lament your lot and ponder how much better things could be, remember the message of Ephraim: how the Al-mighty has blessed you with so much good, how things could be so much worse."

Dead or Alive

*A*S THE RICHEST MAN IN TOWN AND CHIEF EMPLOYER of the townspeople, Refael knew how to throw his weight around. He dictated the comings and goings of the villagers, and the people had no choice but to obey him, as they lived with a fear of displeasing him and losing their jobs. Even the activities of the rabbanim in the town were restrained. Because Refael supported them generously, the rabbanim wouldn't dare to criticize Refael's way of living, for that might incur his wrath — and their possible expulsion from the city.

Among his many idiosyncrasies, Refael had a particular loathing for happy people. In truth, he couldn't stomach the fact that with all his money, he was still miserable, while others, even if they were destitute, were happy. During the Three Weeks, sadness was prevalent; people walked around dejected and gloomy. But during the joyous times of the year, Refael had to exert his influence to make sure that people were not affected by the happiness inherent in the day. Succos, with its eight days of prescribed joy, was especially challenging for him.

Refael was able to wield his power over almost everyone in town. But one beggar was completely unafraid of Refael; he knew that Refael could not fire him, because he didn't work for him. Refael found this beggar, Yossel, extremely annoying — because he was always happy, always smiling, despite his poverty. Throughout the Yom Tov of Succos, Yossel sat in his succah, singing happily with his family and feeling content with his lot.

In desperation, Refael issued a warning to all of his employees that anyone caught providing wood for Yossel's succah would be fired. Yossel went from door to door, searching for scraps of wood with which to build a succah, but he was unable to find any donors. Before long, he found out who was behind the refusals. But Yossel would not be deterred.

He went to the cemetery to search for wood. In those days, the villagers could not afford stone for their monuments, and used wood instead. When Yossel entered the cemetery, he immediately spotted the tall wooden planks, with the distinctive "*Peh nun*," which stands for "*Poh nikbar* — Here is buried," prominently displayed on the top quarter of each one. He took a large pile of the planks, loaded them onto his wagon, brought them to his home, and built a succah.

After his meal on the first night of Succos, Refael went for a stroll around the village. He was pleased that there was very little singing coming from the city's succos. But as he was heading home, he began to hear the distinct sound of singing in the distance. As he walked toward the joyous sound, he discovered that his worst nightmare had come true. Somehow, some way, Yossel had built himself a succah.

Refael had given clear orders that no one should give Yossel any wood. And it was obvious that he could not afford to buy the wood on his own. So how did this happen?

Unable to control his anger, Refael stormed toward Yossel's succah, banged loudly on the door, and pushed it open before anyone had a chance to answer. "What in the world is going on here?" he demanded.

Startled by the outburst, Yossel immediately stopped singing. With his perpetual smile on his face, he welcomed Refael and offered him a seat and something to eat and drink. Refael refused the offer. He just wanted to know how Yossel had managed to build a succah.

At first, Yossel reassured Refael that no one had defied his orders by giving him wood. But then, since he had the wealthy man's attention, Yossel decided to teach him a lesson. "I knocked on everyone's doors and asked for scraps of wood, but I was repeatedly refused. At first, it seemed strange to me, since these were people who had always shared with me whatever they had. Eventually, I realized something was wrong, and one of the people informed me of your strict instructions. I certainly did not want to get anyone in trouble.

"Finally, I met someone who is not afraid of you. In fact, he had come to the city as a visitor and was looking for you."

Refael was surprised. "Really? Who was it?"

"Why, it was the *Malach HaMaves*, the Angel of Death himself!"

Refael was stunned. "And he was looking for me?"

"He most certainly was. And I told him that he should not waste his time, since there is no reason to take you away. After all, you are already dead. Because you're so miserable and depressed, and you make it your business to take away everyone else's joy, you are really dead inside.

"He appreciated that I had saved him so much trouble, and he asked me how he could repay the favor. I told him about your cruel plan, so he told me that he would give me some wood. I took him up on his offer. And just to prove it, look carefully and you will see the trademark of the Angel of Death on the top portion of all the pieces of wood in my succah."

Humbled and embarrassed, Refael apologized profusely for all the wrong he had done. "Please tell me how I can change. What is the secret of your happiness?"

Yossel thought for a moment and replied, "Appreciate what you have, no matter how much or how little it may be, as it is all from Hashem."

Refael was impressed by the poor man's wisdom. Before long,

the two struck up a friendship, and their village became one of the happiest places around.

We are taught in Pirkei Avos (4:1): "Eizehu ashir, ha'samei'ach be'chelko — Who is rich? He who is happy with his lot." But the opposite is also true. "Eizehu samei'ach, ha'ashir be'chelko — Who is happy? One who feels rich with his lot." One who accepts whatever Hashem sends his way is truly a happy person.

When the Klausenberger Rebbe, Rav Yekusiel Yehudah Halberstam, worked in a slave labor camp, his identity was kept a secret from the Nazis, as they were notorious for singling out rabbanim and tormenting them. One day, in the middle of a torrential downpour, which followed many days of rain, the inmates were lined up and given boulders to carry up a steep, slippery slope. If they could not bring the boulders to the top, they would be beaten mercilessly. Time and time again, the inmates failed in their attempts to carry the boulders to the top of the hill. One of the fellows noticed that at a certain point, the Rebbe began mumbling to himself. The man moved closer to hear what the Rebbe was saying.

"Tachas asher lo avadta es Hashem Elokecha be'simchah u've'tuv leivav mei'rov kol — Because you did not serve Hashem, your G-d, amid gladness and goodness of heart, when everything was abundant." Quoting from the Tochachah (Devarim 28:47), the Rebbe identified the source of our suffering: not serving Hashem with joy.

As Rav Moshe MiKobrin stated, "Simchah is not a mitzvah, but it is the pathway to all mitzvos. Likewise, sadness is not a sin, but it is a pathway to all sins."

Smiling Down on Him

THERE ARE TIMES WHEN WE FEEL THE *HE'ARAS PANIM* OF Hashem — the shining Face of the Al-mighty — and there are times when we are unable to see the light, but we must know that it is there. Rav Chaim Stein, the rosh yeshivah of Telshe Yeshivah in Cleveland, would often stress the importance of understanding that everything that happens is all *chesed Hashem*. Even after living through the conflagration of Europe, the bitter cold and fear of Siberia and Samarkand, the illness and death of his child, and the death of his granddaughter, Rav Chaim perceived only the *chesed Hashem*.

On the night of Tishah B'Av toward the end of his life, Rav Chaim had a medical emergency. After the situation stabilized, the family members who were with him in the hospital read *Eichah*. Upon reading the words, *"Chasdei Hashem ki lo samnu* — Hashem's kindness surely has not ended"* (3:22), which expressed the guiding principle of Rav Chaim's life, one grandchild wondered aloud, "What is such an upbeat *pasuk* doing in *Eichah*?" After some contemplation, he surmised that *Chazal* teach us that by the principle of *klal u'prat,* we say, *"Ein be'chlal ella mah she'be'prat* — The only thing included in the rule is that which is stated specifically." Rav Chaim's life was one long *Megillas Eichah*. That was the *klal*. But the *prat* was: *"Chasdei Hashem ki lo samnu."* He saw the *chesed Hashem* in everything. Despite the fact that he had endured so many difficulties, he viewed his life as one of constant kindness.

> *Rashi tells us that when Yosef HaTzaddik was taken to Egypt with the caravan of Yishmaelim, there were sweet-smelling spices in the wagons (Bereishis 37:25). This was a hint to Yosef that the Al-mighty was looking after him. Rav Mottel Pogromansky, a gadol from pre-war Lithuania with whom Rav*

Chaim had a very close relationship, used a beautiful parable to explain what had happened to Yosef.

Once there was a child who was very sick. After consulting the doctors, it was determined that he must undergo a very serious operation. When he was in the hospital preparing for surgery, the intimidating surroundings were too much for the frightened young boy, and he began to cry. The operating room was also very scary, as there were doctors and nurses and all sorts of machines surrounding him, while his parents were not allowed to enter the room. The boy began to scream and had to be held down by the nurses. Suddenly, the curtain covering the window of the room was moved to the side, and the boy calmed down immediately. The nurses turned to see why. The boy's mother was standing at the window, smiling and waving at him. And once he knew his mother was there, the boy was ready for the operation.

Yosef HaTzaddik knew that he would endure loneliness and suffering. When he smelled the sweet spices, he knew that his Mother was smiling at him through the window.

Remarkably, Rav Chaim always saw the shmeichel (smile) of HaKadosh Baruch Hu.

Swimming With the Sharks

ONCE UPON A TIME, THERE WAS A VERY WEALTHY INDIvidual. It seemed as though he owned the entire world. Although he was known throughout his country for his philanthropy and kindness, he did not mingle with the masses and only rarely made personal appearances.

Since the man never married and had no children, he began to realize that at the time of his death, there would be no heirs to inherit his wealth. He thought long and hard about what he should do about this and finally came up with a plan. With hundreds of employees in his business, he decided that they were the ones with whom he was closest. He would choose a beneficiary from that group.

One day, he invited all of them to his resplendent home. Sprawled across hundreds of acres of land, it was a sight to behold. The perfectly manicured lawns were complemented by the rarest and most beautiful bushes, hedged to perfection. He had lakes, streams, and tennis courts, none of which were ever used or occupied. While his workers were awed at the sheer beauty of his estate, they were sad that he had no one to share it with.

Finally, after a long and elaborate tour of the premises, he gathered all his guests to the center of his estate, which was graced by the largest and most magnificent swimming pool they had ever seen. Much larger than a standard Olympic-size pool, it looked more like a miniature lake.

When the employees were standing around the pool, their boss appeared before them and began to speak. "I have gathered you here to deal with something very important to me and very dear to my heart. Even though I don't interact with you daily, you are my most loyal friends and I want to share my wealth and possessions with you. Since I never got married, I have no children but I have much to give. So I devised this contest to determine who will be the beneficiary of my generosity.

"Before your eyes stands a pool, probably the largest one you have ever seen. It is quite a challenge to swim from one end to the other. What makes it even more challenging is the large shark that lives inside these waters. Yes, it is dangerous, but the person who makes it across, an individual with determination and courage, will prove that he is a worthy recipient of my wealth; as my heir, he will know what to do with my assets, how to use his riches wisely.

"So let's see who is willing to take me up on this challenge, for that person will receive half of my estate and half of my cash."

The people looked at one another and stared at the huge pool. That was when they noticed the intimidating shark lurking in its waters. At first, no one dared to take the plunge, as they knew that although there was a fantastic reward waiting for the one who could cross the pool, there was also a tremendous risk. He may never reach the other side. With the menacing jaws of the shark serving as a deterrent, no one was willing to take the plunge.

They waited and waited until suddenly, one man jumped in, wearing his suit and shoes and holding his briefcase. The entire group gasped and watched as the brave man swam frantically toward the other side of the pool, where the shark was waiting for its prey. Ultimately, though, it did not wait for the man to approach but began to swim in his direction and attack. The man thrashed about violently, swinging his attaché case repeatedly at the shark's head, hoping to fight off the vicious attack. But the shark would not relent.

Realizing that his life hung in the balance, the frantic swimmer lashed out in desperation and managed to hit the shark squarely on its head, causing it to retreat to a far corner of the pool. Finally free to swim toward the other side of the pool, the relieved victim swam quickly until he reached the other end. His colleagues met him at the edge of the pool and quickly hauled him out onto dry land.

The wealthy man smiled and congratulated the winner. Still hyperventilating, the victor tried to calm himself. He had been through a terrifying ordeal and was clearly shaken. As the crowd watched him struggle to gain his equilibrium, they knew that he would say it was all worth it. But instead of celebrating his good fortune and thanking his benefactor, he asked a completely unexpected question.

"The one thing I want to know is: Who pushed me into that pool?" The shocked crowd looked at the triumphant individual in astonishment. What a foolish question! He was now the heir to half his employer's wealth, and all he wanted to know was who got him into this mess to begin with.

> *The Al-mighty wants to share His infinite wealth and possessions with us. But he needs us to overcome challenges in order to earn these assets. These trials may come in the form of struggles with health, spirituality, children, or livelihood. The struggles may scare us half to death; we may wish that we never had to face these internal demons and suffocating challenges. As we drown under the weight of their burden, we thrash about, hoping to emerge triumphant. And when we do, the Al-mighty is ready to compensate us with endless rewards.*
>
> *Often, we complain about the tzaros we had to undergo, and all we can wonder is, "Who got us into this mess to begin with?"*

Dancing Into the Book of Life

*M*OSHE GREW UP IN LITHUANIA AND WAS A staunch *misnaged*. He disliked Chassidus and felt that its approach to various aspects of *avodas Hashem* was totally wrong. He had recently moved to Poland, where there was a strong Chassidic presence. At first, he tried to ignore the disparities and nuances of the Chassidic *derech*, but he found himself bothered by what he considered the Chassidim's unconventional behavior. And what irked him most was their constant happiness.

The Chassidim of Lublin were always singing and dancing.

Moshe, who was very serious — even morose — by nature, preferred a more stoic approach to the performance of mitzvos. Occasionally, he felt a bit guilty about his dour attitude and sour mood, but he brushed off the guilt by reassuring himself that his *derech* was the proper one.

With Rosh Hashanah just a few days away, Moshe prepared himself for the inevitable aggravation that came along with each Yom Tov in Lublin; he was certain that the Chassidim would sing excessively. But when word reached him that the Chozeh of Lublin, Rav Yaakov Yitzchak, not only allowed — but encouraged — dancing in his *beis midrash* on Rosh Hashanah, Moshe decided that this was something he had to see with his own eyes. In addition, he was determined, once and for all, to speak to the Chozeh and try to put an end to the Chassidim's inappropriate behavior.

On Rosh Hashanah, Moshe could hear the singing and dancing from down the block. With each step he took in the direction of the *beis midrash,* his anger mounted. By the time he arrived, he was seething. Moshe walked into the building and saw hundreds of Chassidim dancing in elation, the joy radiating from their faces. He also noted that off to the side, there was a handful of lonely-looking Chassidim. Some were brooding, while others just seemed uninspired.

Moshe searched for the Chozeh. When he found him, he approached him and immediately unloaded his many complaints and frustrations regarding the Chassidic way of life. The Chozeh listened patiently to Moshe's tirade and nodded every so often. Although this fit of anger was a clear sign of disrespect toward the Chozeh, he patiently allowed Moshe to finish his diatribe. Upon its completion, instead of immediately offering a rebuttal, he first wished Moshe a *gut yahr*. Moshe was taken aback by the Chozeh's warmth and gentleness.

Then, the Chozeh said to Moshe, "Tell me. What bothers you about the dancing in particular?" Moshe then went into another lengthy harangue. He said that he felt it was highly inappropriate to dance while one's life is hanging in the balance. He wondered how a person could take such a serious day so lightly.

Suddenly, the Chozeh pulled Moshe close to him, and he asked him to close his eyes and allow the Chozeh to place his hand over his face. Moshe granted permission and closed his eyes, while the Chozeh placed his hand over Moshe's eyes. All of a sudden, Moshe began to shake, and he quickly moved away. When the Chozeh asked him what he had seen, Moshe admitted that he had seen an image that portrayed the dancers in the circle, and how they had all been inscribed in the Book of Life. The cynicism with which Moshe had entered the *beis midrash* was quickly dissipating.

The Chozeh smiled and asked him to close his eyes once more. Again, Moshe closed his eyes and the Chozeh placed his hand over Moshe's eyes. After a moment, Moshe pulled away again. But this time, he was visibly upset.

"What is wrong, Reb Moshe?" asked the Chozeh.

Moshe described the second vision he had seen: the Book of Death, and the names of all of those who were sitting in the sidelines were inscribed in its pages. Moshe looked up at the Chozeh, his face ashen. "Rebbe, what about me? If I don't feel like dancing, what does that mean for my future? Is it indicative of my demise, like the rest of those men who are out of the circle?" By now, Moshe had completely lost his negative attitude. He just feared for his life.

The Rebbe was quiet for a moment as he contemplated Moshe's question. "Reb Moshe, let me tell you an important insight. There are two ways to be inscribed in the Book of Life: either with your hands or with your feet. For most, it is their hands, symbolizing their good deeds, which gain them entry into the *Sefer HaChaim*. But even for those who have not gained life through their good deeds, there is still hope. They can be inscribed through their feet, by dancing with *simchah*.

"Perhaps you are not yet worthy due to good deeds, but you can still dance your way in.

"Reb Moishele, *gei mach ah tantzel* — go do a little dance."

He did. And he lived.

Some people may snicker at this story as another Chassidishe maaseh. They may scoff at the narrative and dismiss its authenticity. But its message is priceless. Simchah is a critical component in every mitzvah, and most certainly in the mitzvah of teshuvah.

Happiness is not a superficial emotion. Rather, it is a very deep acceptance of the manner in which Hashem treats us. When we are happy, we convey a high level of emunah.

How can one act happy when he is feeling anything but? The Malbim differentiates between two of the words that depict happiness: sasson and simchah. Sasson is an external expression of joy, simchah is an internal feeling.

When you are not feeling happiness inwardly, fall back on sasson, the outer expression of joy. And if you go through the outward motions, then the internal satisfaction and joy will follow.

A Hostage Crisis

YIGAL YARON SERVED IN THE ISRAELI ARMY FOR OVER twenty-five years. Although many Israeli soldiers serve until their retirement in their mid-to-late 50's, Yigal was ready to retire in his 40's. It had not been a simple decision; he had spent his entire adult life in the Israeli Army and was considered a rising star in its ranks. However, his last mission convinced him that the time had come to leave.

It was supposed to be an easy operation. He was instructed to lead a group of soldiers into an Arab village and evacuate the residents, so that the Israelis could then bomb the village and thereby send a message to the Arabs that using civilian areas for launching missiles would not be tolerated. It was not meant to be a violent mission, and the officials did not want any casualties. When Yigal and his men entered the village, the first few homes did not present a problem. Although the villagers were reluctant to leave, they agreed to do so.

However, before long, fighting broke out. Yigal was shot in the leg and then taken captive. It would take a few hours for the rest of the soldiers to secure the area and disable the gunmen. While he was in captivity, the enemy soldiers beat him and tortured him, trying to get him to reveal secret information. But Yigal was able to keep his silence, and eventually he was rescued.

This harrowing experience gave him pause for reflection, and made him realize that the time had come to retire. After discussing his decision with his wife and children, he informed his superiors. Upon hearing that he would be leaving the service, they were surprised and even taken aback. They offered him a desk job and promised to reward him for all his past efforts, but he was anxious to leave army life altogether. He had three children at home and wanted to be around to spend time with them and with his grandchildren one day.

A few days later, Yigal was taking a walk near his home when a van pulled up right next to him, and a group of Israeli soldiers instructed him to get inside. They said that they had orders to bring him in to headquarters. Although he was curious as to why his superiors had not called him directly, he did not resist and entered the van. But as soon as he got in, he realized he had made a terrible mistake. These were not Israeli soldiers at all — they were Palestinian terrorists, who quickly blindfolded him and tied his hands and feet together. After driving a while, they shouted at him in Arabic. Then they carried him from the van into a concealed basement.

Yigal feared for his life. In all probability, these people had heard about his rescue from captivity and wanted to take revenge. They tied him to a chair and then took off his blindfold. There were five captors in all. They were young and, he feared, blood-thirsty, as well. They began to ask him questions about sensitive information that he had been privy to, and when he refused to answer, they smacked him hard. They kept badgering him with more questions, but he answered none of them. After each refusal, he was "encouraged" to cooperate. But he refused again and again. He noticed that on the table next to him, there were instruments used for torture. Nevertheless, although the kidnapers hit him when he didn't answer their questions, they seemed to be holding back somewhat.

This realization helped him maintain a bit of his stamina, but Yigal soon felt his strength waning; it was getting more and more difficult by the minute. Every time he was about to divulge a secret, he imagined what his parents, his wife, and his children would say if they heard that he had caved in and given away important information. Buoyed by the image of his family, Yigal resolved to remain silent. But he did not know how long he would be able to continue.

Soon, the first round of questioning came to an end. The Palestinians walked out of the room and headed to a nearby area to play cards and relax. But they would soon be back …

Yigal was quite relieved that they had finished for now. He was ready to give his life if he had to, but he was mentally drained. He knew he had some time until his kidnapers returned, so he desperately sought a means of escape. Looking around the room, he noticed that his captors had left the door open a bit. They probably wanted to keep an eye on him while they were in the next room. He heard them laughing loudly. Quietly, he moved his chair over and tried to listen to what they were saying, hoping that he would be able to somehow pick up a clue that would help him escape. As he listened, he was shocked to discover that they were not speaking Arabic, but they were speaking *Ivrit*. He listened to some more of the conversation, and he soon came to the conclusion that these people were not Palestinians — they were Jews!

He then grasped that this was not a real kidnaping, but that the army was testing him, to see if he had given away any secrets when he had really been taken captive. His superiors were taken aback by his sudden retirement, and they wanted to make sure that it was not due to any feelings of guilt he was harboring from giving away army secrets.

At that moment, he felt empowered to withstand anything his kidnapers would do to him, and he knew that nothing would be too terrible to handle. These captors were not the enemy; they were merely testing his loyalty. Infused with a newfound spirit, he was prepared to endure any suffering that came his way. He would persevere.

> *If only we realize that when the Al-mighty tests us, He is doing just that — testing us. He is on our side and backing us every step of the way. The suffering we endure is only to test our faith. And, at the end of the day, we will be rewarded for withstanding each and every challenge.*

Holding Hands

IVKY WAS BORN WITH AN INOPERABLE TUMOR ON her kidney. Shortly after her birth, the doctors explained to her parents that they had no idea how long she would be able to live, given her condition. Her rare illness provided no reliable statistics.

Until she was 6, her devoted and loving parents managed to keep her happy and content. At times, it seemed as though she was just like any other child. But then, the situation became more complex. Although her kidney function had always been deficient, Rivky had been able to manage. Then, she began experiencing more pain than usual, as well as other problems. When there was no sign of improvement, her parents took her to the hospital, realizing that her condition was worsening. Even Rivky sensed that something was very wrong. Since she had been born with this condition, she understood the fragility of life and was more mature than the average 6-year-old.

The blood tests confirmed their worst fears. The doctors informed Rivky's parents that the tumor had grown, and now an aggressive treatment protocol was in order. Rivky's body was already so frail that her parents could not imagine how much more their daughter could tolerate. But they desperately wanted to save her life, and they were willing to try anything to make that happen.

Rivky's father, Michoel, refused to leave her bedside, and her mother, Dina, also tried to be with her as much as possible. However, she was juggling the care of her other children. Eventually, she decided to place them with other families, so she could spend as much time as possible with her sick daughter.

Rivky's big, beautiful black eyes still sparkled, but the dark bags that formed underneath them told a different story. As the treatments wreaked havoc on her body, she became even weaker, until she was able to get around only in a wheelchair. Her emaciated legs could no longer hold her up.

In honor of Rivky's seventh birthday, her parents arranged for a grand party, replete with ice cream, cupcakes, clowns, balloons, dolls, and toys. The doctors and nurses joined family and friends to help Rivky celebrate this special day. Her gratified smile made all their plans and hard work worth it, but her parents struggled to hold back their tears, knowing that this birthday may very well be the last one they would celebrate.

From time to time, Rivky's father would take her outside to smell the flowers and feel the breeze. Rivky loved the time she spent outdoors, and smiled and laughed when she watched others playing on the swings and slides in the park near the hospital. But with her deteriorating state of health and the spread of her illness, the trips to the park became less and less frequent. Her skin turned pale and lifeless, and the beautiful sparkle in her eyes began to dim. It was time for her family to prepare for the worst.

The doctors met with Rivky's parents again and explained everything in a very clear and decisive manner. They told them that Rivky's days were numbered, and the family should prepare for the difficult decisions that lay ahead. While Michoel and Dina cried, they knew that they would have to put on a brave face for their daughter.

They were realistic, though, and realizing that there was little time left, they decided to say their final good-byes to Rivky. When they sat down next to her, they were amazed to see that she smiled at them. How difficult it must have been for her. But she managed, probably because even in her sickly state, she wanted to make her parents happy.

Finally, her father began to speak softly, as he took her frail hand in his. "Do you remember when we would sing *Mizmor LeDavid* at *Shalosh Seudos*?" And he began singing the words, "*Gam ki eileich be'gei tzalmaves lo ira ra ki Atah imadi* — Though I walk in the valley overshadowed by death, I will fear no evil for You are with me" (*Tehillim* 23:4).

Michoel then explained the meaning of that verse to his dear daughter. "Sometimes life is scary and difficult, Rivky. You could be walking down a dark, narrow street, and you look around for us — your Abba and Imma — you want to hold our hands, but you may not find us. But you still have no reason to be afraid. You know why? Because Hashem is with you. He is also your Abba, and He loves you more than anyone else. He waits in the middle of that dark road, and reaches His hand out to you, and He will hold your hand as He takes you to Gan Eden.

"When you get to Gan Eden, all the *tzaddikim* will be there to greet you: Moshe Rabbeinu and Avraham Avinu and Rochel Imeinu, and your bubby and zeidy, too.

"So you see, you have no reason to fear. *Ki Atah imadi.* Hashem will be there with you."

His young daughter didn't die that night. But she closed her eyes and never opened them again. A few weeks later, she passed away.

And no doubt, if she had ever been afraid, she was no longer.

This poignant story was retold by one of Rivky's nurses, who was present at the time of the conversation. She has spent countless hours in that ward, as well as in many others. She has encountered hundreds of people who came face-to-face with death. Many of her stories do not have happy endings.

But she never met a family with such fervent faith, which was rooted in one premise:

Ki Atah imadi…

Hopelessly Hopeful

This classic story was retold by the great baal mechazeik, Rav Yaakov Meir Schechter, from Rav Nachman of Breslov's sefer, Sefer HaMaasiyos. Rav Yaakov Meir has endured great suffering in his lifetime; he has faced seemingly insurmountable challenges, but his smile and constant sense of hope encourage even the most down-and-out individuals. When recounting the tale, Rav Yaakov Meir prefaced his remarks by saying that he was not reading the story directly from the sefer, and it is not exactly as it appears there; in fact, his version is abridged. Nonetheless, the message rings loud and clear, for this is a story that speaks to the power of perspective.

ONCE UPON A TIME, THERE WAS A VERY RICH MAN, THE wealthiest man in his region. He was well known for his wealth, as well as his good deeds; he supported many institutions. One day, this man decided to give a very large monetary gift to the most hopeless person he could find, hoping that he would be able to transform the person's lot.

The wealthy man traveled from town to town and from village to village, but he was not satisfied; he couldn't find anyone who had lost all hope. Finally, he arrived at a certain town and saw a man lying in the street; his clothing was torn and his shoes were full of holes. He had a haggard and lost appearance. The wealthy individual went over to the poor man and spoke to him for a few minutes. He discovered that the man was homeless and had no family.

Who could be more hopeless than this person? thought the rich man. After speaking to him for a few more minutes, he decided that this was his man. And so, he informed the beggar that he was going to give him a tremendous amount of money. But instead of accepting the gift graciously, the poor man reacted in a totally unexpected manner. "You said that you were looking for the most hopeless person, and that is why you are giving me the money. If that is the case, then give it to someone else. I am not hopeless; in fact, I am a most hopeful person. I know that if this is what the Almighty has given me, then this is what I need. So I refuse to accept any money. Go find someone else to give your gift to."

The rich man was shocked. He had come to do a good deed, and he could not understand why he had been rebuffed. He begged the man to accept the gift, since he had traveled throughout the region and had not found anyone as worthy as this person. But no matter how much he tried to convince the poor man to accept the money, he would not give in. Instead, he offered a suggestion.

He told the rich man to take the money to the cemetery and dig a deep ditch. That is where he should place the money, for maybe one day it would find its way into a hopeless man's hands. The rich man did exactly as the pauper had instructed. He went to the cemetery, hired a few of the gravediggers to dig the ditch, and he buried his treasure.

Many years passed, and the wheel of fortune turned. From a state of affluence where he had the ability to distribute charity, the rich man descended to poverty and became himself the recipient of charitable funds. He wandered from place to place and from town to town. Finally, one day he came to the village where he had met the man whom he had deemed hopeless. He recalled that the pauper had told him that one day a hopeless man would find the money. Now he thought to himself, *I am the most hopeless man in the world.* Thus, he was a suitable recipient of his own gift.

He trudged to the cemetery and found the spot where he had buried his treasure. A short while after he began digging, however, two officers came to the cemetery and asked him what he was doing. When he told them his story, they mocked him and accused him of desecrating graves, a criminal offense. Despite his protests, they grabbed him and locked him up in the town's prison.

In this village, the mayor of the town was the presiding judge over all the criminal court cases. And so, the officers brought the formerly rich man before the mayor. They described how they had found him digging in the cemetery, and how he had told them the unlikely story that he had buried a treasure there many years before. They accused him of trying to dig up graves, under the pretense of finding gold or silver valuables. He stood before the mayor and awaited his fate.

The mayor looked at him long and hard. And then he smiled. "This man is telling the truth. Indeed, many years ago he was a wealthy man. He came to this village and offered a gift to the most hopeless individual he could find. But the supposedly hopeless man refused and claimed that he was full of hope. And I know this story is true. Because I am that hopeless man."

The rich-man-turned-pauper took his treasure home and became wealthy once again.

He was hopeless no longer.

We often think that hope and aspiration are determined by whether a person has or doesn't have materialistic acquisitions. We may even make the mistake of thinking that if we have money, then we have hope. The Al-mighty has all the money in the world. He doesn't need us to have money to make us successful. All we need to do is have hope and faith in Him.

Interestingly, the word "to hope" is קַוֵּה, which has the numerical value of 111, or aleph, aleph, aleph, alluding to the Alufo Shel Olam, the Chief of the World. This gematria is laden with meaning.

When you have hope, you have faith in the Chief of the World — and when you have faith in Hashem, you have everything you need. You can be poor and impoverished, with ripped clothing and torn shoes. But if you know that it is He Who has cast you into this lot, you are the most hopeful person in the world.

On the other hand, you could have everything. But if you don't have true faith that He is the One Who has given it to you, then you will be the most hopeless individual.

And nothing — not even the greatest treasure — can save you.

Hashgachah Pratis

Never Left Behind

AVROHOM, LEAH, AND THEIR TWO CHILDREN, ALEX-ander and Sophia, lived in a small village 20 kilometers outside of Odessa. Avrohom was a handyman who made a modest living; the family's needs were met and they were happy with their lot. But when the war began, everything changed.

There was a strong military presence in the region, and the children lived in constant fear. Still, although the Russian soldiers were no great Jew lovers, there was no open persecution of the Jews in the area.

In due time, Avrohom was drafted into the Russian Army to fight against the Nazis, and Leah was left to fend for herself and the children. Food became scarce and rumors of the impending Nazi invasion struck fear in the hearts of the townspeople.

Then one day, a group of Jewish refugees from Poland came into the town, and they told horror stories about the Nazis and the torment the Jews were forced to endure under their oppression. Word of concentration camps and Jews being gassed to death ripped through the town.

Leah, alone and afraid, decided that she had no choice but to head east, far away from the war zone. She knew that leaving the village would minimize the chances of her ever reuniting with her husband, but she was also aware that her husband was, quite possibly, no longer alive. And so, late one night, she packed up her most valuable possessions, plus a change of clothing for each of the children, and hired a wagon to the train station, from where she and her children would travel to Odessa.

The train station was bustling with activity and Leah kept a close eye on her children. It was not easy for her to carry the suitcase, but somehow she managed. While waiting in the station, her children grew hungry, so she gave them some food and water, while trying to ration properly for the long trip that awaited them. Before boarding the Trans-Siberian Railway, she refilled the water canisters.

Still, even with all her planning, by the time the train had been traveling for a few hours, the three of them had exhausted the last drops of water in their canteens. Alex, who was 6 at the time, began complaining that he was thirsty, so Leah tried to soothe him by giving him one last swig from the canteen, hoping that somehow more water would appear. But Alex remained thirsty, and begged his mother for more water. Her heart broke, but there was nothing for her to do except wait until they reached the next station.

Many hours passed as the train rushed eastward. On the one hand, a strong sense of security and peacefulness swept over Leah. She knew that the further east she went, the safer they would be. But on the other hand, she knew that her son was very thirsty. There was nothing in her suitcase that would quench his thirst or soothe his hunger. Finally, after many, many hours, the train slowed down and the conductor announced that they would stop at the station for 15 minutes. Anyone who wanted to fill up his water canisters was allowed to do so. But he also issued a stern warning that the train would be leaving in 15 minutes and would not wait for anyone.

Sophia, who was 9 years old, quickly grabbed as many canisters as she could hold and reassured her mother that she would be back on time. By that time, Alex was sleeping soundly on his mother's lap. Otherwise, she would have gotten off the train and helped Sophia refill the canisters.

Leah was waiting impatiently for her daughter to return when suddenly, the sounds of roaring planes erupted directly overhead. This sudden development caused panic on the train as well as in the station; and the conductor announced that the train would be leaving the station immediately.

Leah screamed for the conductor to open the doors and wait for her daughter. Then she begged him to let her get off the train, but it was already moving slowly. The conductor insisted that as long as they were stationary, they were sitting ducks for any overhead planes, and so they had to move out as quickly as possible. Leah was beside herself. She screamed hysterically, "*Ribbono Shel Olam,* You took away my husband. You took me away from my home and my village. Please…please don't take my daughter away, too."

Leah banged on the train's windows, but it was to no avail. Distressed and exhausted, she collapsed back into her seat on the train and held onto Alex. She hoped and prayed that everything would yet turn out all right. She shuddered at the thought of how lonely and scared her little girl must feel.

Back at the station, Sophia filled up her canisters of water and hastily made her way back to the train. But as she approached, she, too, heard the terrifying sounds of the planes flying above. She moved even more quickly toward the train, but it began pulling away. She called out for the train to stop, but her cries were drowned out by the noise all around her. She ran as fast as she could, but a 9-year-old's legs are no match for a locomotive. In a few seconds' time, the train sped away and Sophia collapsed in tears on the floor of the train station.

Sophia was not your typical 9-year-old girl. She was bright and fearless; she had endured much hardship in her young life and had been her mother's "right hand" after her father had been taken to the army. But this was too much even for her. How would she manage? What would she do? Why did her mother leave her behind? She knew there had to be answers to these questions, but right now she felt so alone. Overwhelmed and fearful, she continued to cry bitterly.

Suddenly, a soldier stood above her. His arm was in a sling and he looked quite bedraggled. "Little girl, what's wrong?"

Sophia looked up and told the Russian soldier of her terrible situation. "I am 9 years old. My family is Jewish and my mother took us away from our village to save us from the Nazis. And now, the train left me behind, and I am all alone in this world."

The sympathetic soldier bent down and smiled at her. "I promise you that you will not be alone. I am part of a group of wounded soldiers who are no longer able to fight. We are on our way to a nearby hospital to seek medical attention. In a few weeks, those of us who can return to the front will do so, but the rest will be allowed to head home. You have my promise. I will not leave you behind."

He took the girl by the hand and led her to the rest of the soldiers. "We even have a Jewish soldier among us," he told her as they walked toward the group. "You can sit with him." Sophia slumped down next to the Jewish soldier who appeared more dead than alive. Although she felt a little better after the kind soldier's reassurance, she started to cry once more. She placed her hands over her eyes and cried for a while. When she stopped, she wiped her tears and leaned over to look at the soldier who lay before her. She could not believe her eyes.

"PAPPA!!!"

Her father was barely conscious, but she could not mistake him. He mustered a smile and hugged his daughter tightly. She would not let go of her father and they cried on each other's shoulders for a long while. The other soldiers stood by and watched in amazement, sensing that something Divinely ordained had just taken place before their eyes.

Sophia nursed her father back to health. Three months later, they were reunited with Leah and Alex in Uzbekistan. Eventually, the whole family made their way to Eretz Yisrael, where they set up their home and rebuilt their lives.

A few generations have passed. Now Avrohom and Leah have many grandchildren and great-grandchildren who give them much *nachas*.

There are times when we feel as though the train has left us behind and we are all alone. But remarkably, there are other soldiers, kindhearted soldiers, who place their arms around us and reassure us that we will never be left behind.

But there is one more lesson to be learned from this poignant story.

All too often, we are certain that something bad or hurtful has befallen us. We may foolishly question why we are forced to face these difficult challenges. But if we allow the Master Plan to unfold, we will see the magnificent and glorious hand of Hashem, as He reveals His Hashgachah.

And ultimately we will realize that what we were so sure was a tragedy turned out to be a blessing in disguise.

A Stitch in Time

I N 1937, RAV AHARON KOTLER'S 19-YEAR-OLD SON SHNEUR experienced several bouts of severe abdominal pain and was in need of immediate medical attention. However, the doctor who serviced the city of Kletzk was out of town. Since the city was on the border and there were a large number of troops stationed at a nearby base, Rav Aharon set out to find an army doctor; he located one, who agreed to come at once. After a thorough examination, it was determined that Shneur was in need of an appendectomy.

Rav Aharon and his rebbetzin ordered a taxi to take them to the railroad station, where they were to board a train to Vilna. Vilna, which was a five-hour train ride from Kletzk, was a much larger city, where they hoped to obtain the services of an expert surgeon. The trip was a lengthy one and Shneur needed to lie down in order to minimize his discomfort. Therefore, Rav Aharon booked a sleeper compartment equipped with a bed. However, much to their chagrin, they were unable to open the door of the sleeper compartment; the lock seemed to have jammed. Other passengers tried, too, but were also unsuccessful.

Left with no alternative, they went into the next compartment, where there was an occupied bed, as well as an empty one. Rav Aharon laid his son down on the empty bed, and left the room. When he went back to the original compartment and tried getting the door to open, he was able to open it without any difficulty. Rav Aharon was well aware that nothing in this world is coincidental. He merely waited for the story to play itself out, so he could see the hand of Providence on display.

Shneur's roommate, who was sleeping in the adjacent bed, was a famous Jewish Polish attorney by the name of Chernikov. When he awoke and saw the young Jewish fellow sleeping in the bed next to him he began to complain. But as soon as he noticed the ice pack on Shneur's abdomen, he realized that the young man must be sick. When he asked what was wrong, Shneur responded that he needed an appendectomy, and was traveling to the city of Vilna to have the surgery done there.

The attorney pointed out that traveling five hours would be too risky for a young man in such a condition, and he suggested that the operation be performed in a hospital only two hours away, in the city of Baranovich. Shneur explained that they had tried to get an appointment in the hospital in that city, but were unable to.

Mr. Chernikov said that he would pull a few strings to arrange the operation in Baranovich. And as soon as the train stopped, that is what he did. Then he rushed back onto the train and declared that the doctor was waiting to perform the procedure. A few hours later, the operation was completed and Shneur was no longer in danger.

As he was wont to do, Rav Aharon sent a letter to the attorney, thanking him for the arrangements he had made so that his son could receive the proper medical care:

There is really no way that I can adequately thank you for saving the life of my son. However, there is one thing I can do for you that can be immensely beneficial, and that is to point out to you how clear the hand of Providence is in every aspect of our lives.

And since you were a part of that, you should remember it forever.

A Bullet's Target

THE YEAR WAS 1948. MOSHE KAMARA AND HIS FELLOW soldiers were fighting for their very lives as the Jewish people were desperately trying to return to their homeland. Moshe was a medic in the army. During the past few months, he had seen it all. Soldiers had died in his arms, but many had been saved because of his heroic efforts, and Moshe had earned the respect of his fellow soldiers.

Working with nothing more than his small bag of medical supplies, Moshe excelled at making the most of a difficult situation. While many of the wounded he treated really needed a hospital and a full team of doctors, Moshe managed to do wonders with just a few sterile instruments. But his past experiences paled in comparison to the danger and casualties that lay ahead.

There is a well-known Russian monastery right near Gush Etzion. Moshe's group formed a battle station in the monastery, where their mission was to prevent the Jordanians from traveling the road from Chevron to Yerushalayim and transporting ammunition and other supplies that might help the enemy's cause.

If the lookouts noticed any oncoming vehicles, they immediately warned everyone to man their positions and prepare for battle. So prepared were they for war that they slept in their clothing and their shoes, ready to spring up at a moment's notice. Moshe normally slept with his *tefillin* and *siddur* in his pockets, next to his grenades. He never placed them in his knapsack, as he wanted them as close as possible. In a sense, one could say that his *siddur* and *tefillin* were weapons of battle just as much as his grenades. Some would provide physical protection, while the others would provide spiritual protection.

When the alarm was sounded, Moshe would run to battle with his submachine gun and his medic case in his hands, and his spiritual protection in his pockets. When he needed to shoot, he shot, and when he needed to heal, he healed. One night, while they were sleeping, the alarm sounded. Immediately, the soldiers jumped up and manned their positions. The Jordanians were trying desperately to deliver reinforcements and ammunition to their soldiers. The skies, which were lit up from gunfire and bombings, indicated that they were in for the fight of their lives.

Moshe's commanding officer warned him beforehand that he would need every drop of supplies he could bring along. Moshe filled his bag with everything he had: bandages, medical tape, scissors, surgical knives, and morphine. If and when a soldier was shot, Moshe would have to do everything he could to save that soldier's life. And if, G-d forbid, he was unable to, he had the morphine to make sure that the fellow's last few moments were as painless as possible.

Moshe even filled his pockets with medical equipment. But because of this, for the first time ever in battle, two mainstays had to be removed from his deep pants pockets: his *tefillin* and his *siddur*. Left with no choice, he placed his *tefillin* inside his knapsack. Then, holding his *siddur* in the palm of his hand, he thought for a moment and then placed it in his shirt pocket. Ensconced in a small leather case, it fit snugly inside the pocket.

The battle against the Jordanians was even bloodier than expected. Bombs and gunfire continued to explode all around them. The casualties piled up quickly. One by one, Moshe's comrades were pummeled relentlessly by enemy gunfire. Moshe tried to save those he could, but he was one man fighting the angel of death. All too often, he lost the battle.

The soldiers slowly crept closer to the enemy. Suddenly, Moshe was shot in the chest. The force of the bullet knocked him to the ground. This time, his fellow soldiers ran to his aid, hoping to save his life. But a few seconds after hitting the ground, as Moshe's fellow fighters feared the worst, Moshe sprang to his feet and continued to forge ahead.

Many soldiers died on the battlefield that night, but those that remained eventually captured Gush Etzion. After the bloody battle was complete, his comrades approached Moshe and asked him what had happened. Why had he fallen as if hit by a bullet and then, only seconds later, jumped up and resumed fighting?

Moshe looked at the friends with whom he had shared the most dangerous battle of his life. He then removed the treasured *siddur* from his chest pocket and showed it to them. The bullet had punctured the leather protective case and ripped through the wooden cover of the *siddur*, stopping halfway through. He kissed his tiny protector, and quickly whispered a meaningful prayer to the Al-mighty, thanking Him for saving his life.

Somehow, the bullet had been stopped and had not killed him. He wished that there was a more reasonable explanation, but that is what had happened. It was nothing short of an open miracle. Had the bullet not been stopped by the *siddur*, it would have pierced Moshe's heart, killing him instantly.

The stunned soldiers reached out to hold onto this miraculous *siddur* and gently caress its pages. The *siddur* passed from hand to hand, with each soldier kissing it and shaking his head incredulously.

Tragically, only four soldiers survived from the group at the

Russian monastery. Moshe Kamara was one of them. While the main contingent headed toward Gush Etzion, Moshe withdrew to Masu'ot Yitzchak. The inhabitants of Gush Etzion and all the soldiers stationed there were brutally murdered after raising the white flag of surrender. Moshe was taken captive with a much smaller group. Somehow, he survived captivity and returned to Yerushalayim.

All the while, his *siddur* never left his side.

Sixty years later, Moshe's grandson told the story to his professor, a *baal teshuvah*. Deeply moved by the story, he asked the young man at which word the bullet had stopped. The grandson called his mother to find out. She went to check the *siddur,* which was in her possession. And when she opened it up, she shuddered in amazement.

The bullet had stopped at the words of *Shemoneh Esrei*, "*Melech meimis u'mechayeh u'matzmiach yeshuah* — A King Who causes death and restores life and makes salvation sprout."

> *This incredible story was sent to me by Rabbi Raphy Garson, the director of the Hertfordshire Learning Experience in England. He heard it directly from one of his congregants at the Ohr Yisrael Federation Synagogue in Elstree. His congregant is none other than Uri Kamara, Moshe's son.*
>
> *While there are many lessons to be learned from this story, one thought struck me. During Moshe's time of crisis, he placed his siddur next to his heart — and it saved his life. When we face a crisis in our lives, we must pray from our hearts. If we do, it can save our lives.*

A Divine Destination

ALTHOUGH CHAVI HAD A LOT ON HER MIND, SHE VERY much wanted to visit the *kever* of Rabbi Meir Baal HaNes in Teveriah. She went to the taxi station, where a *sheirut* was waiting; seven passengers boarded the car, the majority of them *chilonim*. Chavi was wrapped up in her own thoughts as the taxi began the trip. The drive from Yerushalayim would certainly take a good few hours, and she figured she would catch up on some davening and *Tehillim* along the way.

The first hour was uneventful; most of the people in the taxi kept to themselves. But a little over an hour after the trip had begun, the conversation turned louder and highly inappropriate. In a polite and respectful way, Chavi asked the passengers to keep the conversation down or change the subject matter, but her request fell on deaf ears. The other travelers even made some snide remarks about religious people before continuing with their offensive discussion. But Chavi would not relent. She felt that the conversation was not for public consumption and asked the driver to help her with her reasonable request. The driver apologized but insisted that the people in the car were allowed to discuss whatever they wanted.

Finally, Chavi asked the driver to stop the car and let her out. The driver informed her that he would let her off at the next stop, but Chavi was adamant that he let her off immediately! She said that every extra moment in the car was detrimental to her spiritual health, and she had to get out right then.

The driver pulled over and Chavi stepped out of the car. The rude passengers felt somewhat remorseful that they had caused the girl such discomfort. They didn't really intend to hurt her like that, but comforted themselves that she was overreacting and should not have left the car just because of the conversation.

Chavi had made up her mind, and she now stood on the side of the highway, all alone. Almost immediately, a car pulled up to where she was standing. An older woman stuck her head out of the window and asked Chavi if she knew the way to the *kever* of Rabbi Meir Baal HaNes. As she explained later, she usually went together with her brother to the grave to commemorate a special miracle that happened to their family. But now her brother was in the hospital, and she needed directions. Chavi told the woman, who introduced herself as Mrs. Scheiner, that she was heading that way; if there was room in the car, she would direct her to the exact place of the *kever*. Mrs. Scheiner invited her into the car, and they drove toward the *kever*.

After they arrived, the two of them spent some time davening at the grave of Rabbi Meir Baal HaNes. Then the older woman thanked Chavi for her assistance and showered her with praise and *berachos*. But before parting, she asked her for one more favor.

"There is one more thing that we do to commemorate our family's miracle," explained Mrs. Scheiner. "We always make it a point to find an orphan girl who is about to get married and we pay for her wedding. Would you happen to know of one?"

Chavi fell silent. When Mrs. Scheiner pressed further, she reluctantly admitted that she had lost her father a few years before and had recently gotten engaged. However, there was no money to pay for the wedding expenses. She had come that day to pray at the grave of Rabbi Meir Baal HaNes to ask for a miracle.

The older woman smiled broadly. "Worry no longer, my dear *kallah*. Your prayers have been answered." Chavi hugged her "Heavenly angel" and thanked Hashem for answering her prayers.

Mrs. Scheiner's family paid for Chavi's entire wedding and even insisted on completely furnishing her apartment: from appliances to linen and everything in between.

This story teaches us many lessons. We learn about the indomitable spirit of a young woman, who was unwilling to

compromise even one iota on her standards of propriety in
speech. She placed her faith and her life in the hands of the Al-
mighty, confident that it would all work out for the best — if
she did the right thing.

And we also witness the machinations of the ever-watchful
and loving hand of the Al-mighty. Yeshuas Hashem ke'heref
ayin — Hashem's salvation can come in the blink of an eye.

We never know exactly how things will work out. But
when we truly believe, we know that they will.

A Text From Heaven

AFTER A LONG AND ARDUOUS SEMESTER OF LEARN-
ing, four boys who attended Yeshivah Derech Avrohom
decided to go on a hike, in order to refresh themselves
before the upcoming *zman*. Aware that the hike would entail some
challenging climbing and difficult maneuvering, they packed
accordingly. Each boy took a backpack filled with climbing gear,
compasses, water canteens, and other small odds and ends. However, since none of the boys in the group were experienced climb-
ers, they knew they would have to follow a route that accommo-
dates beginners.

They headed up north early in the morning and set out for a
trail that would challenge them, but would not overwhelm them.
Shortly after they embarked on their hike, they came to a crossroads. It was impossible to tell from the fork in the road which path
was the easier one. Assuming that the two diverging paths were
equally challenging, they chose the one toward the left. They did
not notice a small marker indicating that this path was reserved
for army training.

Before long, they noticed that this part of the trail was much harder than the first part they had completed. Their inexperience was beginning to show. A few hours passed, and the supply of water in their canteens was dwindling quickly. They had anticipated a three-to-four-hour hike, yet now they were at the five-hour mark with no end in sight. The trail grew more and more difficult by the minute, and a strong sense of worry and panic began to set in. When would this end? They began to feel dehydrated. When would they be able to get more water? They checked their cell phones to see if there was service in the area, and were terribly disappointed to discover that there was no reception at all. Left with no other option, they continued to climb higher and higher, hoping that their ordeal would soon be over. Unfortunately, this was not to be.

The four boys finally reached the peak of the mountain. They expected that a trail downward would lead them to the end of their journey. But as they peered over the side, they saw that it was nothing more than a dangerous cliff, with no way down. They tried to suck out the last droplets of water in their canteens, while the sun beat down mercilessly on their backs and necks. The horrific reality began to set in, and they tried to figure out where they went wrong. Just this morning, they had set out for a relaxing and enjoyable *tiyul*. And now, unless help arrived very soon, they were not going to live much longer.

The boys sat down on the edge of the cliff, contemplating their options. One boy began to whimper softly and the others followed suit. Realizing that the time had come to do *teshuvah*, they began reciting *Viduy*. Suddenly, one of them heard a buzz coming from his pocket. At first, he thought his mind was playing tricks on him. But then, he pulled out his phone and saw that a text message had somehow found its way through. It was a random text message, but it made him realize that there was a signal. Ever so carefully, he maneuvered his phone into the exact position as before and texted his contacts that he and his friends were stranded, and he indicated their approximate location. Almost immediately, there was a response. Although they were still in desperate need of water, the boys knew that help was on the way. Within a few hours, a rescue team arrived and saved them from catastrophe.

After making their way down the mountain and being treated for dehydration, the boys were made aware that the path they had taken was meant for army training and could only be completed by those in excellent shape and prepared for battle. It was certainly not intended for yeshivah boys looking for a relaxing and enjoyable hike. The head of the rescue mission informed them that a few times each year, he and his crew find people on the mountaintop who wander off and get lost. But the vast majority of those individuals are either dead or unconscious by the time they are found.

When the young men returned to their dormitory that night, they called their parents and tearfully told them of their frightening experience. Then they went to visit their rebbi, who shared a powerful lesson, perfect for the Elul *zman* they were about to enter.

"Throughout the year, each of us goes on a journey. We think it is going to be an enjoyable trip, but before long we recognize that we must have taken a wrong turn. We find ourselves on a harrowing path, one that is dangerous to our spiritual lives. When we look over the other edge of the cliff, we think that there is no way to be saved. But at the last moment, we hear a buzz, a text message from Heaven, which comes in the form of the trembling sound of the shofar. Although previously we thought that the lines of communication were gone, we realize that the lines are indeed open. Hashem is anxiously awaiting our response — which will help us find our way home."

The young men heard their rebbi's message loud and clear. They were now prepared for the necessary guidance and direction to lead them on the proper path.

Patient With the Plan

We often struggle to find the fingerprints of the Al-mighty within a tragedy. When we hear about a fire, a car accident, a debilitating or fatal illness, or the sudden death of a young person, the suffering boggles our minds. We want to understand; we want to believe that the Al-mighty's kindness is evident in everything that He does.

But most of the time, we are left with nothing but our faith. Living in an "olam" (world), which is rooted in the word "ne'elam" (hidden), we are not always able to perceive Hashem's open kindness. We need to believe — and we must believe — because more often than not, we will not be able to see the complete picture.

RECENTLY, A 6-MONTH-OLD BABY DIED SUDDENLY IN her mother's arms. Exhibiting incredible strength, the young parents accepted the decree without any qualms or questions. At the funeral, one of the rabbanim delivered words of comfort in his eulogy, as he shared a very personal anecdote:

Just a few years ago, I went to Eretz Yisrael and did the most difficult thing I've ever done in my life: I buried my grandchild with my bare hands. After the funeral, as I was about to leave the cemetery, Rav Tzvi Kaplan, rosh yeshivah of Yeshivas Kodshim in Yerushalayim, took me by the hand and told me something that made a tremendous impact on me and gave me a great deal of comfort. He said that when *he* lost someone who was very close to *him*, Rav Shmuel Auerbach, the rosh yeshivah of Yeshivah Maalos HaTorah, approached him at the cemetery. And he said that when *he* lost someone who was very close to *him*, he heard something from his father, Rav Shlomo Zalman Auerbach, which Rav Shlomo Zalman had heard as a tradition handed down from the Vilna Gaon.

An elderly couple living in Vilna did not have children for many years. Finally, they were blessed with a child. This child was their entire world. They doted on him and gave him all of their love. And then, suddenly, he died. Everyone in the community tried to find the proper words to give the couple some sense of comfort. But they were too old to have any more children, and no one seemed to find the right words to say to them.

The Gaon, who was not known for his pastoral visits, came to the home of the elderly couple and shared a very powerful thought. "As you know, not long ago, there was a great tzaddik in our town by the name of Avraham ben Avraham. This holy convert fled from his family of Polish noblemen and came to our city to immerse himself in the holy words of the Torah. After an endless search, his Catholic family discovered that he was hiding in our city. The Catholic Church strictly forbids anyone from leaving their religion and converting to Judaism, so they offered him the chance to give up his conversion — or be killed. He chose to sanctify the Name of the Al-mighty and was burned at the stake.

"Let me tell you what happened when his soul ascended to Heaven. He was given the greatest honor and taken to the highest levels; every door was open for him. Ascending higher and higher, he opened door after door, until finally, he came to one door that would not open. As much as he tried, he could not gain entry into this room. Wondering why he was unable to do so, he asked and was told that his soul had nearly reached perfection. There was only one thing missing — he had not been born to a Jewish mother. Hence, he was lacking that last drop of perfection. And that is why the door remained closed."

The Gaon now addressed the broken couple. "I came here to tell you that the soul of your child was the soul of Avraham ben Avraham. Its sole purpose in this world was to perfect the

last element that needed perfection. You enabled Avraham ben
Avraham to open that last door."

The Gaon's visit concluded.

The elderly couple now understood.

"This is the story," explained the rav at the infant's funeral, "that I heard at my grandchild's funeral, from Rav Tzvi Kaplan, who heard it from Rav Shmuel Auerbach, who heard it from Rav Shlomo Zalman."

The rav now directed his remarks toward the broken young parents. "I wish I could tell you that I know the precise reason that your child was taken from you at such a young age. But I am not the Vilna Gaon, and I am not privy to such information. But I can promise you this: your child's death served a purpose. It perfected a soul that was lacking very little. I hope that you can gain some comfort in that."

We may try to understand the plan of the Al-mighty, and we
will still lack the clarity and comprehension we so eagerly
desire. Of course, it can take months, years, and even a life-
time for us to see the wisdom and kindness in everything the
Al-mighty does. Along the way, there may be unanswered
questions and countless loose ends that remain untied. But we
must believe that there is a plan.

And we must be patient with the plan.

The Consequences of the Commissar

WHEN THE BOLSHEVIKS INVADED BERDITCHEV, THEY placed the Jewish Communists, called the *Yevsektzia,* in charge of the city. These Communists, although Jewish by birth, were completely removed from any semblance of Torah observance, with an insistence that there is no G-d. Immediately, they made life miserable for the religious population. They closed the shuls and locked up the *mikvaos.* All kosher butcher shops were closed and *shechitah* was outlawed, as it was considered cruel and unusual punishment to animals. The children's schools and *chadarim* were also closed indefinitely. Even the yeshivah, under the leadership of Rav Shmuel Weintraub, was shut down and the *bachurim* were placed in prison for illegal activities against the government.

Although the Jewish police tried to clamp down on all religious activities, the observant Jews still managed to observe the mitzvos. The kosher butchers somehow found a secret place to slaughter the animals; the people in charge of the *mikveh* sneaked out in the middle of the night to open the *mikveh* when necessary; and the rebbeim risked imprisonment and exile to Siberia to ensure that the children were able to learn Torah. Indeed, the townspeople were quite a resilient group.

Frustrated with the inability of the Jewish police to stop all religious activity, the commissar, who himself was a Jew, decided to take matters into his own hands. He called a meeting of the town's residents in the town square, and announced that anyone who did not show up would immediately be sent to Siberia.

By 4 in the afternoon, the town square was filled with men, women, and children, hundreds of people awaiting the commissar's next move. At 4:15, the commissar appeared, wearing an impressive, long black coat. His assistant pulled out a metal stool, which the commissar stood upon, so he could be seen by the entire crowd.

"It has been brought to my attention," the commissar began, "that despite our best efforts, you people have been acting in a stubborn manner and have been making it difficult for us to remove all religious practices from this city. We tried to save the animals from inhumane slaughter, but you insist on slaughtering the animals anyway to make sure your meat is kosher. We don't want you to fill the children's minds with silly religious beliefs, but you have been teaching them anyway. You don't seem to understand that we are only trying to make life better for you.

"What is everyone afraid of? Who's going to do anything to you if you commit any of these sins? Are you afraid of G-d? What is He going to do to you? You should be afraid of us. Because if you don't listen to us, you will be sent to Siberia, or you will be locked in prison, or you will be killed!

"Now, I will demonstrate that G-d will not punish you if you sin."

The crowd did not have to wonder what this wicked man had up his sleeve, for he proceeded to pull a long piece of ham out of his pocket, and he raised it high in the air.

"Ladies and gentlemen, I am holding before you a piece of pig. And I know that according to the Torah, it is forbidden to eat this. But I will prove to you that even if I do eat it, nothing will happen. Or do you think that I will be struck by lightning?"

The commissar, who was quite amused with himself, let out a bellowing laugh. But the people of the town were miserable. What a horrible *chillul Hashem*! Then, much to their horror, he placed the meat in his mouth and began to chew on it, as he screamed, "Look! I'm still alive!"

All of a sudden, there was a commotion at the opposite end of the square; a tram was coming from the other direction. The sea of people quickly parted to make way for the trolley. Realizing that he was directly in its path, the commissar quickly jumped off the stool, barely avoiding the moving tram. But then he felt a strong pull on his long coat, for it had gotten caught in the tram's wheels. Before he knew it, he was being dragged along by the trolley. He screamed in terror and the crowd gasped in shock. But there was nothing anyone could do. By the time they were able to stop the tram, the commissar was nearly dead, and all the people could hear were his last words: *"Shema Yisrael, Hashem Elokeinu, Hashem Echad."*

With this stunning display of *Middas HaDin* and *Hashgachah*, the townspeople were given a clear idea of what happens to those who challenge the greatness of the Al-mighty.

> *In truth, these miraculous demonstrations are few and far between. Still, everything in this world happens for a reason; nothing is happenstance. In the words of the late Lieutenant Meyer Birnbaum, "There is no such thing as a coincidence. Everything is a 'Kah-incident.'" Everything that happens is orchestrated by Kah, the Al-mighty.*
>
> *It is our job to open our eyes and see His Providence.*

Faith in the Strength of Torah

Forgotten and Remembered

The decree of the Cantonists was one of the most horrific ever enacted against the Jewish people. At the beginning of the 19th century, the czar decreed that Jewish children be snatched away from their homes at a young age. Many were taken when they were merely 5 or 6 years old. These children were taken to schools where they were indoctrinated with the Russian worldview and trained to be tough soldiers. At the age of 18 they were sent to the czar's army, forced to serve for 25 years. So hopeless was their situation that their parents would often pray that their children should die instead of being forced to abandon their faith.

By the time they were free to leave the army, these unfortunate souls were usually completely alone in the world. Their families had long ago given up on them, because the Russian authorities would send forged letters to the children's families, which were ostensibly written by the children, describing how they had forsaken Judaism and converted. In return, their parents sent them angry letters, telling them they were no longer welcome in their homes and villages. Thus, even the few who were able to hold onto some semblance of Yiddishkeit were often ostracized. They moved to far-off towns where they lived out their lives, lonely and miserable.

*R*EB YOEL AND HIS WIFE DEVORAH LIVED IN A SMALL village. Reb Yoel learned much of the day, while Devorah dedicated her life to performing acts of kindness for others. But they were missing the one thing that would make their lives complete: a child. Then, after 15 years of pouring their hearts out to the Al-mighty, they were blessed with a baby boy, whom they named Mordechai. Their world revolved around little Mordche'le. When he smiled his first smile, and then took his first step, they were elated.

Reb Yoel often held his infant son in his arms while he learned. Even as he got a bit older, Reb Yoel enjoyed having Mordche'le play in the room in which he was learning. *"Amar Rava, amar Rav Huna…"* Reb Yoel sang the sweet melody and Mordche'le hummed along as he played with his toys.

But one day, the unthinkable happened. The czar's soldiers came to their village, broke into Reb Yoel's home and ripped the 5-year-old child out of his screaming mother's arms. Devorah tried desperately to grab her child back, but the soldiers knocked her to the ground and stormed away. Reb Yoel, who was not home at the time of the abduction, arrived shortly afterward to find his wife on the floor, crying hysterically. Realizing what had happened, he joined his wife and they both sobbed uncontrollably.

Years passed. Devorah could not come to terms with her devastating loss. All her life, she had dreamt of having a child; her dream had been fulfilled and now it had been shattered. Although her husband was also broken by the loss of their child, he was able to find some solace in the words of Abaye and Rava, as he lost himself in the world of Torah.

Yet when he learned, he could not help but think of the days when his Mordche'le had sat and played at his feet. He tried to be as strong as possible for his wife, and he assured her that their son would be able to hold onto his faith. In truth, he had no idea how that would happen. How could a child so young possibly maintain his faith in a world where brainwashing and beatings were used to make him forget his past? Nonetheless, he tried to encourage his wife to be strong.

After several desperate attempts to find out more information about their son's whereabouts, Reb Yoel and Leah were warned by the authorities to stop searching for answers. But they would not give up.

One day, a group of soldiers appeared at Reb Yoel's door. They instructed him to gather some basic necessities, as he was going on a trip. Reb Yoel was painfully aware of what this meant. Obviously, they were eliminating the problem he represented. Then they grabbed him roughly and threw him into the back of their wagon, which transported him up north — to a Russian prison.

Even in his prison cell, Reb Yoel was not forlorn. He had his most prized possession; his Gemara *Bava Basra* was among his belongings and kept him company. *"Lulei Sorascha shaashu'ai az avadti ve'anyi* — Had Your Torah not been my preoccupation, then I would have perished in my affliction" (*Tehillim* 119:92).

Though alone in the frozen tundra of Siberia, he knew that the Al-mighty always had a plan. Somehow, this was for the best.

His captors pressed him for information about his treasonous activities, but Reb Yoel denied all wrongdoing. He thought that perhaps he had pushed too hard in trying to find his son, but who could blame him?

In their demand for answers, the authorities subjected Reb Yoel to many harsh beatings. Their frustration grew as Reb Yoel displayed unusual self-control and refused to allow any sort of scream to issue from his mouth. Instead, he focused on the *sugya* of "*gud o agud*," a famous discussion in *Bava Basra* (13b). There were some questions he wanted to clarify. He knew that the Rashba addressed those questions, but there was no Rashba to be had in the wasteland of Siberia.

One day, the inevitable occurred. One of the Russian guards entered Reb Yoel's prison cell and informed him that his superiors had instructed him to ask Reb Yoel for his final wish, for he was going to be shot for treasonous activities. Reb Yoel accepted the news with equanimity. He had known all along that this day would come. However, at this moment, his mind was elsewhere. He thought of his son, Mordche'le, and wondered if he was still alive. And if he was, was he still aware that he was a Jew? Was he, even to a small extent, able to be *shomer Torah u'mitzvos*?

Generally, Reb Yoel did not look at the faces of the soldiers, but when he was about to state his final wish, he looked the soldier in the eyes. And he recognized something there. He knew that look from somewhere. Could it be? Could this soldier be his son, Mordche'le? Was his mind playing tricks on him? He called out Mordche'le's name but the soldier merely looked at him like he was crazy. *Maybe I am,* thought Reb Yoel. *Perhaps in my desperation, I am trying to imagine something that does not exist.*

Reb Yoel then put in his last request. "I need a Rashba. I must clarify something in the *sugya* of *gud o agud*." The soldier looked at him in disbelief. He did not know what he was asking for, but the czar insisted on allowing prisoners one final request. So someone was sent to a faraway village, with Jewish inhabitants. A few days later, the man appeared with a Rashba.

Could it be? When Reb Yoel opened the *sefer,* he found a page torn out of a *siddur* with the words of *Viduy.* No doubt, some Yid had realized that the man requesting the Rashba was also in need of the final prayers a Jew must recite.

Reb Yoel opened the Rashba and devoured the words that elucidated the *sugya* and gave Reb Yoel a clear understanding of the matter. The soldier watched incredulously; he had never seen anything like it before. Reb Yoel sat bent over the *sefer* and learned with concentration for about a half-hour. Suddenly, his eyes lit up, and he smiled and began to sing and dance. The soldier in charge of guarding him was amazed. Reb Yoel caught his gaze and called out, "Mordche'le, *mein ti'ere* Mordche'le [my dear Mordche'le], please remember. My time is precious; in a few minutes, I will be gone, and I need you to remember that you are a Yid."

But the soldier's expression remained unchanged. Time was quickly passing and the soldier instructed his prisoner to prepare for his final moments as he walked him toward the execution wall. Reb Yoel said *Viduy* with tears coursing down his cheeks, crying not only for himself but for his son who was lost forever.

The soldier stood him against the wall and walked back to his place among the other soldiers. The officer in charge of the execution awaited his orders. Suddenly, Reb Yoel began to sing the tune that he always used when learning. It was the sweet melody that had comforted him for so many years — at first through the childless ones and then after he lost his son.

His eyes locked on the soldier who had escorted him. The tears rolled down his cheeks. "*Amar Rava, amar Rav Huna. . .*"

The order was given.

The shots rang out.

"Pappa!"

In one moment, the memories came flooding back. Mordche'le rushed to his father, who was bleeding profusely.

"Pappa, I remember!"

Mordche'le held his father tight, tears streaming down his face as his uniform soaked up his father's blood. During his last few moments on this earth, Reb Yoel asked his son for a promise to return to the ways of old, to live out his life as a Torah Jew.

Mordche'le promised and held onto his father until he breathed his last breath.

Mordche'le fulfilled his promise, for the very next day he disappeared from the army and lived the rest of his life as Rav Mordche'le, the *tzaddik* of Cracow.

This moving story should give us pause for reflection. We must ask ourselves: What is the song that our children will remember? When they are struggling, what will make them change their ways? What song will speak to the depths of their souls?

The Right Address

This story took place in 1970. Much has changed since then, but the power of Torah and our belief in its ability remain unchanged.

REB SHMUEL RUBINSTEIN WAS BEAMING WITH PRIDE. And he had every right to. His son, who had just turned bar mitzvah, had completed the entire *Seder Nezikin* of Gemara. Had he merely finished the entire *Seder Nezikin* of *Mishnayos*, that would have been a tremendous accomplishment. But completing a whole *seder* of Gemara is something that many people do not accomplish in an entire lifetime.

Many dignitaries came to the festive *siyum*. Rabbanim and roshei yeshivah marveled at the young man's abilities. Finally, after many speeches, Reb Shmuel got up to speak. He did not hold anything back. He told his son how proud he was, and how he felt he could do anything he set his mind to. At the end of his speech, he offered his child a reward: a public offer for anything he wanted.

The boy's response shocked the audience. He stood up and boldly requested, "Abba, promise me that you'll live."

It was well known that Reb Shmuel was not a healthy man. Although he was still in his early 30's, he suffered from congenital heart failure. Even after numerous procedures and treatments, his heart remained weak and unstable. In fact, that is what made this gathering so special, for who knew how long Reb Shmuel would live? Who knew if he would ever be able to celebrate with and participate in his son's future *siyumim*?

The young man's plea broke the hearts of the people attending the *siyum*. Many wiped tears from their eyes. Indeed, how could Reb Shmuel possibly promise his son something that was beyond his control? But Reb Shmuel had promised his son anything he wanted, and there was nothing in the world that the boy wanted more than a living, breathing father.

Reb Shmuel nodded and meekly promised he would live. An audible gasp was heard from the crowd. Many must have thought, *How can he possibly promise?*

The following day, Reb Shmuel went to Hadassah Hospital to undergo a battery of tests to prepare him for his upcoming surgery. Pricked with needles and connected to machines, Reb Shmuel contemplated the severity of his situation, and how the outcome of this next surgery could very possibly determine his future.

After he finished the tests, Reb Shmuel walked out of the hospital. At the entrance, he sat down on a bench and gathered his thoughts. He knew his prognosis was bleak. Reb Shmuel had dealt with his illness his entire life, and as it grew progressively worse, he understood that in all probability, it meant he would have a shortened life; his doctors had told him that he had only a 10 percent chance of living a long life.

But now, he had an additional challenge. He had promised his son. Promised. How could he go back on a promise? Is that a way to reward a child who has just finished *Seder Nezikin*? Overwhelmed by it all, he broke down crying.

Suddenly, a man tapped him on the shoulder. He looked up into the kind eyes of Dr. Gottesman, a religious doctor who had just been leaving the hospital. The doctor asked him if he was all right and what he could do to help him. Reb Shmuel unburdened himself to the doctor. He shared his medical history and then told him about the promise he had made to his son.

The doctor listened carefully. When Reb Shmuel finished his monologue, the doctor asked one question. "So then what are you doing here?"

Reb Shmuel did not understand what Dr. Gottesman could possibly have meant. "Where should I be, if not the hospital? I am preparing for an upcoming surgery that will determine the outcome of my life. Could you suggest a better place for me?"

Reb Shmuel's frustration was clearly evident. But he did not mean to take out his anger on Dr. Gottesman. He quickly apologized but Dr. Gottesman maintained that there was no need for apologies; he hadn't taken Reb Shmuel's words personally. This wasn't the first time a very sick patient had raised his voice at him, and it wouldn't be the last.

Then the doctor explained, "Yes, there is a better place for you to go to: 10 Rechov Rashbam, in Bnei Brak." Reb Shmuel knew of no specialized heart hospital in Bnei Brak. All of his doctors, the best in the country, were based in Hadassah.

"I am talking about the home of Rav Yaakov Yisrael Kanievsky, the Steipler Gaon," clarified Dr. Gottesman. Reb Shmuel, of course, had heard of the Steipler but had never gone to see him. In those days, Yidden didn't visit with and speak to *gedolim* so readily. "I guarantee that you will find what you are looking for when you go to the Steipler," insisted the doctor.

Reb Shmuel's surgery was scheduled for later that week, and he felt like he had to do something. He hoped that this spontaneous meeting with Dr. Gottesman was really a message from Heaven. He immediately hopped into a taxi and headed to Bnei Brak to meet with the Steipler Gaon.

Forty-five minutes later, Reb Shmuel knocked on the door of the Kanievsky apartment. After a few minutes, he let himself in. Reb Shmuel had been informed that the Steipler was very hard-of-hearing, so if he did not answer the door, Reb Shmuel should walk in on his own.

The Steipler was immersed in a *Teshuvos HaRashba*. After Reb Shmuel caught the Steipler's attention, the Steipler handed him a piece of paper and said, "*Shreib voss ihr villt* — Write down what you want."

Reb Shmuel wrote one Hebrew word on the paper. "*Lichyot* — To live."

Then, Reb Shmuel explained his predicament to the Steipler. He told him about his heart ailment and the promise he had made to his son in honor of his finishing *Seder Nezikin.* As he spoke, the Steipler listened closely and then blessed Reb Shmuel that everything would be all right.

But Reb Shmuel was quick to respond. "Rebbi, I didn't come here for a *berachah,* a blessing; I came here for a *havtachah,* a promise."

The Steipler thought for a moment. "A *havtachah*? Then you must go back to Yerushalayim. There is a Yid who lives there named Rav Yosef Shalom Elyashiv. In *Shamayim,* they listen when he gives a *psak,* a halachic decision. Tell him that I said he should *pasken* that you are going to live."

Reb Shmuel did not hesitate for a moment. Immediately, he set out for Yerushalayim and headed to the home of Rav Elyashiv. When he arrived, he told Rav Elyashiv the entire story: his promise to his child that he would live in spite of his weak heart, his meeting on the steps of Hadassah Hospital, and his encounter with the Steipler — which brought him here.

Rav Elyashiv looked up at Reb Shmuel and asked, "The Steipler said I should *pasken*?"

Reb Shmuel nodded.

Rav Elyashiv stood up. "I, Yosef Shalom Elyashiv, am *gozer be'koach haTorah,* that Shmuel ben Sarah, *yavri ve'yamshich lichyot,* should become healthy and continue to live."

Reb Shmuel listened with his eyes closed and answered *Amen* to Rav Elyashiv's *havtachah.*

Forty-three years later, Shmuel ben Sarah's weak heart continues to beat strongly.

Much to the delight of his son and the rest of his children and grandchildren.

Nachas From the Kinderlach

Rav Meir Shapiro was the rosh yeshivah of Yeshivas Chachmei Lublin and the founder of Daf Yomi. Once, when he was walking in the courtyard of his yeshivah with a talmid, he heard the thunderous sounds of Torah study emanating from the yeshivah. Rav Meir, who was not zocheh to children of his own, looked up at the windows of the beis midrash. Turning to his talmid, he stated, "Ich hub tzvei kinder: Yeshivas Chachmei Lublin un Daf Yomi — I have two children: Yeshivas Chachmei Lublin and Daf Yomi."

Those who learn Daf Yomi are the spiritual heirs of Rav Meir, as they perpetuate his legacy.

R AV YOSEF FUCHSMAN OF BARANOVICH RECORDED A heartbreaking incident that occurred during the German occupation, involving a group of Slonimer Chassidim who were *Daf Yomi* learners.

Although the Nazis posted an edict forbidding use of the shuls and *batei midrash*, these Chassidim were determined to learn the *daf* — especially on this day, the seventh of Cheshvan, 1942, the day of Rav Meir Shapiro's *yahrtzeit*. These heroic individuals sat in Yagiche's Kloiz, learning with *hasmadah*. Suddenly, a number of Jewish policemen (known as *Judenrat*) barged in and demanded that they leave the shul immediately. But the Chassidim remained steadfast and refused to leave; they continued to learn with spirit and passion.

The Chassidim's defiance infuriated the *Judenrat*, who began to beat them with rubber truncheons. Shielding their faces from the blows, the Chassidim continued to learn. With each additional line, they were rewarded with another fierce, painful slap. The blows continued to rain down upon them, the Chassidim were bruised, bloodied, and beaten, but the sacred words of the *daf* glowed as never before.

Rav Meir's children had made him proud.
The daf lives on.

The Dreams of the Old and the Dreams of the Young

RAV SHMUEL TZVI KOVALSKY, WHO SERVED AS THE RAV of the Sochatchover Chassidim as well as their rosh kollel, delivered a *Daf Yomi shiur* in Bnei Brak. He was privileged to finish the *Daf Yomi* cycle numerous times with his *shiur*. About 30 years ago, on the day that they were beginning a new cycle, the weather was scorching hot and the air-conditioning, which needed to be replaced, was failing to make the room comfortable. A kindhearted fellow brought in cold bottles of soda and placed them on one of the tables, and a number of people got up to quench their thirst. For many, it was not their first time learning the *Daf Yomi*, but there was still a sense of excitement in beginning once again; perhaps this time they would add more fervor to the learning and spend more time reviewing each page.

An elderly gentleman, Reb Chaim Licht, walked into the *beis midrash* to daven *Minchah*. Having a very difficult time with the heat, he sat down with a deep sigh; someone offered him a drink of cold soda, which he accepted gratefully. Reb Chaim had suffered through the horrors of the Holocaust, and had rebuilt his life in Israel. When someone asked him to join the *shiur*, Reb Chaim began to talk.

"Unfortunately, I have never been able to commit to the daily schedule of learning the *Daf*. When I lived in Afula, someone used to pull me to a *shiur,* but I never came close to finishing Shas." He looked around the table and saw how a large crowd had come for the beginning of the new cycle. He saw the eagerness and excitement on their faces. One of the older members chided him, "Come on. It's never too late to begin. We're starting fresh today. Why don't you come and join us?"

Reb Chaim waved off the offer. "It really is a shame. I can no longer think the way I once did. My legs hurt me, and it is difficult for me to keep to a schedule of learning every day. In truth, if I knew that I would be able to finish the cycle, then I would have the strength to begin. But I'm old, and I don't even know what tomorrow will bring. And you expect me to make a commitment for the next seven years?"

Rav Shmuel Tzvi stood off to the side. As the old man spoke, Rav Shmuel Tzvi saw that the man had a desire to learn, despite his refusal. Reb Chaim looked up for a moment, and his eyes locked with Rav Shmuel Tzvi's. He stood up and walked toward him. Rav Shmuel Tzvi took him by the hand, and the two of them walked outside to the courtyard of the shul.

The sun was setting and for a split second, a cool breeze blew against their faces. "I have a proposition for you, one which you can't turn down," Rav Shmuel Tzvi offered the elderly fellow. "If you accept upon yourself to learn every single day — aside from any time you are not well — I will pray on your behalf that you should live to finish the *Daf Yomi* cycle and that no harm will befall you."

Reb Chaim grabbed the rav's hands, and with blazing eyes, asked, "Are you promising that I will live if I pledge to learn every day?"

Rav Shmuel Tzvi assured him that indeed it was a promise. "Well then, I ask you to sign a piece of paper recording our deal so that we will remember the terms."

The two of them went to the back of the room, and a small crowd gathered around them. They drank a *le'chaim* to seal the deal, with shouts of "Mazel tov!" filling the air. The document was signed by two witnesses to ensure its legality. And then the whole group sat down to begin the first page of many.

For the next seven-plus years, Reb Chaim came every day to learn from his rebbi, Rav Shmuel Tzvi. And after 2,711 days, they were both present at an unforgettable *siyum haShas*. At the *siyum*, Reb Chaim held up the document, and with great emotion in his voice and tears in his eyes, he called out, "*Morai ve'rabbosai*, I want you to know that the Torah is like the *Aron,* which was *nosei es nosav,* it carried those who were carrying it. We have to set aside time for the learning of Torah. And if we do, then we will see success in all our endeavors, and we will live long, happy lives.

"And if you don't believe what I am saying, just look at me."

This story teaches us how our dreams can carry us to fulfill the seemingly impossible. But we must be willing to dream. When we do, nothing stands in our way.
And, of course, we are never too old to dream.

The Dreams of a Child

AS A CHILD, MEIR SHAPIRO WAS ALREADY KNOWN AS a genius who was way ahead of his peers. One day, his *melamed* told his father that he was no longer able to teach his son. He felt that Meir could reach much greater levels in learning than he was able to provide. Meir's father asked Rav Sholom Moskowitz, the Shatzer Rav, who was the rav of the city, to learn with him. The rav agreed to teach him, along with his two sons, in his home. Although Meir was much younger than the

Rav's sons, as they were already 18 and 19 years old, the rav felt that Meir would be able to keep up with them.

And so it was.

Meir grew by leaps and bounds, skyrocketing in his learning. But since he was still a child, he would speak to the younger members of the household about childish things, as well. One of the things he would discuss was his dream that one day all the Jews in the world would learn the same page of Gemara, and all Jews would share a common bond as they discussed the same *daf*.

But as children often do, they teased him about his far-fetched ideas. "Meir, what a shame that you are wasting your talents and your brilliance on dreams that will never amount to anything. No one else has ever done this, and you think that you will? Why don't you just do what you're supposed to do and learn, and one day you'll be a big *talmid chacham*."

But Meir was resilient, and from time to time, he would still talk about his dream.

Many years passed. As is well known, in 1923, with the approbation of the Chofetz Chaim and other *gedolei Yisrael,* Rav Meir Shapiro introduced the idea of the *Daf Yomi* at the Knessiah Gedolah. This time, no one laughed at him. His idea swept across the world and caused a revolution in the way Torah is learned and Jews are connected.

One time, as he was waiting for a train, a man came over to Rav Shapiro and introduced himself as the son-in-law of the Shatzer Rav. He said that his wife was very pleased to hear about his success, and she gave over her good wishes and blessings for continued *hatzlachah*. Rav Meir accepted the wishes. Then he asked the fellow to arrange a meeting with his wife, as he had something important to tell her.

Although it was unusual for him to ask to speak to a woman, Rav Meir walked over to where she was and spoke to her. "Do you remember when we were small children and I used to speak to you and your brothers about my dream to start the *Daf Yomi*? You and your brothers used to make fun of me; you told me that I should stop being such a dreamer, and I should focus on my learning. I am not upset with you, because we were all children. But I have one request. You are a renowned *mechaneches*, and you are entrusted with teaching young children. Promise me that you'll never belittle the dreams of a child!

"If I would have been like many other children, then I would have dropped my dreams. Can you imagine what the Jewish people would have lost? The dreams of children can change the world."

Rav Mishkovsky told over this story to a large crowd. At the end of the speech, a prestigious *talmid chacham* approached him and told him that he doesn't believe the story. He felt that it was grossly exaggerated.

A while later, that fellow met Rav Moshe Halberstam, and he complained that many speakers exaggerate and tell stories that are not true. And just to prove his point, he told over this story.

A big smile spread across Rav Moshe's face and he remarked, "Actually, I know that this story is true, because the daughter of the Shatzer Rav is my mother."

> *Indeed, the dreams of children build our future. In their innocence and idealism, they envision a world that adults, with their jaded vision, cannot relate to. Look at what the dream of a child can accomplish.*
>
> *If Rav Meir felt as strongly as he did over 80 years ago when he met the woman who had teased him, then what would his reaction be today, when hundreds of thousands of participants learn the daf, creating such a kiddush Hashem?*

The Circuitous Route to Torah

*A*RYEH LEIB BAKST WAS BORN IN THE CITY OF DELATY-cze, Lithuania, in 1915 (5675), to Rav Yaakov Yehoshua and Rebbetzin Rivka. When he was very young, his mother would walk him to *cheder* every morning. Like many young children, he wanted to spend the day with his mother and not in *cheder*. On the first and second day, he left the school a few minutes after she left him there and walked home on his own. On the third day, however, his mother came up with a novel idea.

Instead of following a direct route, she walked him to school in a roundabout manner, crossing busy streets with horses and carriages and even a few cars. After his mother left, Aryeh Leib considered running home again, but he was afraid he would get lost. He decided to remain in *cheder* and learn there.

> *It must have been hard for his mother to leave him, but in doing so, she provided an invaluable lesson: There would be times in his life when he would long and yearn for his home, but Rebbetzin Rivka Bakst had demonstrated to her son that his life must be linked to Torah study.*

After Aryeh Leib finished *cheder,* his father was advised by Rav Chaim Ozer Grodzenski to send Aryeh Leib to Lida to learn by Rav Avrohom Tropp (the son of Rav Naftali Tropp) and Rav Yaakov Neiman. Aryeh Leib was very homesick in Lida. Nevertheless, anchored by his *hasmadah*, he overcame this challenge and began to acclimate to his new surroundings — until the yeshivah became his new home. And he remained a *yeshivahman* for life, eventually becoming the rosh yeshivah of Yeshiva Gedolah Ateres Mordechai in Oak Park, Michigan.

Years later, it was this lesson that Rav Leib, as he was affectionately called, conveyed to the fledgling American boy searching for direction in life: Anchor yourself to Torah. There will be times in your life when you need to take the roundabout passage, the circuitous route; especially during these times, hold onto the Torah.

Embrace it, learn it, love it. This will ensure a safe journey.

A Sefer for Safekeeping

*I*N 1942, RAV MOSHE STERN, A *POSEIK* AND *DAYAN* IN THE city of Debrecen, Hungary, was herded into the ghetto, along with the rest of the Jews of the city and its surrounding villages. Together with his young family, Rav Moshe joined over 10,000 Jews, who carried nothing more than their basic necessities, having left behind their homes, furniture, and possessions.

Rav Moshe noticed that one of the rabbanim in the ghetto had in his possession the *sefer Gevuras Ari* on *Maseches Taanis,* written by Rav Aryeh Leib Ginzberg, known as the Shaagas Aryeh.

At Rav Moshe's request, the rav gladly lent him the *sefer.* Having never seen this *sefer* before, Rav Moshe felt as if he were receiving manna from heaven. All of the *sefarim* of the Shaagas Aryeh had always been very dear to him, but in those times, there were many *sefarim* that never reached certain regions.

Rav Moshe felt it appropriate that the *sefer* was specifically on *Maseches Taanis,* which deals with fasting and times of anguish. As he entered the ghetto, he found himself in a situation of *taanis* — suffering and persecution. Rav Moshe reasoned, "What better *masechta* to learn at a time like this?" The illuminating thoughts of the *Gevuras Ari* lifted his spirits and gave him hope. He studied its words and delved into their meaning.

One day, the accursed Nazis liquidated the ghetto. They stormed into apartment buildings and emptied them one by one. Accompanied by their vicious German shepherd dogs, the Nazis quickly organized the hapless Yidden into large groups. Thousands of Jews were forcefully ushered onto cattle-cars, which were headed to Bergen-Belsen. The vast majority of them died there, or later on in Auschwitz.

When the Germans arrived at his door, Rav Moshe walked to the threshold of his makeshift apartment with his toddler son, Mordechai Nissen, in his arms. Hot tears streamed down his face as he took leave of his home. The Nazi guards screamed at Rav Moshe to hurry, but he was completely oblivious to their words. He was in a world of his own. His thoughts were focused on his precious *sefarim*.

Rav Moshe was thinking about two specific *sefarim*: his *Maseches Taanis,* and the *Gevuras Ari* that he had borrowed; he promised the Al-mighty that if he would make it out of the camps alive, he would reprint the *Gevuras Ari* and include some of his own original thoughts.

Although Rav Moshe did not bring the actual *sefer Gevuras Ari* along to the camp, it never left his side, for he carried it in his heart. At night, as he lay in the lice-infested barracks, he would think about his promise. When he was physically broken and emotionally crushed, this promise became his lifeline.

By the end of the war, Rav Moshe had lost so much. But he held onto his pledge.

Years later, Rav Moshe Stern established the Debrecen congregation in Brooklyn, New York. And when the right time came, he kept his word. He reprinted the Gevuras Ari, together with the thoughts he had originated, under the name Be'er Moshe.

A record of these events appears in the introduction to this magnificent volume.

As we say when making a siyum, "Hadran alach… ve'hadrach alan — We will return to you, and you will return to us."

Finding Hope

RAV MICHEL YEHUDAH LEFKOWITZ, ROSH YESHIVAH OF Yeshivah Ketanah of Ponovezh, was a beloved leader of the Jewish people. Rav Michel Yehudah gave advice and guidance to thousands and always managed to find the proper words.

But there is one story that stands out. For in this story, Rav Michel Yehudah revealed a personal secret — in order to help another Yid.

A *yungerman* came to Rav Michel Yehudah with a whole slew of problems. He had made numerous mistakes in his life, constantly causing himself difficulties. His repeated failures left him without any confidence and broken beyond measure.

There was only one area in which he was successful: *limud haTorah*. He learned well and thoroughly enjoyed it. But the myriad of challenges he now faced overwhelmed him entirely. Rav Michel Yehudah encouraged him never to give up hope, and he pushed him to immerse himself in his learning, and to find solace and comfort in the words of Torah.

The *yungerman* wanted to accept the advice, but the look on his face revealed that he was confused with Rav Michel Yehudah's response. His problems had nothing to do with his Torah studies; it was the other aspects of his life that were weighing him down.

Rav Michel Yehudah then related a story:

Almost 70 years ago, a young married fellow endured an unimaginable tragedy. He was carrying a samovar of boiling water, as his baby daughter was crawling at his feet. Not noticing that she was there, he tripped over her and the scalding water spilled all over her tiny body.

The man killed his daughter.

He was completely inconsolable. Nothing anyone said or

*did brought any comfort. Days passed, and the young fellow
was losing hope on life. Someone suggested that he speak to
the Chazon Ish, Rav Avraham Yeshayah Karelitz.*

*He walked into the home of the gadol hador and burst out
crying. Utterly shattered, he begged for some sort of chizuk
and encouragement that would enable him to move forward.
But instead of giving him words of chizuk, the Chazon Ish
began speaking to him about a discussion in the Gemara. The
young fellow was taken aback. That is not what he had come
for. But slowly, he became involved in the conversation and
responded to the Chazon Ish's question on the Gemara.*

*They went back and forth for half an hour, until the broken
father caught himself.*

*"Rebbi, I didn't come here because of a shverkeit in learn-
ing. I came because I am a broken man. My daughter died,
and I am the one responsible. And I need chizuk because I am
losing hope."*

*The Chazon Ish looked directly into the fellow's sad eyes. "I
know why you are here. By learning with you, I am giving you
a message: If you become completely engrossed in Torah, then
you will find comfort in its words. And if you don't, then you
will never find nechamah."*

Rav Michel Yehudah then stated, "I know the story well,
because I was that *yungerman*. I was the one who dropped the
samovar on my daughter. And if not for Torah, I would have been
one of those old men sitting on a park bench feeding pigeons."

The stunned man thanked Rav Michel Yehudah for his penetrating words of *chizuk* and left with a new appreciation and commitment to the learning of Torah.

*We may falter and fail, time and time again. But the Al-mighty
has given us the gift of Torah to help us heal from our wounds.
Battered and broken, we may search for other remedies to help*

us escape our inadequacies. But there is only one solution: Torah.

"Toras Hashem temimah meshivas nafesh — The Torah of Hashem is perfect, restoring the soul" (Tehillim 19:8).

The Cure for Everything

OSHE WAS AN ENERGETIC 14-YEAR-OLD BOY, healthy as could be. But one day, in the middle of *Shacharis*, his left leg fell asleep. At first, he was not concerned since this is a common occurrence. But when the numbness did not go away by the end of breakfast, he became a bit unsettled. He went to his classroom and tried to paid attention to *shiur*, but by now, the lack of sensation in his leg was consuming his thoughts.

Finally, he approached his rebbi and told him about the problem. The rebbi was concerned and called Moshe's parents, Dovid and Malka. They picked him up and took him to Ichilov Hospital in Tel Aviv. Upon his arrival, Moshe was sent for various tests. Since by now Moshe was unable to walk, Dovid placed his child in a wheelchair and pushed him through the halls of the hospital. On the way to the lab, they met a neurological specialist who agreed to take a look at Moshe. He checked for feeling in his legs and even inserted a needle, but the young man was unable to feel anything. The doctor admitted that he had no idea why this had happened.

Thus began a difficult time for Moshe and his family. Moshe was admitted to the hospital and was seen by one doctor after another, but they were all confounded. The daily grind took its toll on the family. After several days, Dovid's brother Bentzion came to visit. Seeing the parents' distress, Bentzion recommended that they go to Rav Chaim Greineman for advice. It didn't take much convincing, as they had exhausted all other options.

That day, Dovid and Malka traveled to Bnei Brak, and Dovid detailed the events of the past few days to the great rav. Upon hearing their dilemma, Rav Greineman recommended that they see an expert in the field by the name of Dr. Constantinos, in Rechovot. Moshe's parents thanked Rav Greineman and immediately traveled to Rechovot to ask the doctor to examine their son. The doctor agreed, but requested that the child be brought to the hospital in Asusa. By that point, the paralysis was spreading.

After examining Moshe, Dr. Constantinos decided to operate on Moshe's back, so he could examine his spine and see what was wrong. This terrified Moshe and his parents, but they really had no choice. Moshe's uncle Bentzion, however, who had accompanied them and encouraged them to begin this exploratory journey, recommended that they receive a blessing from Rav Chaim Kanievsky.

It was Friday afternoon and there was no time to waste. When they arrived at the Kanievsky household, the *gabbaim* insisted that Rav Chaim's visiting hours had already concluded, and he was preparing for Shabbos. But the father's heartfelt tears moved them, and they agreed to let Dovid in to see Rav Chaim. After listening to every word, as Dovid explained the situation, Rav Chaim asked him one question. "Do you keep Shabbos?"

Dovid, a very religious man, was shocked at the question. He answered with an emphatic "Of course!" Rav Chaim did not appear apologetic and instructed him to learn the laws of Shabbos in a consistent and thorough manner. And then he uttered four words: "*Likras Shabbos lechu ve'neilchah* — To welcome the Shabbos, come, let us go (literally, walk)."

Moshe's father was dumbfounded but did not say a word. He and Bentzion thanked Rav Kanievsky for his time. However, when they stepped out of his inner chamber, Dovid turned to his brother-in-law and asked, "Why did you bring me here? He didn't even give us a blessing!"

After overhearing the conversation, Rebbetzin Kanievsky asked them what happened. They told her the entire story, and Dovid explained his bewilderment that Rav Chaim had not even offered a blessing.

But the rebbetzin corrected him. "You don't understand; he did give you a blessing. He told you clearly, *'Likras Shabbos lechu ve'neilchah.'*" They thanked her for her explanation, wished her a good Shabbos, and went right back to the hospital. With just a few moments to the arrival of Shabbos, Dovid stepped into the hospital chapel and sat down to learn several of the halachos of Shabbos.

He returned to his son's room, intending to learn more from the *Mishnah Berurah*. As he sat next to Moshe's bed, he was overwhelmed with emotion. Lying in front of him was his child, who was now paralyzed from the waist down. The doctors had no idea what was wrong, and there was no telling when this would end — or if it would end. As he cried, his tears drenched the open page of the *Mishnah Berurah*.

That night, Dovid dozed off in the chair. In the middle of the night, he heard movement coming from his son's bed. He looked up and saw Moshe sitting up. *"Abba, ani rotzeh lakum ve'laamod —* Abba, I want to get up and stand." Dovid looked at him in puzzlement. The room was dark and it was very late. For a moment, he wondered if he were dreaming. "Moshe, I also want you to get up and stand, but you can't do it. Go back to sleep."

But a short while later, Moshe called out to his father again. Once more, his father opened his eyes. And he started to cry. Moshe was standing.

Likras Shabbos lechu ve'neilchah

I know of three other instances in which someone experienced a health complication and Torah healed it. One fellow suffered from terrible pains in his legs, and his doctor was unable to diagnose the problem. Rav Chaim Kanievsky recommended that the fellow learn Hilchos Regel Be'regel — the laws of the regel: Chol HaMoed. (Regel means leg, but also refers to the holidays in which we go up to Jerusalem.) The fellow did as he was told. A short while later, his foot ailments went away.

Another individual was unable to walk. Rav Chaim suggested he learn Perek Keitzad Haregel. (Regel here also means leg.) Once more, the problem went away.

On a third occasion, a young man experienced weakness in his hands, and again the family enlisted the advice of Rav Chaim Kanievsky. He advised the bachur to learn the subject matter dealing with the washing of one's hands, Maseches Yadayim.

Klal Yisrael is faced with countless problems.

If only we realized that Torah can solve them all!

Staying Awake

Three stories. In each, there is a powerful message about the importance of learning Torah, and more specifically, about the importance of fighting off sleep in order to learn. But while the behavior of the protagonists of the first two stories may be somewhat predictable, the third story is about a mere 12-year-old.

RAV DOVID POVARSKY, THE LEGENDARY ROSH YESHIVAH of Ponovezh, who was a great *masmid,* had an unusual *hanhagah.* The first time he stirred in the middle of the night, he would not go back to sleep. Instead, he would wake up, get out of bed, and immediately head to the *beis midrash* to learn. It didn't matter if it was 2 or 3 o'clock in the morning. The Gemara was waiting for him, and Rav Dovid could not wait to get back to it. This practice continued for many decades, and Rav Dovid never missed a day.

One night, when Rav Dovid was already in his 90's, he wasn't feeling well. His family suggested that the next morning, instead of adhering to his regular practice, he grab a few more hours of sleep. But no matter how much they tried, they were unable to convince him to take time off from his learning.

The next morning, Rav Dovid awoke at the first stir. As he always did, he went to the *beis midrash* at a time when even the early risers were still sleeping. When asked why he was so insistent about adhering to this practice, Rav Dovid gave a classic response. "It is not about this morning. But it is about tomorrow morning and the morning after that. There will always be an excuse not to get up in the morning. But one should never break a *kevius*."

The second story has a similar ring to it. But this time it is about a kevius at night.

Rav Moshe Soloveitchik learned in the Lomza Yeshivah with Rav Chaim Kanievsky. Recently, Rav Chaim recalled Rav Moshe's diligence. He told how during the day, Rav Moshe learned for many hours and covered numerous *blatt* of Gemara. But even though he learned all day, he had a practice to learn an extra *blatt* before he went to sleep at night. No matter how tired he was, he would push himself and even exert his last ounce of strength to learn that extra *blatt*.

One night, Rav Moshe attended a friend's wedding. After spending the night dancing for the *chassan,* he was thoroughly exhausted. He came back to the yeshivah at 2 in the morning. After sleeping very little all week, he couldn't keep his eyes open. He sat down in his room and struggled mightily, but was unable to stay awake. Finally, he jumped up, and after continually nodding off, he finished his one *blatt* of Gemara.

When asked why he insisted on staying up to learn that extra *blatt*, he explained, "I couldn't skip one night. Because if I did that, I would break the *kevius*, and what would happen the night after that? And the night after that?"

Menachem Mendel Pfeiffer, who passed away at the age of 13, had always been an unusual boy. He was a Satmar Chassid and his Rebbe, the Beirach Moshe, Rav Moshe Teitelbaum, remarked that there was no bachur like him. Mature and wise beyond his years, Menachem Mendel displayed extraordinary diligence in his learning. Deeply admired by his family, friends, and rebbeim, he finished a number of masechtos prior to his bar mitzvah. A sefer titled Menachem Meishiv Nefesh was written in his memory; it includes the following story.

Menachem Mendel was learning in a *beis midrash,* and the hour was late. Suddenly, he walked over to the *bimah* and took hold of a thick *gartel.* He rolled up the sleeve of his frock and began wrapping the *gartel* around his arm as if he were donning *tefillin.* A young married fellow who witnessed this scene sensed that this was not just any 12-year-old pretending to put on *tefillin,* so he approached the young man and asked for an explanation.

The more Menachem Mendel attempted to dodge the question, the more curious the *yungerman* became. Finally, Menachem Mendel relented and explained. "It is late and I am very tired. I really want to learn some more, but I am struggling not to fall asleep. It is not *assur* to fall asleep while one is learning. But it is *assur* to fall asleep when one is wearing *tefillin.* I am trying to get the feel of wearing *tefillin,* so I can carry that over to my learning."

The *yungerman* watched in amazement as the 12-year-old walked back to the bench and continued to learn.

I once heard that learning while one is tired is considered yissurin shel ahavah, and can save a person from suffering and difficulty. Additionally, the drool of one who falls asleep on his Gemara may serve as the tal shel techiyah, the dew that will revivify us at the time of techiyas hameisim.

These stories provide us with the inspiration to push ourselves as far as we can and then even farther — to learn even more.

Faith in the Strength of Mitzvos

Digging for Diamonds

WITHIN A VERY SHORT PERIOD OF TIME, THE NAZI invasion of Poland completely overturned the lives of Polish Jews. Reb Efraim Londner and his wife, who were Gerrer Chassidim, were the proud parents of a beautiful girl. Soon after the Nazis took over his town, Reb Efraim was walking outside with his young daughter. As he passed an acquaintance walking with his daughter, the two of them exchanged glances, knowing that in all probability they would not be afforded the luxury of strolling with their children for much longer. For the vultures were already circling; the Nazis walked freely around the town and on a whim decided who should live and who should die.

One day, the Nazis marched from building to building and emptied the apartments of their occupants. When they came to Reb Efraim's apartment, they were ready to whisk Reb Efraim and his wife away. But his beautiful daughter, Baila Gittele, was in her grandparents' home at that time. Reb Efraim and his wife begged the Nazi monsters to allow them to stay and wait for their daughter to return home, but their desperate pleas fell on deaf ears.

Reb Efraim and his wife would never see their daughter again.

Reb Efraim would often recall that awful day. One time before reciting *Yizkor*, he stated that he had long ago accepted all of the horrific tragedies that had befallen him and his family, but two images would always haunt him.

The first was the moment that his daughter had come back into their apartment. He could only imagine the little girl skipping up the stairs and bounding into their home. She had probably opened the door and yelled out, "Mommy, I'm home!" And when there was no response, she had most probably gone from room to room, looking for her mother and father. And with each passing moment, her hysteria could only have grown. No doubt her cries increased, until she finally gave up looking. What a terrible scene.

The second image was the picture he had in his mind of his beloved child walking off the cattle-cars that headed into Auschwitz, holding on to her zeidy's hand, until they were taken to the gas chambers.

These two images filled Reb Efraim's mind for the rest of his life.

And yet, he never let go of his faith.

Throughout his tenure in the concentration camps, he sought various ways to hold onto his belief. Occasionally, he would meet someone who would share a page of a *Chumash* or a *siddur*. Reb Efraim drank in those words of Torah and *tefillah* like a thirsty soul in a desert.

But his most prized possession was the *tefillin shel yad* he had acquired. Although he risked his life every time he donned them, Reb Efraim knew that the *tefillin* watched over him and protected him; they were his connection to the Al-mighty.

On the day he was liberated, Efraim was informed that his wife was alive and had also been liberated in a camp for women some 20 kilometers away. He quickly hitched a ride with a group of soldiers. His reunion with his wife, whom he had not seen since the beginning of the war, was bittersweet. Although they had both survived, their Baila Gittele, as well as the rest of both their families, had not.

They spoke for hours and cried together for what they had lost. Finally, as they prepared to go to sleep, Efraim realized that he did not have his *tefillin*. He had left them behind in the camp. He did not know what to do, since he surmised that there were no *tefillin* in the women's camp. On the one hand, how could he not put on *tefillin* the first morning after his liberation? What type of display of *emunah* would that be? On the other hand, what could he do about the situation now? It was very late at night and there were no rides from one camp to another.

As he was discussing this problem with his wife, a young woman approached and explained that she had overheard their conversation. She mentioned that originally, this camp had not been just for women. As such, she recalled that when she had first arrived at the camp, there had been a large pile of confiscated religious items, including *tefillin*. The woman knew where they were buried. Perhaps, she suggested to Reb Efraim, if he dug, he would be able to find himself a set.

With faith pulsating through their veins and urging them on, Reb Efraim and his wife joined the woman and spent their first night of freedom digging for a possible pair of *tefillin,* although it seemed highly unlikely that they would succeed. To a stranger, the whole scene made no sense. How could it be that there were still people so bound to their belief? With nothing more than the light of the moon to guide them, the three of them dug steadily for over an hour. At a certain point, Reb Efraim stopped, wondering why he should continue. What were the chances that he would find anything?

But then, he marshaled his inner strength and persevered. And a short while later, they found a pair of *tefillin!* His perseverance had paid off.

After brushing off the dirt, Reb Efraim held the set of *tefillin* in his hand. Much like him, it had been buried and left for dead. But much like him, it was part of the world of the living.

Reb Efraim held onto this pair of *tefillin* for the rest of his life. Eventually, he and his wife moved to Eretz Yisrael and rebuilt their lives.

As for the woman who helped them, she merited to become the wife of the Gerrer Rebbe, Rav Yisrael Alter, who was known as the Beis Yisrael!

A Chanukah Miracle

*I*N THE LATE 1940'S, AS THE GERRER REBBE, RAV AVRAHAM Mordechai Alter, the Imrei Emes, aged, he became so weak that he needed constant assistance. Although he spent most of his time in his private quarters, he tried his best to see and meet with his beloved Chassidim whenever he could.

The fewer appearances he made, the greater the desire of the people to see him. During the instances that he made public appearances, the crowd pushed and shoved to try to get as close as possible in order to catch a glimpse of the Rebbe. There were times when the situation became so uncontrollable and dangerous that his *gabbaim* had no choice but to recruit some of the strongest Chassidim to form a protective wall around the Rebbe, to prevent him from getting injured.

It was the last Chanukah of the Rebbe's life. Despite his weakness, he insisted on lighting the menorah in the *beis midrash*. Aware that he did not have much time left in this world, he hoped his efforts would give his Chassidim inspiration. As word spread that the Rebbe would be lighting publicly, throngs flocked to Yeshivas Sfas Emes to catch a glimpse of him.

No matter how hard they tried, the Chassidim were unable to form a protective wall around the Rebbe that would allow him to make his way safely from his home to the *beis midrash*. The *gabbaim* tried to maneuver the Chassidim to the side, but the crowd was simply too large. The *gabbaim* thought that perhaps it would be wise to cancel the public lighting and have the Rebbe light in his home; it was dangerous for the Rebbe to expose himself to a crowd like this. After some discussion, one *gabbai* announced that the Rebbe would stay where he was until the crowd settled down.

Naturally, though, this caused another tumult, as hundreds try to push their way to the front. The *gabbaim* erected a makeshift blockade, warning everyone to stay behind the line. Somehow, someway, one young man, Elimelech, made his way to the front of the crowd. And he had no intention of giving up his spot. But one *gabbai* had other plans.

The *gabbai* tried to move everyone out of the way, but Elimelech, with his slight build, held his own. The *gabbai* gave the defiant young man a menacing look and warned him that he must vacate his place, but the strong-willed *bachur* would not budge.

Once more, the *gabbai* tried to explain that if the young man would not move, others would follow his lead and the Rebbe would not be able to emerge from his home. But Elimelech insisted that others could move as well as he. Suddenly, the *gabbai* reached out and smacked Elimelech across his face!

Everyone was stunned. For one split second, the shoving and pushing, the hustle and bustle and chaos stopped. Clearly, what the *gabbai* had just done was very inappropriate.

A moment later, the Rebbe emerged and kindled the menorah. Just like that, everyone forgot about the slap and focused on the lighting of the menorah. Everyone, that is, except for Elimelech, who was ashamed and hurt by the incident.

Shortly after the *hadlakah* concluded, Elimelech received word that the Imrei Emes wanted to speak to him. The shocked boy thought there must be some sort of mistake. The Rebbe wanted to speak to him? What could he have possibly done?

The Rebbe welcomed him warmly and Elimelech stood in awe, hardly able to believe that he was having a private audience with the Rebbe. The Rebbe then opened the *sefer Chok Le'Yisrael,* to the section pertaining to Thursday of *Parashas Mikeitz.* There it quotes a famous selection from the *Zohar:*

The Zohar tells the story of Rabbi Abba who was sitting at the gate to Lod. He noticed a man sitting on a small ledge that was sticking out of the side of a mountain. The man, who was very tired from traveling, was sleeping and unaware of a venomous snake that was about to bite him. Suddenly, an insect bit the snake and killed it. The man awoke shortly thereafter and noticed the dead reptile at his feet. Then he stood up to continue his journey. The moment he stood up, the ledge broke off the mountain and fell into the valley beneath it. Had he still been sitting on the ledge, he would have fallen along with it into the abyss and been killed.

Rabbi Abba, who witnessed the entire scene, went over to the man and asked him what he had done to merit these two miracles. The man replied that all his life, if anyone ever wronged him, he immediately made peace with the person and forgave him. And even if he wasn't able to reconcile with the person, he did not go to sleep before forgiving him, along with all those who had caused him pain. And he never bore anyone a grudge; moreover, from that day onward, he tried to do favors for those people who had wronged him.

Rabbi Abba began to cry. "Indeed, you are worthy of having Hashem perform many miracles for you."

Elimelech understood the Rebbe's message and decided that he would go to appease the *gabbai* for what he had done. He went straight to the *gabbai*'s home and brought along a bottle of wine. The *gabbai* answered the door and was shocked to discover Elimelech standing there. He struggled to find the right words as he invited Elimelech in. But before he was able to say anything, Elimelech blurted out his apology. He explained that he had been out of line and stubborn, and because of that he had instigated a fight.

The *gabbai* was speechless. Elimelech poured a *le'chaim* for the two of them, and he promised that he would never cause trouble again. The *gabbai* thanked Elimelech for his forthrightness and expressed his amazement that Elimelech was apologizing when, in fact, the *gabbai* was the one at fault. But Elimelech repeated his point. He was at fault and he would never let it happen again. The *gabbai* thanked Elimelech and wished him well.

Elimelech returned to his dormitory, feeling empowered. With his adrenaline pumping, he could not fall asleep. At first he twisted and turned, and then he decided that he would try to learn a little bit. He did not want to wake up his roommates by turning on the light so instead he lit a small candle and began to learn by candlelight.

After a short while, Elimelech became very tired and fell asleep on the *sefer* he was learning. The candle continued to burn while Elimelech slept soundly. Suddenly, the table moved and the candle fell onto Elimelech's bed. Within seconds, his pillow and blanket were engulfed in flames, and the room filled with smoke. Elimelech started to cough and woke up. Startled, he awakened his roommates and they ran out of the room.

By the time the fire was brought under control, the entire room was destroyed. Elimelech and his roommates had escaped in the nick of time. Elimelech's clothing and possessions were ruined, but he was very grateful that he was alive.

Only then did Elimelech realize the magnitude of the Rebbe's message. Just as had happened to the man observed by Rabbi Abba, Elimelech's vatranus — his appeasement and apology — had saved his life.

All because he was man enough to say, "I'm sorry."

The Strength of a Tear

DURING THE LATE 1800'S AND EARLY 1900'S, CON-scription into the Polish Army was the equivalent of a spiritual death. Living together, side by side, with non-

Jewish soldiers exposed these young Jewish souls to the worst spiritual dangers. They were forced to work seven days a week and desecrate the Shabbos. There were no kosher meals. Unless one was prepared to starve, he would have to eat *chazer* to survive. Perhaps a young man could manage for a month or two, but after five years, the fellow who left the army bore no resemblance to the one who went in. If a young man received his draft notice, he had to resort to extreme measures to avoid being taken into the army.

Anyone who weighed less than 45-50 kilograms (100-110 pounds) was given an exemption from serving. Some of the young men were so determined to earn an exemption that they went on extreme diets. Others, who had the means, would bribe the local officers to receive an exemption.

Anyone who could not manage these two scenarios was left with two undesirable options: flee or serve. Fleeing the country prevented these young boys from having any contact with their family and ever returning to their villages. If they were ever caught, they would be put in prison for twenty-five years. In many cases, the young men had no choice but to serve and pray that they would find the strength to hold onto their faith.

Heshy, a young Gerrer Chassid, came home one day and received the terrible news. Since he was a heavyset fellow, losing a large amount of weight in such a short period of time was not an option. Furthermore, his father was not a man of means, so he was unable to bribe the authorities. Therefore, he was forced to choose between leaving his family or serving in the army.

Heshy went to the Rebbe, the Imrei Emes, Rav Avraham Mordechai Alter, for advice. He shared his dilemma and nervously awaited the Rebbe's response.

"Hust nisht der moss — You don't have the minimum-weight requirement?" the Rebbe asked.

Heshy responded that he was above the minimum-weight exemption.

And then, strangely, the Rebbe repeated his question. *"Hust nisht der moss?"*

Again, Heshy responded that he did not, wondering if he had spoken clearly enough the first time, or if the Rebbe had not heard him properly.

Once more, the Rebbe looked at Heshy, this time more intensely, as he asked him the same question a third time. *"Hust nisht der moss?"*

Heshy shrugged his soldiers and reaffirmed his negative response yet again.

The Rebbe shook his head and walked away.

There were times when the Chassidim struggled to understand the Rebbe's response to their queries and would turn to his brother, Rav Moshe Betzalel, to gain clarity and understanding.

Rav Moshe Betzalel, keenly aware of the predicament, revealed a powerful lesson that was taught by the Rebbe's cryptic response. "The Rebbe is aware of the different options facing a young man who is drafted into the army. The first time he posed the question, he was wondering if you fulfilled the minimum-weight requirement. So he asked you if you had the *'moss* — measure.' When you responded that you did not, he asked you about your second option: if you have the *'ma'os* — money.' When you replied that you did not have the money either, he reminded you that there is a third option, one you did not think of: Do you have *'de'maos* — tears'? That is an option which, regardless of your weight or your financial situation, you can and should employ."

Upon hearing these words from Rav Moshe Betzalel, Heshy lowered his head and burst out crying. He cried bitterly for the rest of the night. The next morning, he stood in front of the draft review board. The doctors examined him and weighed him; then he waited to hear the dreadful news.

It never came.

"Dismissed."

They didn't give a reason.

He didn't have the weight. He didn't have the money. But he had something much more precious. He had *de'maos*. And there's no telling what they can accomplish.

Over the course of his long life, Rav Michel Yehudah Lefkowitz educated generations of *talmidim*. Through his keen sense of intuition, he was able to project the path of his students.

In one family, three of the *bachurim* were known as the best students in their respective *shiurim*. But a fourth brother, Eli, had a reputation as a troublemaker. Many times, the yeshivah thought about asking him to leave, but somehow he managed to remain.

His parents were at their wits' end; they had no idea how to deal with his antics. His mother cried bitterly, praying that he would turn himself around and become more like his brothers. During this time, Eli's parents frequently sought advice from the yeshivah. Most of the *hanhalah* members shared the parents' worries and were very concerned, but Rav Michel Yehudah constantly reassured them that Eli would find his way and would bring them much *nachas* one day.

About twenty-five years later, the four brothers attended a Yarchei Kallah event. The three exceptional brothers had all fulfilled their potential and each was a leader of his own yeshivah. But Eli, the fourth brother, outshone them all.

The father of these brothers, a zeidy many times over, mentioned to Rav Michel Yehudah how grateful he was that Eli had become so successful. Rav Michel Yehudah smiled and reminded the father of his constant reassurance. When asked how he knew, Rav Michel Yehudah responded with one word, "*Treren* — tears."

And then he went on to explain. "Your other sons were all outstanding, but none of them had the power of their mother's tears. Since they were all so well behaved, your wife never had to expend tears on them. But Eli's antics caused his mother to cry, and I knew that those tears would bear fruit."

There is a beautiful thought that connects to these two poignant stories. The numerical value of the word דִּמְעָה, tear, is the same as the numerical value of מְעַט, less, as in the pasuk in Tehillim (8:1): "Va'tichasreihu me'at mei'Elokim — Yet You made him but slightly less than the angels." Elokim in this pasuk refers to angels, but it can also refer to Hashem, in the capacity of Judgment. When Hashem is characterized by the Middas HaDin, then tears — represented here by the word מְעַט, which has the same gematria as דִּמְעָה — can mitigate the pain and the effects of the Din.

What Won't a Mother Do

In the following story, we learn of the tears of a despondent woman and their tremendous power.

RAV YISRAEL BAAL SHEM TOV USUALLY CONDUCTED HIS Pesach Seder in the company of many of his closest disciples. Among them were the Toldos Yaakov Yosef of Polnoya, Rav Dov Ber of Mezritch, Rav Zev Wolf Kitzes, Rav Yechiel Michel of Zlotchov, the Shpolya Zeide, and the Baal Shem Tov's brother-in-law, Rav Gershon Kitover. Celebrating the Exodus from Egypt brought the Baal Shem Tov great joy, as he found within its story the yearly salvations of the Jewish people.

But this year it was different, for something was troubling the Rebbe. Beginning less than thirty-six hours before the Seder, as he attended to the necessary preparations for the Yom Tov, the Baal Shem wore a worried expression. He set out the ten pieces of bread and conducted the search for them. However, even after finding the pieces, which represent the *se'or she'be'isah* — the evil inclination hidden within all of us — he was still troubled. He then told his disciples that he planned on conducting a special *Tikkun Chatzos* service that night, hoping to bring about some sort of redemption.

The disciples sat with their master as they prayed fervently and cried bitterly. But even after their long prayer session, nothing seemed to have changed. As the holiday drew closer, the pained expression remained on their Rebbe's face. A heavy cloud hung over their master and over the entire city, whose inhabitants all sensed that something was wrong.

The Baal Shem Tov and his students went to shul and exalted in the recital of *Maariv* and *Hallel,* but the heaviness remained. The Rebbe arrived home, donned his *kittel,* and set up the Seder plate, yet his deep, mystical thoughts could not break the sadness. During the Seder, the Baal Shem would generally discuss mystical topics and sing joyously. But now, he seemed to be going through the motions without the usual celebration.

When they came to the section of the *Haggadah* that speaks of the decree that every male be cast into the sea, the master suddenly smiled. Then he began to sing and share deep thoughts. The dark cloud was lifted and the ebullient joy of the holiday was restored.

One of his closest disciples mustered up the courage to ask his teacher what had happened. The Baal Shem closed his eyes and tears began to stream forth, as he recounted the following.

> *Hashem had decreed that anti-Semites would stage a pogrom against the people of a nearby village, and all of its Jews would be murdered in cold blood. I tried desperately to alter the decree, but to no avail. Then tonight something happened, and it was able to accomplish what all of our prayers could not.*
>
> *A couple in that small village had not been blessed with children. Although they have prayed for many years, they are still childless. As they conduct their Seder, it is difficult for them to overcome their feelings of loneliness. There are no children to ask the Four Questions and no children with whom*

to share the story of the Exodus. Yet, they have accepted their fate with faith; they don't question the Al-mighty's actions.

Tonight, the woman listened as her husband read about the decree that every male baby was thrown into the river, and she cried out, "How could He do it? How could the Al-mighty allow His children to be drowned in the river? Why didn't He protect them? The Al-mighty is their Mother, and a Jewish mother doesn't allow her children to be tortured and killed in that manner. Why didn't He stop it? Why? Why?

"If I will ever be blessed with children, I will make sure to protect them. I will never let anyone touch my children — they would have to kill me first. I don't understand how He let it happen."

The childless woman cried bitterly not only because of her pain and suffering from so many years of childlessness, but also because of her anguish over Pharaoh's cruel decree to throw the babies into the river. Her husband tried to calm her and reassure her that the Jewish people were saved and the Al-mighty took them out of Egypt. Still, she continued to protest and continued to cry.

In Heaven, a great debate ensued. The decree had been issued that the Jews of the village were to be wiped out in a terrible pogrom. However, this woman insisted that a Yiddishe mamma must protect her children. And if that was the case, the decree should be abolished; the greatest Mother of all, the Ima Ila'a, must protect Her children from the pogrom.

Finally, the decree was abolished. The childless woman saved her village. With her heartfelt tears, she accomplished what we were not able to with our deep and mystical prayers.

That night, the Seder continued in the manner in which the Baal Shem had always conducted it: with great joy, deep insights, and beautiful singing.

The following year, the couple in the nearby town once again sat down to their Seder. But this time, after 20 years of being child-less, they were joined by their newborn baby.

This woman was sure of one thing: she would protect her baby from any harm. Because that is what a Yiddishe mamma does for her children.

A Timeless Derashah

WHEN ARI WAS 21 AND STUDYING IN YESHIVA UNI-versity, he came home to spend Rosh Hashanah with his parents in New Jersey. After graduating high school, Ari had learned in Israel for a few years and had made enormous strides in his observance. But his parents, worried that he would "flip out," had brought him back before he became too fanatic for them.

Although his family was not on the same religious level as Ari, he was very happy to spend Yom Tov with them. His newly married sister and her husband would be joining them, too, and his parents were happy to have everyone together for the Jewish New Year.

Arriving shortly before sunset, he realized that he had for-gotten to bring his *machzor* with him. He was hoping his parents had an extra one, but all the *machzorim* in his house were already being used by other family members. His parents encouraged him to run over to the rabbi's home and borrow a *machzor* from him. The rabbi apologized that he did not have any *machzorim* with English translation available, but he told Ari that he was more than welcome to take a look in the library to see if one of the older *machzorim* appealed to him.

After rummaging through the bookcase, Ari took an old, dusty volume off the shelf. The *machzor*'s brittle yellow pages indicated that it was a *machzor* with a history. He took a quick peek inside and decided it was suitable. Ari was already of the age when most of the words of davening were familiar to him. For the more difficult words, he would either look on with the fellow next to him or manage on his own.

Early on Rosh Hashanah morning, Ari arrived in shul and began davening with intense fervor. In the middle of davening, a piece of paper fell out of the back of the *machzor*. Realizing that many years must have passed since this paper was last read, he unfolded it and scanned its top. It said: *Rosh Hashanah derashah mei'eis Rav Yoel Teitelbaum, 5686, Karaly* (Rosh Hashanah speech by Rav Yoel Teitelbaum, 1925, Carei, Romania).

Ari had heard of Rav Yoel, the Satmar Rav, although he presumed this speech must have been delivered prior to his appointment in the city of Satmar (which was in 1934). Fascinated at the history of the paper, Ari read through the document, which was penned in legible handwriting. He was surprised that the *derashah* did not contain any thoughts pertaining to the Yom Tov; rather, the speech focused on the importance of married women covering their hair. It spoke about the concept of *tzniyus* and cited numerous halachic sources about the seriousness of the prohibition of a married woman not covering her hair.

Ari knew virtually nothing of the city where the rav had served, but he assumed that the level of *tzniyus* in those days must have been better than the *tzniyus* in his community. As he continued to read, Ari discovered that he was not permitted to make *berachos* and *bentch* in front of his mother and sister, both of whom were married but did not cover their hair.

The issue weighed heavily on his mind. He could not dismiss it. He knew that everything in this world is Divinely ordained, and that forgetting his *machzor*, borrowing one from the rabbi, and then discovering this document inside it were all part of a message from the Al-mighty.

Following davening, Ari came home to a beautifully set table. He knew that his mother loved him very much and was willing to make accommodations for his sake. Though his father also loved him, Ari knew that he would be less understanding. So when his father was out of earshot, Ari asked his mother if she could cover her hair. Intrigued, she asked him what had brought on this sudden request, and Ari told her about the *derashah* of the Satmar Rav.

In the middle of the explanation, Ari's father walked in and asked what was going on. As soon as he heard the topic of the conversation, he dismissed the rav's *derashah* and mumbled something about a radical view. When Ari cited the sources from *Shulchan Aruch,* his father grew more and more agitated.

Ari had no intention of upsetting his parents. When his father instructed him to let the matter go, he acquiesced but refused to come to the table for *Kiddush* and insisted that he would not *bentch* at the table either. Furious, Ari's father said he would ask his rabbi if this reaction is correct. However, Ari knew that the rabbi usually said what his congregants wanted to hear. He apologized for his stubbornness and lack of respect, but explained that he just wanted to do what is right.

Suddenly, his mother spoke up. "Ari, if it means that much to you, I will cover my hair for the meal." She left the room and came back a few moments later with a head covering she rarely, if ever, wore. Following her mother's lead, Ari's sister also went to retrieve a hair covering.

From that day onward, Ari's mother and sister kept their hair covered.

Over eight-five years had passed since the Satmar Rav delivered his derashah. It is hard to imagine that many people in his city were lax in covering their hair. Nevertheless, he felt it necessary to strengthen the commitment and adherence to this mitzvah.

But his words would not be forgotten. Stashed away inside

*a machzor, they remained silent until a young man was stirred
and decided to do something about it.*

*When Rav Gamliel Rabinovitch told this story, he noted
that there will be times that we stand up for what we know is
right, yet we feel that nobody has taken our words to heart.
But those words will not go to waste. They will be heard, and
someone will be inspired.*

It may take over eighty years, but it will happen.

Living for the Sake of Living

W HEN HE WAS 15 YEARS OLD, YOSSI, A BRITISH native, was diagnosed with an aggressive form of cancer, which was slowly destroying his body. After eight months of grueling treatments, Yossi was told by his doctors that there was nothing left to do but go home.

In an odd way, Yossi was relieved to hear the doctors' verdict. He had been through so much over the past year, and he had had enough. He wasn't a fool. He had seen the looks on the doctors' faces as they updated his parents on the progress of the chemotherapy and radiation treatments. The cancer had spread, and even these powerful treatments were powerless against it.

But his parents were not willing to give up hope. They continued to do research and consult with the biggest experts in the field. Soon enough, they discovered an experimental treatment that was being administered overseas, in Memorial Sloan-Kettering Hospital in Manhattan. Pleased that there was still some chance for their son, they informed him that there was one more treatment available, which could possibly extend his life. Although it would be quite painful, they wanted him to give it a try.

But Yossi wouldn't hear of it. He knew that the chances of the treatment's success were slimmer than slim, and he had suffered so much already. He just wanted to live out the rest of his days in peace. No more pain, no more needles, and no more suffering.

Yossi's parents were at a loss. How could he not go ahead with the treatment? Yet, ultimately, it was his life and his choice. They turned to Rav Ezriel Tauber and asked him to speak to Yossi, to try to convince him that he should agree to the treatment.

When Rav Ezriel arrived, Yossi respectfully asked his parents to leave the room; he wanted to speak with the Rav privately. "I know that my end is near, and I have no complaints against the Al-mighty," he told Rav Tauber. "The doctors told me that the next treatment is going to take about four weeks, and I can decide whether to go ahead with it or not. But why should I? What will I possibly gain? Over the past months, I have been connected to all types of machines, and my body has been pricked countless times. I can't concentrate for more than five minutes at a time, and I can't perform mitzvos. I understand why my parents want me to go through these treatments; they don't want to give up on me. But is that really a reason that I should suffer for another month? They need not worry; I don't think they have given up hope. Still, I don't want to suffer anymore, just to live for the sake of living."

Yossi spoke with great maturity and intelligence, and his argument was impressive.

Rav Ezriel waited for him to finish his piece and then asked Yossi, "What is the greatest positive mitzvah one can perform? Is it keeping kosher? Shabbos? Learning Torah?"

Yossi admitted that he did not know which mitzvah was the greatest.

"The greatest mitzvah one can perform," replied Rav Ezriel, "is the mitzvah of life itself, as it says (*Vayikra* 18:5), '*Ve'chai ba'hem* — And by which he shall live.' How do we know this? If we are told to transgress every single commandment in the Torah, except for the three cardinal sins of idolatry, immorality, and murder, in order to live, we must do so. If someone tells us that we must eat nonkosher meat in order to live, we must eat it. Not only are we allowed to do so, but we have to.

"Imagine an old man lying in bed in a hospital in a vegetative state. The doctors have informed the family that they can extend his life for one more minute, but in order to do so, every single Jew in the entire world must transgress Shabbos. What are we required to do in such a situation? The answer is that the entire Jewish nation is required to transgress, just for one added minute of life for a man who is 100 years old and can no longer perform any commandments. That is how important one minute of life is."

Yossi smiled, but did not know what to answer.

"Think about that," continued Rav Ezriel. "The Al-mighty created the world in order for us to do His commandments. And if one person can gain one more minute of life, the Al-mighty says, 'I want you to nullify all of those commandments so that he can live one more minute.'

"David HaMelech writes (*Tehillim* 150:6), '*Kol haneshamah tehallel Kah* — Let all souls praise God.' This *pasuk* can also be read, '*Kol haneshimah tehallel Kah* — Let every breath praise God.' With every second of life, we breathe another breath with which we praise the Al-mighty. And that gives Him immeasurable joy.

"Millions of souls are situated in Heaven and are basking in the *Ziv HaShechinah*, the glow of the Divine Presence of the Al-mighty. But there is one thing they can't do: they cannot add to the honor and glory of His kingdom. This gift is given only to those who are living. David proclaims (ibid. 118:17), '*Lo amus ki echyeh* — I shall not die! But I shall live.' And what will he do with his life? '*Va'asaper maasei Kah* — And I will relate the deeds of God.' "

Yossi listened to every word Rav Ezriel said. When he finished, Yossi knew what he had to do. He called his parents in and told them that he was willing to try the treatment. His parents were overjoyed that their child would have one last chance. However, Yossi requested a recording of Rav Ezriel's words. He wanted to review his talk over and over again.

Although he was deathly ill at the start of the new treatment, over the course of the month he began to feel a bit better. Every day, he listened to Rav Ezriel's thoughts and gained strength and encouragement from their profound lessons. The doctors even allowed him to leave the hospital for a few days.

Although the reprieve was brief, Yossi displayed considerable courage and *simchas hachaim* over the last month of his life. To the amazement of the doctors and nurses, and with his parents at his side, Yossi smiled through the pain and suffering, sanctifying Hashem's Name, until he breathed his last breath on Shabbos HaGadol.

With a smile on his face.

From One End of the World to the Other

IT STARTED LIKE ANY OTHER DAY. JOSEPH SASSON, A 9-YEAR-old boy who lived in London, left his house in the morning, and his parents packed him a delicious lunch and helped him with his backpack. He scampered out of the house and ran toward the bus.

But when they came to pick him up later that afternoon, they were shocked to discover that he had never made it to school. At first, they thought Joseph had played hooky, although that kind of behavior was out of character; he was usually well behaved. Of course, they were concerned about this misdemeanor, but they planned on admonishing him and hoping it would never happen again.

However, an hour later, when they still had not heard from him, they began to panic. They called the school to ask the staff members to check if perhaps Joseph had hidden somewhere inside the school. After a thorough search, the school administrators came up with nothing.

Mr. and Mrs. Sasson alerted the police. Before long, a full-blown search was underway. Joseph's mother and father sat in their kitchen, shedding bitter tears. Where was he? Where could he have gone? Why did he run away from home? He was always so happy at home. Something was wrong. Something did not make sense.

The local investigators in London met with Mr. and Mrs. Sasson and then determined that Joseph had not run away. In fact, they feared he was kidnaped. This caused Joseph's parents to become more alarmed. Who kidnaped him? What could the motive possibly be?

The London police met with Joseph's parents and encouraged the Sassons to send out search teams. They also recommended that Mr. and Mrs. Sasson appear on television and other media sources and offer to pay a ransom for their son. They hoped that Joseph's father, Mr. Benjamin Sasson, a man of means, would be able to pay the ransom. Of course, that was assuming that the sole reason for kidnaping Joseph was for the money.

Before Benjamin agreed to appear before the media, someone suggested that he fly to Israel to meet with the great Baba Sali, Rav Yisrael Abuchatzeira. As a Sephardic Jew, Mr. Sasson had sought guidance from the pious leader before. Perhaps the sage would be able to help the distraught father.

A few hours later, Benjamin was on a flight to Israel. From the airport, he took a taxi to Netivot, the home of the Baba Sali. He cried his heart out as he told his story and described his dilemma. What should they do? Should they appear before the media and offer a ransom? Although Joseph's father was hysterical, Baba Sali maintained his composure as always. After listening carefully, he recommended that Mr. Sasson go to the Baba Sali's son, Baba Meir, who lived in Ashdod. He assured him that his son was a very righteous individual and that he was the one who could help him. Confident in the reassurances he had just received, Mr. Sasson took a taxi to Ashdod.

He repeated his tale to Baba Meir and asked him for a blessing that he find his son immediately. However, instead of giving his blessing, Baba Meir opened a map of the city of London, a city which he had never visited, and he closed his eyes. After concentrating deeply for a few moments, he placed his finger on the map and began moving it to a specific location. Finally, he opened his eyes and indicated the spot where his finger was placed. "Your son is right here, and you don't have to worry. He is safe."

Mr. Sasson looked incredulously at Baba Meir. He had so many questions. But none of them were important at the moment. Only one thing mattered: finding his son. He quickly picked up the phone and called his wife in London, and spoke to the authorities who were standing right near her. Within a few short moments, Joseph was discovered, exactly where Baba Meir had said, safe and sound. Soon, Joseph was reunited with his mother, and she held him tightly in her arms. Although he was terrified, he was finally safe.

When he had calmed down enough to speak, Joseph told his story. He was on his way to the bus that he always boarded at the end of his street, when a car with two men pulled up next to him and asked him if his father's name was Benjamin. When he replied in the affirmative, they grabbed him and shoved him into a car. They brought him to a nearby warehouse, where the thugs gagged him and tied his hands. They warned him that he better stay put, but then they went into the next room and drank lots of whiskey. Before long, they were completely drunk. Joseph described how he was able to wiggle free and then run for his life, until he had come to an alleyway where he found an empty building and managed to slip inside. Since then, he was just waiting there quietly, hoping that someone would find him and save him.

Benjamin listened on the phone from Baba Meir's house as Joseph described what had happened. When Joseph finished speaking, Benjamin told his son that he loved him and that he would see him very soon.

Afterward, Mr. Sasson asked Baba Meir how he knew that Joseph was hiding in the empty building — if he had never even seen the streets of London before. Baba Meir shrugged, and dismissed it as nothing.

But when Rav Shabsi Yudelevitch, a famous maggid, retold this story, he explained, "Is it any wonder that he was able to see from one end of the world to the other? When someone keeps his eyes clean and pure, there is no limit to the distance he can see."

This dramatic story contains several lessons. First, we must have faith and belief in the power of our righteous and G-d-fearing leaders.

In addition, we must realize that our own shortcomings are what limit us. Our eyes can see only a limited amount, because we don't guard them the way we should. If we watched the way we spoke, our words would be more potent and our prayers would be more powerful.

With a little more care, there is no telling what we could accomplish.

Believing in Mashiach

Waiting for Yankel

"Achakeh lo — I wait for him [Mashiach]." These two words, which we say every weekday at the end of davening as part of The Thirteen Principles of Faith, are very potent and laden with meaning. But do we really understand how to wait for Mashiach?

The Chofetz Chaim, Rav Yisrael Meir Kagan, was an example of a Yid who waited for Mashiach. Rav Avraham Kalmanowitz, the Rakover Rav, who later became the rosh yeshivah of Yeshivas Mir in Brooklyn, was once asked by the Chofetz Chaim, "Rakover Rav, are you waiting for Mashiach?" Rav Avraham responded that he was. The Chofetz Chaim repeated his question two more times, and each time Rav Avraham answered in the affirmative.

But the Chofetz Chaim was still not satisfied. "Nein, nein, Rakover Rav. Mir darfen varten far Mashiach vi der mamma hut gevarten far Yankel — No, no, Rakover Rav. We must wait for Mashiach like the mother who waited for Yankel."

And then, the Chofetz Chaim proceeded to explain.

*T*HERE WAS ONCE A COUPLE WHO DIDN'T HAVE CHILDREN for many years. With great concern, they went to various doctors to see what could be done, but the doctors were unable to help them.

The couple then traveled to *"gutte Yidden"* for *berachos*, and the Al-mighty had mercy on them. Finally, after many tears were shed and many prayers were offered, they were blessed with a baby boy.

Who can imagine the *simchah* of this couple? In fact, the entire town was overwhelmed with joy. The *bris* was like a wedding, with a band and a sumptuous meal. Friends and family traveled from far and wide to take part in the celebration. The couple named their child Yaakov, but he was called Yankel by everyone who knew him.

After thirty days, the couple celebrated again with a lavish *pidyon haben*, as they handed the Kohen five silver coins and redeemed their child. He was finally theirs. From that moment, every event in Yankel's life was cause for celebration. When he took his first steps, his parents rejoiced. When he began learning *aleph-beis*, his parents treated that day as a Yom Tov. When he became a *Chumash yingel* and then a *Mishnayos yingel*, his parents were overwhelmed with joy.

Before long, he became old enough to attend yeshivah. This was the first time he would be separated from his parents. When he took leave of them, they were filled with heartache. But they knew that this was what was best for him, and they were so proud that he was ready to grow as a yeshivah boy.

Yankel developed into a young scholar and gained an excellent reputation. But then one day, tragedy struck. The police arrested him on the grounds that he had been involved in criminal activity. Word reached his parents only a few days later, and his mother and father did not waste a moment. They boarded a train and traveled to the city of his yeshivah, to try to prevent him from languishing in prison.

His mother went to the arresting officer, who absolved himself of all wrongdoing and sent her to his commanding officer. When she went to the commanding officer, he sent her to the regional director. Eventually, she had an audience with the mayor, the top elected official in the city. She contended that her son had done no wrong: he was an exceptional boy and a budding scholar, who had never caused harm to anyone.

The mayor had no interest in arguing with a distraught mother. He agreed to release the boy, but informed her that it would take three weeks for Yankel to come home from the prison camp where he had been sent. Although she was disappointed that it would take so long, she agreed to return to her hometown until then.

At first, three weeks seemed interminable, but eventually, one week had passed. At that point, she was no longer counting the weeks; now she was counting the days. Only 14 to go. Another week passed and she could hardly control her excitement. She thought of her son day and night and eagerly awaited his return. Now Yankel's mother was no longer counting the days. Instead, she was counting the hours. When there were less than 24 hours left, she began counting the minutes until his arrival.

She made her way to the train station, so she could be there the minute he arrived. With only one hour left, she stopped counting the minutes and began counting the seconds until she would be able to hug her child.

At 12, she heard the sound of the train whistle, which alerted the people in the station of the train's imminent arrival. She jumped out of her seat and ran to catch a glimpse of her son. The train stopped and the passengers began to disembark. She waited and waited and waited some more. But her Yankel never emerged. In a state of panic, she ran over to the conductor to inquire about her son's whereabouts. After the conductor looked carefully at the train schedule, he informed Yankel's mother that she had made a mistake.

Yankel would be arriving on the next train, at 6, in another six hours.

The Chofetz Chaim turned to the Rakover Rav and told him,
"Imagine the anticipation of Yankel's mother during those

*next six hours. That is the feeling of anticipation we must
have for Mashiach's arrival."*

*Although the Jewish people have waited and waited and
waited for Mashiach to arrive, those six hours have never
ended.*

Achakeh lo. . .

Just like Yankel's mother.

The Song of Mashiach

*This story touched me in an unusual way. It speaks to
the manner in which we accept our fate: with dignity and
strength, but perhaps even more impressive: with song and
serenity.*

REB AZRIEL DOVID FASTAG WAS ONE OF THE MOST PRO-
lific songwriters among the many composers of Modzhitz.
But this was no time for singing, as thousands of Jews
were being rounded up from the Warsaw Ghetto and forced to
gather at the *Umschlagplatz* (loading zone). From there, they were
headed for Treblinka, an infamous death camp, where nearly
900,000 Jews met their end.

Only 60 kilometers separated the vibrant metropolis of Warsaw and the eerily silent Treblinka. Nevertheless, the trip by cattle-
car could take three days; guards, food, and ammunition had to
be taken on at various stops along the way. Those in the crowded
cattle-cars were well aware that this was most likely their final
journey, and the length of the trip only prolonged their agony.

Reb Azriel Dovid boarded the train with dignity. As the German
shepherds barked and the soldiers shouted orders and shoved the

helpless Jews into the cattle-cars, jabbing them with their rifle butts, Reb Azriel Dovid tried to maintain his calm. He managed to find himself a corner in the car and settled in for the long and torturous ride.

During the initial leg of the journey, the car was filled with the sounds of children screaming and mothers trying to calm them. Others pushed their way around, trying to find another inch or two to breathe. But after the first few tumultuous hours, silence descended, as many people simply collapsed from physical and emotional exhaustion. In addition, one could detect a deep sense of reckoning, a *cheshbon hanefesh,* as many became lost in thought, with just the rhythmic sound of the train speeding down the tracks as background noise.

Suddenly, a tune could be heard. Initially, it was nothing more than a faint humming sound, but soon enough, one could make out the unmistakable words of the haunting melody: *"Ani maamin, ani maamin, ani maamin. . .be'emunah sheleimah. . .be'vias haMashiach. . .ani maamin* — I believe, I believe, I believe...with complete faith...in the coming of the Mashiach...I believe."

At first, those who heard the singing thought the singer had lost his mind. Singing? At a time like this? But it wasn't long before those around him began to hum along softly, the meaningful words igniting a fire inside their broken souls. The song transported them from their dreary, hopeless situation, to one where This World and the Next World merge: the days of Mashiach. And if only for a few moments, they connected emotionally to this melody, which gave them reason for hope.

As the sound of the newly composed song resonated throughout the car and beyond, the disgruntled guards traveling on top of the cattle-cars began shouting and threatening in order to silence the inmates. Suddenly, Reb Azriel put up his hand and the crowd grew silent. "*Ti'ere Yidden,* dear Jews, we all know where this journey will end. Soon we will reach the *Olam HaEmes.* But what will become of this *niggun*? How can we keep it alive, to be *mechazeik* others and give them hope for the coming of Mashiach? I promise to give half of my *Olam HaBa* to anyone who will jump off the train and somehow find his way to the Modzhitzer Rebbe, to teach this song to him."

Two men took Reb Azriel Dovid up on his offer. Both jumped from the train. One of them was immediately shot and killed by the German soldiers. But the second fellow made it to safety, dodging bullets as he ran into the forest. He survived the war and eventually arrived in America. Remembering his mission, he went to the Modzhitzer Rebbe, Rav Shaul Yedidya Elazar Taub.

"Rebbe," he began, "I have regards for you from the *Olam HaEmes*." The Rebbe looked at the survivor, who was gaunt and skeletal, but whose eyes were ablaze. Without hesitation, the survivor began singing the stirring melody of *Ani Maamin*. Since his escape from the cattle-car, he had sung this song countless times. It was now part of him, a piece of his *neshamah*. As the man sang the song over and over, the Rebbe sang along, tears streaming down his face: "*Ve'af al pi she'yismahme'ah, im kol zeh achakeh lo be'chol yom she'yavo... ani maamin* — And even though he may delay, nevertheless I anticipate every day that he will come...I believe..."

After singing the tune for a long while, the Rebbe looked up, his eyes red. "I want you to know something. The *kedoshim* walked to the gas chambers singing this song, and they will rise from the ashes and greet Mashiach singing this song, as well."

Meeting Eliyahu HaNavi

THROUGHOUT THE GENERATIONS, EXALTED INDIVIDUALS have merited *giluy* Eliyahu HaNavi, a revelation of Elijah the Prophet. Those who had this opportunity performed specific deeds to earn this unique privilege. Some fasted for 40 consecutive days, while others learned through the night for 1,000 successive nights. These people rarely, if ever, divulged exactly how they met Eliyahu.

One day, Aharon, a simple Chassidishe Yid, came to the Baal Shem Tov and asked if there was any way he could meet Eliyahu HaNavi. He realized that the action necessary to warrant such a meeting was probably above his capabilities, but he asked nonetheless. Thus, he was surprised when he was told that he could meet Eliyahu. The Baal Shem Tov instructed him to purchase a large basket, fill it with food for Shabbos, and bring it to a town that was two days away by wagon. When he expressed doubt that such a simple assignment could bring about such a lofty goal, the Baal Shem assured him that if he would do this, he would meet Eliyahu.

Aharon bought a large basket and filled it with all the food a person would need for Shabbos. He placed the basket in a wagon and set out on his trip on Wednesday. As expected, he reached his destination on Friday. After davening in the shul on Leil Shabbos, he waited for an invitation, but none was forthcoming. He had no choice but to knock on a door with a *mezuzah* and ask for a place to eat. A widowed woman and her young son answered and invited him in for the meal. He happily handed them the basket of food, assuming that now he would meet Eliyahu. He waited the entire Shabbos, but was disappointed that Eliyahu did not come.

He thanked the widow and her son for hosting him and traveled back to his hometown. Upon his return, he approached the Baal Shem and told him that he had followed all of his instructions, but did not meet Eliyahu. Once more, Aharon asked his Rebbe to arrange a meeting with Eliyahu. And once more, he was instructed to prepare a large basket of food and head out to the same village. This time, he was told, he was guaranteed to meet him.

Aharon followed the instructions perfectly. He purchased the food and brought it to the city. Once again, he was not invited for a meal, so he went back to the home where he had eaten the previous Shabbos. Certain that he would meet Eliyahu, he was very disheartened when no one came. As he passed people on the street, he imagined each one could be Eliyahu, but nobody revealed himself as the great prophet.

For the second time, he headed back home and went to the Baal Shem to express his disappointment. He told the story of his travels and his Shabbos, which had not resulted in the revelation he desperately craved. For the third time, he asked the Baal Shem for a meeting with Eliyahu. He was given the exact instructions again.

This time, he did not waste his time going to the synagogue to wait for an invitation, since he knew none would be coming. Instead, he brought his package of food to the home where he had spent the past two Shabbosos. He walked up to the door and was about to knock, when suddenly, he heard a conversation through the door.

"Mamma," cried the young orphan, "I am so hungry and we have nothing to eat for Shabbos. What are we going to do?" From outside the door, the guest listened as tears welled up in his eyes.

"*Mein ti'ere kindt,*" his mother replied, "the past two weeks, we also had nothing to eat. But each time, Eliyahu HaNavi brought us a package of food. Don't worry. I'm sure he will come again."

Aharon listened to the mother and her son crying softly. He waited a few minutes, knocked on the door, and then presented them with the food they needed so badly.

As he walked out of their home, they thanked him profusely.

Aharon finally got the message the Baal Shem was trying to convey.

In a small way, there is a bit of Eliyahu inside each and every one of us. Whenever a person is the bearer of good news, he becomes a mevaser tov, one who proclaims good tidings, heralding redemption and salvation for those in need.

"HaRachaman Hu yishlach lanu es Eliyahu HaNavi zachur

la'tov vi'vaser lanu besoros tovos yeshuos ve'nechamos —
May the compassionate One send us Eliyahu, the Prophet —
who is remembered for good — to proclaim to us good tidings,
salvations, and consolations."

A Perfect Perspective

*I*N DECEMBER 1971, RAV SHLOMO KOOK, THE CHIEF RABBI
of Rehovot, was driving his car when it was hit by an oncoming train. Rav Shlomo, who was 42, was killed, along with his
40-year-old wife, Yehudis, and two of their children, Menachem,
10, and Nachman, 3. The tragedy rattled the entire country, as the
rav was beloved by both the Ashkenazi and Sephardi communities
and was respected by Knesset members, as well.

Thousands came to the funeral, and a steady stream of people
visited his home during the week of *shivah*. When Rav Elazar Menachem Shach, the rosh yeshivah of Yeshivas Ponovezh, entered
the house, he spoke to all the *aveilim* and delivered a meaningful
message.

"History has taught us that our greatest misfortunes lead us to
a better understanding of Hashem's kindness and goodness. We
have no idea what is good for us and what is not."

To illustrate this point, he cited a prime example. "When World
War II broke out, the Russian authorities announced that anyone
who wished to leave the country would be permitted to do so.
Although the Russians were generally rigid about allowing anyone
to leave, they seemingly relaxed their exit-visa requirements at
that time. Thousands of Jews grabbed hold of this opportunity and
prepared to leave the country. However, some people were suspi-
cious of this supposed benevolence on the part of the infamously
cruel government, and they decided to remain put.

"Shortly thereafter, the police arrested all those who had tried to leave and charged them with treason; they were exiled to the frozen gulags of Siberia. This appeared to be a horrible decree. Siberia was an unforgiving land, which had claimed the lives of thousands. Those exiles stood little chance of survival. Their relatives mourned their fate.

"But in retrospect, not only was this not a tragedy for those families, it was their salvation, because they were no longer within the deadly clutches of the Nazis. Most of the people who were sent to the Siberian wasteland survived. Of those who remained behind, thousands were either captured by the Nazis or killed in the bombings."

Rav Shach concluded. "You see, we are unable to determine what is good for us and what is not. Although you are suffering, you must trust the *Ribbono Shel Olam.*"

Most of the *aveilim* accepted Rav Shach's words. But Rav Avraham Yitzchak Kook, Rav Shlomo's brother and a *talmid* of Rav Shach, was still not satisfied. "This is true when a tragedy contains no loss of life. Then you can hope that everything will turn out for the best. You can believe that this suffering is a small exchange for a greater good that will happen. But when lives are lost, when a father, mother, and two children die, where is the goodness?"

Rav Shach listened to his *talmid*'s question and felt his pain. Then he replied, "Life is not the most valuable commodity for a human being, even for a non-Jew. Think about it. People are willing to sacrifice their lives for a greater good. This holds true for everyone, but even more for a Jew. We know of the *aveiros* one may not transgress, even if it means giving up his life. So we see clearly that there are values greater than human life. And because of that, we are prepared to sacrifice ourselves for those values.

"If this tragedy will bring about *kiddush Sheim Shamayim*, then that is greater than life. If the manner in which these deaths are accepted, and the merits accumulated as a result, bring a *kiddush Sheim Shamayim*, then these deaths will not be viewed as a bad thing, but as something that caused immeasurable good, in this world and the Next.

"I am certain that if the deceased were asked if they were willing to do this for *kiddush Sheim Shamayim,* they would have agreed wholeheartedly. And for this reason, we can proclaim, '*Gam zu le'tovah!*' "

Rav Shach then cried together with the *mishpachah,* as they accepted the *gzar din* with love.

Sometimes, events seem so tragic that it is difficult to grasp how good can come from them. But we must believe that everything the Al-mighty does is for the good.

The Sfas Emes (Vayeitzei 5658) quotes a Midrash (Bereishis Rabbah, Vayeitzei 70), which states that the Al-mighty looked at the language of our Avos and from their words, He created a key for the redemption of their children. Yaakov said, "Ve'hayah Hashem li leiLokim — And Hashem will be a G-d to me" (Bereishis 28:21). The promises for our salvation also come with the word, "ve'hayah," as in, "Ve'hayah ba'yom hahu yitaka be'shofar gadol — And it shall be on that day that a great shofar will be blown"(Yeshayah 27:13).

The Sfas Emes points out that the letter vav at the beginning of a verb can change the past tense to the future, and the future tense to the past. Hayah means: it was. The vav at the beginning of ve'hayah changes the tense to the future, changing the meaning to: it will be. Perhaps we can take this insight and extend it to better appreciate the meaning of the Midrash.

The letter vav can represent the word vav, which means a hook. The past presents many difficulties and questions. However, the vav, the hook that symbolizes our unbreakable connection to the Al-mighty, will enable us to appreciate the transformation of the past to the future — and the revelation that will accompany it.

What a revelation it will be!

Believing in Others

Knocking on Doors

*I*T WAS NOT THE TYPE OF SEND-OFF SHMUEL WOULD HAVE expected from the Steipler Gaon, Rav Yaakov Yisrael Kanievsky. Shmuel had come to Bnei Brak to discuss a number of issues with the Steipler. Then, as Shmuel was ready to leave, the Steipler told him, "*Shick ah grus tzu Yitzchak Stollman* — Send regards to Yitzchak Stollman," since he knew that both Shmuel and Reb Yitzchak lived in the Rechavia neighborhood of Yerushalayim. Reb Yitzchak, who had been a rabbi in Detroit and a contemporary of Rabbi Leizer Levin, had made *aliyah* and settled in Yerushalayim in 1965.

Shmuel was shocked. It was completely out of character for the Steipler to send regards to anyone. Curious as to what lay behind this message, he relayed the regards to Reb Yitzchak. Perhaps what was even more startling was the manner in which Yitzchak accepted the regards. He was not surprised in the least bit. It seemed like this was not the first time he had been given regards from the great *tzaddik*. This piqued Shmuel's curiosity even more. Unable to control himself, he asked Reb Yitzchak for an explanation.

Reb Yitzchak smiled and told the following story:

When he was a young man, Yitzchak had learned in the Novaradok Yeshivah, which was led by the Alter of Novaradok, Rav Yosef Yoizel Horowitz. The Alter often instructed his *bachurim* to spread the word of Torah by establishing yeshivos throughout the region. Two young men would set out to a town in order to open a yeshivah there, armed with nothing more than their idealism. They were searching for *neshamos*. And indeed they would find them, even before a framework was in place.

"We came to the town of Hornosteipel," said Reb Yitzchak, as he told his personal tale. "Immediately after we arrived in the city, we began knocking on doors, asking families to entrust their children to us and send their boys to our yeshivah. Most were unwilling to do so. But some were willing to give it a try. The Kanievsky family agreed to send their son, Yaakov Yisrael."

Reb Yitzchak finished his story and humbly concluded, "The Steipler sends me regards because I am the one who convinced his parents to send him to the yeshivah we were establishing in his town."

Shmuel was amazed. Had he not heard this story with his own ears, he never would have believed it.

Reb Yitzchak Stollman was the one who had found the Steipler Gaon!

What would the Torah world be without the Steipler Gaon? Without his brilliant set of *sefarim*, the *Kehillas Yaakov*? Without his son Rav Chaim Kanievsky? Without Rebbetzin Kanievsky? It is truly hard to fathom.

When Reb Yitzchak Stollman knocked on the home of the Kanievsky family in the town of Hornosteipel, he altered the course of Jewish history.

What a lesson to be learned. There are millions of Jewish children waiting for someone to knock on their doors. But it takes idealism to make it happen. And even once we find those children and they enter our classrooms, we still must knock on the doors of their neshamos.

Imagine if we knew that a child in our class will become the next Steipler Gaon. We would stop at nothing to find that kernel of greatness. No stone would be left unturned.

Every child can be the next Steipler Gaon. We just have to believe in him.

Sharing the Wealth I

RAV YONASAN EIBESCHUTZ, ONE OF THE GREAT *ACHAronim,* was born in Moravia in 1690. His *sefarim,* including *Urim VeTumim, Keraisi U'Pleisi,* and *Yaaros Devash,* are studied in *batei midrash* around the world. Rav Yonasan was proficient in matters of halachah and Aggadah, and his Torah thoughts and halachic decisions are highly regarded even today.

When he was just 20 years old, he became the *darshan* and rosh mesivta in Prague. Until his *petirah* in 1764, Rav Yonasan served as one of the foremost *marbitzei Torah* of his time: in Prague, in Metz, and in the tripartite *kehillah* of Altona, Hamburg, and Vandsbeck.

Rav Yonasan possessed a strong sense of *achrayus* for Klal Yisrael; this is what motivated him to keep producing his Torah writings. It also drove him to defend and help Yidden with all the means at his disposal.

While Rav Yonasan served as a *darshan* in Prague, the members of the Christian clergy poured forth their anti-Semitic rhetoric on all Jews and their religion. He was often forced to speak at public debates against the church's leaders. Because he always emerged victorious, he was hated by the church, and its members looked for ways to make his life miserable.

At one point, they decided to construct a large church opposite the study hall where he spent most of his day. In front of the building, they erected a statue of Yoshke. Although this vindictive act did not bother him, a fellow with whom he learned did not react so passively. He was infuriated at the disrespect the clergymen had shown and decided to protest against the church.

That night, the zealot took a sledgehammer and broke the statue, but he was caught in the act. He was thrown into prison and sentenced to die. Immediately, the community was thrown into turmoil as they searched for ways to free the man. It was discovered that the prison guard could be bribed for 10,000 rubles. The community activists got to work, but after a week they were able to come up with only 2,000 rubles. They turned to Rav Yonasan for advice.

Upon hearing the details, Rav Yonasan responded that he was ready to give the 10,000 rubles from his wedding dowry. In fact, he insisted on donating the entire sum; the activists could take the additional 2,000 and use it for another cause.

However, there was still one problem. He knew that his wife would be upset when she discovered that he had given away the money. So he decided to go out of town for a few days. By the time he returned, he hoped that her anger would have subsided.

Rav Yonasan gave the community members the money and the prisoner was set free. Rav Yonasan then left town for several days. When he returned, his wife greeted him, but it was not the greeting he expected; he thought she would still be at least slightly perturbed, but she was anything but. With great excitement, she explained that the prison guard had brought over two bags of money. The first bag contained the original 10,000 rubles, along with an explanation that the authorities had discovered his plan. The second bag contained the rest of the guard's own money, since he had insisted that he could not be caught with any money on him.

Although his wife expected him to be thrilled by the unexpected windfall, Rav Yonasan was devastated. He cried and fasted for three days, hoping that Heaven would reveal to him the true reason that his money had not been accepted for the great mitzvah of *pidyon shevuyim.*

After three days, he made a *she'eilas chalom,* and the answer was shocking: The Al-mighty had not accepted his money because he had insisted on performing the entire mitzvah by himself. And for a mitzvah to have a *kiyum,* it must come from a collective effort, with everyone's participation.

Sharing the Wealth II

AV SHIMON SOFER, THE SON OF THE KSAV SOFER AND the rav of Erlau, was married to his cousin, Malka Esther, the daughter of Rav Shlomo Zalman Spitzer. Rav Spitzer was the son-in-law of the Chasam Sofer and the first rabbi of the Schiffshul in Vienna.

Once, while sitting at his Shabbos table, Rav Shimon suddenly let out a *krechtz*; he was pained that he was unable to publish the *kesavim* and *chiddushim* of his father, the Ksav Sofer, and his grandfather, the Chasam Sofer. Although their sacred writings were in his possession, he did not have the money to bring them to light. He felt that soliciting funds for the publication of their works would not befit *gedolim* of their stature, and would constitute a lack of *kvod haTorah*.

His rebbetzin, who was a young woman at the time, heard his painful cry. Immediately, she collected all the jewelry she had inherited from her parents, Rav and Rebbetzin Spitzer. She placed the jewelry in front of her husband, and with profound simplicity and incredible sacrifice, she said, "I am donating all of my jewelry for the publication of my uncle's and grandfather's *chiddushim*."

Rav Shimon was so amazed at her *mesirus nefesh* that he left instructions that this story be inscribed on her *matzeivah*.

And it was.

A Grave Sin?

The Talmud Torah of Kelm was founded by Rav Simchah Zissel Ziv, in order to strengthen the study of mussar. Its students were constantly striving to improve their avodas Hashem. To

*this end, they worked with one another to discover their weak-
nesses and bolster their strong points.*

THE FOLLOWING STORY WAS TOLD OVER BY RAV MOSHE
Weinberger, rav of Aish Kodesh in Woodmere, New York.
When Rav Elyah Lopian learned in the kollel of Kelm, he
and a group of his friends, all *bnei aliyah* (men interested in growth),
decided to form a unique *chaburah*. Once a week, they would get
together, and each one would take a turn admitting his sins in front
of the others. At the initial meeting, a *talmid chacham* of impecca-
ble character, who was humble and refined, stood up to confess. He
stood there silently, eyes closed, contemplating, uttering only a word
or two. Then he said, "I can't. I'm too embarrassed," and he promptly
sat down. Seeing how difficult the confession was for this *tzaddik,*
they realized that their plan was unrealistic, and the group disbanded.

Rav Elyah approached the fellow and said to him, "I would like
to know what your transgression was."

"I can't say… I'm just too embarrassed."

But Rav Elyah persisted and finally got it out of him. "One evening, while davening *Maariv,* I had a distracting thought," said the
man. "After a long afternoon *seder* of learning, I was hungry and I
thought to myself, *I hope that my wife cooks potatoes for supper*."
This was the grave sin of this Kelmer *yungerman.*

That was the greatness of Kelm.

The Last Kaddish

*In 1965, a woman named Mrs. Ravitz, who was originally
from the city of Ravko, entered the Jewish Documentation Center of Simon Wiesenthal in Vienna, to testify about war crimes
she had witnessed.*

*S*HE TOLD THE STORY OF A CHILD NAMED SAMMY ROSEN-baum. Sammy was a fragile child, pale and thin, with dark eyes, who appeared to have grown up well before his time — like many other children in the war years. Sammy was a good boy in every sense of the word. He and his sister lived with their G-d-fearing parents in a small two-bedroom house, with a tiny kitchen and eating area. But they were very happy with their life. Every Friday night, after his mother lit Shabbos candles, Sammy walked with his father to shul. Sammy was only 9 years old when the Germans entered Ravko and turned his life into a nightmare.

In 1940, the SS officers set up a training center in Kasraktin, a city right near Ravko. While being trained in these centers, the soldiers were taught how to harden their hearts to the heartrending cries of women and children; the Nazi war machine had to work effectively, with maximum efficiency and minimal commotion. In the earlier stages of the war, the Nazis would kill 50, 100, and sometimes 150 people a day — relatively small numbers compared to the mass killings in the later stages of the war.

The commander of the training center was a brutal and sadistic officer named Wilhelm Rosenbaum, from Hamburg, Germany. He always carried a riding whip in his hand, and his appearance frightened all those in his proximity.

In the beginning of 1942, Rosenbaum instructed all of the Jews of Ravko to come to the training center and sign their names. The sick and old would be sent to their deaths, and the others would be allowed to work for the *Vermacht*, the German armed forces. All of the Jews did as they were told and signed their names on the list.

Rosenbaum then read through the list. When he came to the letter R, his face turned beet-red. He began screaming hysterically and struck his whip on the table, terrifying the crowd. They felt as though he had whipped their bodies. "What is this? Rosenbaum? Jews?! How can you be so impudent to carry my good German name and use it for yourselves? This family must be killed immediately!"

Frothing at the mouth like a mad dog, he threw the list onto the table and stormed out of the room. His instructions were clear. It was only a matter of time before his soldiers found the Jewish Rosenbaums.

> The SS guards would carry out most of their executions in the clearings of the forest. When they would come back from their animalistic shootings, their boots were always full of blood. Mrs. Ravitz was chosen to carry out the gruesome chore of removing the blood and polishing the boots. That was how she witnessed the beginning of the story. She would hear the rest of it from the Jewish kapo.

On Friday morning in early June 1942, two SS guards escorted Sammy Rosenbaum's parents and his 15-year-old sister to the back of a building. Behind them stood the commander, Wilhelm Rosenbaum. Mrs. Rosenbaum and her daughter were shot immediately. But the commander whipped the defenseless Mr. Rosenbaum, all the while screaming, "You filthy Jew! I will teach you a lesson about stealing a German name!" Finally, he removed his revolver and shot the Jewish man three times. While the victim lay there in a pool of blood, Wilhelm commanded the *kapo* who had watched the entire scene to go and get Sammy Rosenbaum.

Although the *kapo* had never displayed much heart, he dreaded fetching the innocent boy, knowing what the boy's fate would be. But he felt that he had no choice. He traveled in a horse-drawn wagon and stopped in the work area, searching for Sammy Rosenbaum. When he found him, Sammy was holding a large rock, much larger than his emaciated body could hold. With all eyes on him, he looked at the approaching *kapo* and asked him where his family was. The *kapo* could only lower his head. Sammy murmured, "They're dead. Aren't they? I already heard about it. They killed my parents and my sister because our name is Rosenbaum. And now you've come to kill me." He wasn't kicking or screaming; he was simply relating what had happened.

The *kapo* had hoped that Sammy would run away. But now it was too late. The SS guards were watching his every move. He recounted all the details of what he had witnessed that morning. Sammy accepted the report and then requested to be brought to his home for a few minutes. The *kapo* agreed to grant Sammy his last request, and brought Sammy to his house. He watched as Sammy cleared the kitchen table, which was filled with glasses of milk that were half-finished and cereal still in their bowls from breakfast. It was already 3:30 in the afternoon, getting close to Shabbos. Sammy took out of a cabinet six candlesticks: two for his father, two for his mother, and two for his sister. He lit the candles and closed his eyes, as his lips began to move. The *kapo* could hear the sounds of *Kaddish*. Sammy was saying *Kaddish* for his family. When he finished, he stood for a moment longer and stared at the flickering flames.

As he made his way back to the wagon, Sammy suddenly stopped and turned back toward the apartment. He took out two more candlesticks and lit two more candles. And then he recited the sacred words of *Kaddish* once more.

When Sammy came back to the wagon, the *kapo* was unable to contain his curiosity and asked Sammy why he had lit two extra candles. Sammy stated simply, "I lit those candles for me. And I said *Kaddish* for myself."

Unable to control his emotions, the *kapo* began to cry. But Sammy did not. Instead, he wiped the tears from the Jewish policeman's face and put his hand on his shoulder, assuring him that he forgave him for what he was about to do.

They traveled together to the clearing in the forest where Wilhelm Rosenbaum and his Nazi underlings awaited him. Within moments, shots pierced the air and then, Sammy Rosenbaum, the *kadosh,* fell to the ground.

When Simon Wiesenthal related this story, he concluded with the following sobering thought: "There is no monument that bears the name of Sammy Rosenbaum or his family. If it were not for this woman walking into my office, there would be no memory of him whatsoever. But every year in the beginning of the month of June, I light two candles and I say Kaddish in his memory."

The Letters of a Legacy

Through his actions and his words, every parent hopes that he is modeling proper behavior for his children, thus leaving them a lasting legacy. The following two stories, juxtaposed by Rav Moshe Mordechai Shulsinger to teach us a lesson, each tell of a legacy that a father left his child, yet with different messages.

THE FIRST STORY WAS TOLD BY THE STEIPLER GAON, RAV Yaakov Yisrael Kanievsky. In 1914, when Yaakov Yisrael was a young boy learning in the Novaradok Yeshivah in Bialystok, he had occasion to travel to another city. While there, he met the father of a fellow student. The father was overjoyed when he saw Yaakov Yisrael, since he wanted to send a letter to his son. In those days, the postal system was inefficient and unreliable, so finding a courier to take one's letter was reason for great joy. After confirming that Yaakov Yisrael was returning to yeshivah shortly, the father found a piece of paper and quickly drafted a letter to his son. It was not a long letter, but the man emphasized that it was important. Eager to do a favor for another Jew, Yaakov Yisrael assured the father that he would deliver the letter to the boy.

But soon after, World War I began its rumblings. Uncertainty caused chaos; roads were closed and people ran for freedom. During that time, Yaakov Yisrael was unable to deliver the important letter to the boy learning in his yeshivah.

Eight years passed, but Yaakov Yisrael did not forget the letter. He kept it in his pocket, close to his heart. He knew how much it meant to the father and could only imagine how much it would mean to the son.

Unfortunately, during this period of time, the boy's father suffered many difficulties and ultimately died of a heart attack. For Rav Yaakov Yisrael, this only increased the value of the letter. Having been forced to flee from his home, the man's son had very little with which to remember his father. This letter would help fill that void and even provide an ethical will.

With all this in mind, Rav Yaakov Yisrael sent a message to the young man, who had since married and even had a child, whom he had named after his father. Rav Yaakov Yisrael informed the young man that he had a letter for him from his deceased father.

The young man and his entire family were very excited about this new development. In order to give this special letter the honor it deserved, the family purchased an ornate frame in which to display it. The night before the letter arrived, the young man could not sleep. He was filled with anticipation, and feelings of gratitude overwhelmed him. He felt that he was about to receive a message from another world, from the *Olam HaEmes*.

Finally, the day came. There was a knock at the door; the letter had arrived. The young man took the letter, thanked the messenger, and with his family surrounding him, he geared himself to read the letter and treasure every word. He opened the envelope very carefully. A chill came over the young man, as he recognized his beloved father's handwriting.

After reading the first few lines, however, he lowered his head and began to cry. His brother, also standing at his side, could not contain his curiosity and exclaimed, "Tell me what it says! What does it say?" But there was no response.

No longer able to control himself, his brother grabbed the letter and began to read:

My dear son,

How are you? How is your learning? Please do me a favor. When you come home from yeshivah, don't forget — make sure to bring us the sardines.

Love,

Your father

The second story was told by Rav Isaac Sher. Before becoming the rosh yeshivah in Slabodka, Rav Isaac headed a yeshivah in Halisk, where the students learned with great diligence and few distractions.

Since they did not travel home often, the *bachurim* looked forward to the letters they received from their parents. Upon receiving a letter from his father, one *bachur* immediately went to his rebbi and showed him its contents:

Dear son,

How are you? How are you learning?

Please remember that whenever you must make a decision, stop for a moment and think: what would I decide if this were the last day of my life?

The letter was signed, "Nosson Tzvi."

It was written to his son, Eliezer Yehudah.

Rav Nosson Tzvi Finkel, the Alter of Slabodka, was the greatest pedagogical master of the past century, and arguably the father of the yeshivah world.

His son, Rav Eliezer Yehudah — affectionately known as Rav Leizer Yudel — became the rosh yeshivah of Yeshivas Mir in Europe and later in Yerushalayim.

Two letters. In one, the father entrusts his son with the legacy of delivering sardines, and in the other, the father gives his son the tools with which to make decisions for the rest of his life.

As parents, we must ensure that our children know what is valuable and important. Let us not allow our children to think that a can of sardines, or sushi, is the most important thing in the world.

A Crack of Kedushah

THE RADOSHITZER REBBE, RAV YITZCHAK SHMUEL ELIyahu Finkler, was among the thousands of Jews who were forced into the ghetto in Piotrkov when the Nazis invaded his town. During that difficult time, the Rebbe was a source of encouragement and hope to his fellow Yidden.

The Nazis abhorred the concept of holiness and sought to remove all connection to it. Knowing the importance of family purity, and *kedushah* and *taharah* in general, the Nazis worked assiduously to close up all the *mikvaos* in the ghetto; one by one, they locked the doors and cemented them closed.

Like most Chassidim, the Rebbe was accustomed to immersing in the sacred waters of the *mikveh* on a daily basis. The absence of this ritual left the Radoshitzer feeling spiritually deprived. Yet, compared to the horrific emotional and mental difficulties most Yidden confronted each day, Rav Yitzchak Shmuel Eliyahu knew that his desire for a *mikveh* was relatively inconsequential. Still, with the Yamim Noraim fast approaching, he simply could not imagine being unable to immerse himself.

On Erev Yom Kippur, at 3 in the morning, there was a knock on the Rebbe's door. When Rav Yitzchak answered, he saw a young boy, 8 or 9 years old, standing before him. His breathing was heavy, and he seemed excited to deliver his message. "Rebbe, I have some very important news for you. A group of *askanim* have risked their lives to open a *mikveh* for *yechidei segulah*. I was asked to inform various rabbanim and roshei yeshivah of its availability."

The Radoshitzer could not contain his emotion. He was overwhelmed, overjoyed, and relieved that a *mikveh* would be available. He bent down and kissed the young messenger on his forehead and quickly followed him to the *mikveh*.

The streets were deadly silent. There was a strict curfew in place; anyone caught outside would be shot immediately. Cognizant of the risk to his life, the Radoshitzer moved stealthily, led by the fearless young boy. They darted in and out of alleyways, until they finally arrived at their destination. They could see that this *mikveh* had been cemented shut by the Nazis. But apparently, a desperate group of men — yearning for spirituality and purity — had chiseled away at the closure and created an opening that was just wide enough for someone to slip through.

Knowing that any noise could result in their immediate death, the Rebbe and his young companion worked quietly. After a struggle, the Rebbe managed to squeeze inside the opening and let himself down. The boy, whose slight build allowed him easy access, followed soon after. The building housing the *mikveh* was quite large, with long corridors. The darkness was pervasive, but there were a few candles lighting the way; any additional light would have attracted too much attention. Without a word, the Rebbe and the boy began walking along the corridor. The Rebbe could hardly control his excitement as he approached the *mikveh*.

Just a bit further and the Rebbe was ready to turn the corner. When he did, he saw something he would never forget: hundreds of Chassidim. Not roshei yeshivah or rabbanim, but simple Jews who could not stay away, who were ready to risk life and limb to taste the sweetness of *taharah* one more time.

There was very little noise coming from the *mikveh* on that Erev Yom Kippur, but the image of hundreds of people who had flocked to the tiny crack in the wall — for a chance to purify themselves amid a sea of impurity — made an indelible impression on all those who were privileged to witness this *kiddush Hashem*.

Nowadays, we are no longer hampered by the enemy without, but by the enemy within. However, we all yearn for a chance to try to make ourselves a bit better, a bit holier, even as we dwell in a world of impurity.

Is it possible to imagine the sight of millions of Jews, who are trying to draw closer to Hashem and to holiness on Erev Yom Kippur, then and even now? What a tumult in Heaven they, and we, can cause!

How holy we are! How great we can become!

The Whole World Holds of Me

The following story may seem trite, but it carries a powerful message. It is very important for every person to feel that he has others backing him; it is scary to feel alone. Even knowing that one person is behind you can change the way you view yourself, and your standing in this world.

ELI SAT DOWN IN THE BACK OF THE *CHUPPAH* ROOM AND was minding his own business, when an old man sat down next to him. Eli had had a hard day at work and had a lot to think about; he was looking forward to a few moments of quiet, but the man began speaking to him immediately. "Do you know who I am?"

The truth is that he didn't know who the man was, and he really didn't care. But Eli tried to be polite, and he responded that he did not recognize the old man.

"My name is Naftali Green."

Eli was no more informed now than he had been a moment ago. The name Naftali Green meant nothing to him. But Naftali wasn't finished, for he added, "And do you know that the whole world holds of me?"

It seemed odd for someone to say that about himself, and Eli realized that he was not going to get those few moments of peace and quiet he had hoped for. He gave the old man his full attention.

Naftali did not wait for Eli to ask him any questions, but went on to explain. "Okay, so you don't know who I am. But perhaps you've heard of my roommate, Chaim Kanievsky."

This last statement caught Eli's attention. Naftali noticed that he was more interested now and carried on. "That's correct. When I was learning in the Lomza Yeshivah, he and I were roommates. In fact, a number of years ago, I went to visit him in Bnei Brak. When I walked into the room, I asked him, 'Reb Chaim'l, do you remember me?'

"At first, he looked at me in a strange way. Clearly, he did not remember me. And who could blame him? It had been over 60 years since we had last met, but when I told him that I was Naftali Green, he smiled and gave me a very nice *shalom aleichem*.

"He asked me where I lived and what I did for a living. I told him a bit about myself, and then I said to him, 'What an *olam hafuch*, upside-down world, it is. We were together in one room. And now the entire world holds of you, and no one holds of me.'

"I wasn't complaining or anything. I was just stating the obvious and remarking how differently two roommates can turn out. But he took it much more seriously than I did, and he said, '*Nisht emes* — It is not true.'

"I looked at him quizzically. What was not true? Rav Chaim said, '*Ich halt fun dir* — I hold of you. *Un der gantze velt halt fun mir* — And the whole world holds of me. *Memei'le, der gantze velt halt fun dir* — Therefore, the entire world holds of you.' "

Having finished his story, a huge smile spread across Naftali's face. "So you see, the entire world holds of me."

It is easy for someone to go through life thinking that no one feels he is important. But every morning when we wake up, we say, "She'hechezarta bi nishmasi be'chemlah, rabbah emunasecha — You have returned my soul to me with compassion, abundant is Your faithfulness." What do we mean when we address the Al-mighty and say, "Abundant is Your faithfulness"?

The Al-mighty believes in each and every one of us. Imagine a father who gives his child a beautiful suit to wear. And time after time, the child dirties the suit. At a certain point, the father will probably feel that the child is not yet worthy of having a suit. He will lose faith in his child and no longer allow him to wear it.

But the Al-mighty is different. Every single day of our lives, He places our soul within us. And every day of our lives, we sully it and hand it back dirty. One may think that at a certain point, Hashem will no longer trust us and He will lose faith in us. But that's not what happens.

Instead, every morning when we wake up, He gives it back to us, cleaned and ready to be worn again. Because He believes that no matter how many times we have stained our soul, today we will do a better job of keeping it clean. Today will be different, because today, He believes we are destined for greatness and purity.

If we can internalize that outlook, it will give us a feeling of empowerment, which will enable us to reach the heights and expectations the Al-mighty has for us. Lest we feel that no one believes in us, the Al-mighty tells us not to fear: "for the whole world believes in Me, and I believe in you, so the whole world believes in you."

Can you imagine the entire world cheering for you, knowing that you can overcome any obstacle that stands in your way?

With this in mind, we can smile at our neighbor, knowing that "der gantze velt halt fun mir."

Beneath the Surface

ONE TIME, THE HOLY RAV BARUCH'L OF MEZHIBUZH traveled to Zhitomir. When he arrived, the entire community came out to greet him. A huge crowd was gathered on the right-hand side of the street, while only one Jew stood on the left. Rav Baruch'l noticed this and asked the wagon driver to let him out on the left side of the street.

The man who stood on the left was clearly shocked that the *tzaddik* had stopped for him. He began to run away, fearing for his life. Over the past few years, this man had been accosted and beaten for confessing to terrible sins, some of which had incriminated the community and caused its members a tremendous amount of trouble. On one occasion, he admitted to stealing from an inn, and on another occasion, a group of men in the community had beaten him for acting in an inappropriate manner toward several rabbis in the community. It seemed as though he was the man behind every wrongdoing, since any time a sin was committed, he was the one who stepped forward and confessed to the transgression.

Rav Baruch'l saw that the man was running away and chased him down. When he caught up with him, he asked him if he had any children. The man answered that he had one child, a 16-year-old girl. Rav Baruch'l smiled and asked the man if he would be willing to have his daughter marry Rav Baruch'l's son. The beleaguered individual seemed confused. "You want your son to marry my daughter?

Do you have any idea who I am?" But the great rabbi ignored the man's protests, and a *le'chaim* was immediately arranged.

That evening, the townspeople were very confused. On the one hand, they were very happy to hear the wonderful news that Rav Baruch'l had seen fit to marry off his son to a young lady in their community. But on the other hand, they were shocked to hear who the bride was, who her father was. Had the Rebbe not heard the terrible rumors swirling around about this man? Knowing that they must never question the actions of the illustrious rabbi, they swallowed hard and accepted the news.

Toward the end of the evening, one fellow could no longer hold himself back and called the Rebbe aside to notify him of the iniquities perpetrated over the past few years, which had caused his *mechutan* to be viewed as an outcast. The Rebbe thanked him but insisted that he was able to sense a *gutte neshamah*. And rumors notwithstanding, he was happy to be *meshadeich* with this man.

Nevertheless, the next morning, Rav Baruch'l went to visit the rebbetzin of the author of the *Ohr HaMeir*, Rav Zev Wolf of Zhitomir, who had passed away the year before. When the rebbetzin wished Rav Baruch'l a *hartzige* mazel tov on the exceptional *shidduch*, Rav Baruch'l expressed his slight hesitation and asked the elderly rebbetzin about his new *mechutan*. The Rav sensed that the man was *ehrlich*, but everyone in the village seemed to think otherwise.

The rebbetzin acknowledged the negative reports. She knew what people were saying, as the *mechutan* had admitted to numerous misdemeanors over the past few years. "But," she explained, "each time the man confessed, my husband told me that he is a *tzaddik* and that he admits to others' sins to salvage their reputations. 'And to prove it,' my husband said to me, 'a *tzaddik* will come to town in a few years and he will pick up on the truth. He will even arrange for his son to marry the man's daughter.' "

Rav Baruch'l was pleased with what he heard. The *mechutan* was truly a *tzaddik*, willing to endure embarrassment and suffering so as not to bring shame to others.

"Ve'ameich kulam tzaddikim — Your people will all be righteous" (Yeshayah 60:21).

Indeed they are. We just have to train our eyes to see their righteousness.

One Holy Goy

REB MOSHE YAAKOV KANNER GREW UP IN ANTWERP after World War II. Most of the members of the small *shtiebel* where he and his father davened were Holocaust survivors. One of them was Reb Yechezkel Goldshtuff, whose father, Reb Chaim, had been a Gerrer Chassid and a well-known wine merchant in Crakow. His brother, Reb Shlomo, was a son-in-law of the Tchebiner Rav.

Reb Yechezkel was an *ehrliche, pashute* Yid. He was not a big *talmid chacham,* nor was he from the sharp Chassidim whose witticisms were often repeated. Many of the young members of the shul had no grandparents, and since Reb Yechezkel had no children of his own, he interacted with the children and *bachurim* in the *shtiebel* and they adopted him as their zeidy. He spoke to them about this, that, and the other, and inquired about their lives and their learning; most of their interactions were limited to small talk.

When Moshe Yaakov's father became ill, Reb Yechezkel looked after him. He gave Moshe Yaakov encouragement and even shared jokes with him that he could pass on to his father to cheer him up. During those difficult times, Moshe Yaakov developed a close relationship with his adopted zeidy. However, when Moshe Yaakov went to yeshivah in Eretz Yisrael, the relationship waned. On the 27th day of Iyar, 1976, Reb Yechezkel passed away.

About 35 years passed. One day, Reb Moshe Yaakov was reading through the *sefer Mekadshei Hashem,* by Rav Tzvi Hirsch Meisels, the Veitzener Rav. The *sefer* discusses various halachic questions that arose during the war years. In the introduction, he relates several incredible stories that took place in the concentration camps.

Along with the millions of Jews who passed through the gates of horror, there were some non-Jewish prisoners of war. Their fortune was considerably better than that of the Jewish inmates. One of them, a fellow named Winneartchik, introduced himself to the Veitzener Rav as a former Shabbos goy. He knew the ins and outs of Jewish life and helped the Jews whenever he could. In fact, he was incarcerated for trying to save Jews. He became known in Auschwitz as an oheiv Yisrael who helped the Jews on countless occasions. At times, he was willing to sacrifice his life for them. The Jewish inmates marveled at this man; they were sure he was one of the chassidei umos ha'olam.

He once approached the Veitzener and asked him why he does not continue the minhag of eating eggs and onions on Shabbos morning. The Veitzener was surprised that he asked such a question. "Here we struggle to find a morsel of bread, and you want to know about egg and onions?" But Winneartchik insisted that he would get the rare treat for the Rav and his followers. And he did! The Veitzener was moved beyond measure at the man's level of self-sacrifice, and he thanked him profusely for his dedication.

Toward the end of the war, the Nazis tried to flee as the Russian Army advanced. Thus, they headed inward, deeper toward Germany, bringing the inmates along. The Veitzener and many others, including Winneartchik, were dragged toward Braunschweig, a city in Germany.

At that point, the Nazis did their utmost to make life miserable for the remaining Jews. During one of those freezing winter nights, when the inmates were shivering in the open fields, Winneartchik approached the Veitzener and asked him about the Jewish custom of lighting Chanukah candles. The Veitzener smiled and said to the kind gentile, "Indeed, there is a mitzvah to light candles each night of Chanukah. However, in this kind of situation, it is impossible to get what is needed to fulfill that commandment."

Once again, Winneartchik came to the rescue. Somehow, in Braunschweig he managed to obtain the necessary materials: oil, wicks, and matches. It wasn't even a one-night event. Every night, the Rav and his fellow Jews added another light, just as Jews had done for thousands of years. Once again, the inmates were overwhelmed by the sacrifice this gentile had made for them.

Soon after the war, the secret was revealed. Winneartchik was not really a gentile. He had disguised himself as one in order to survive the war. While he was in Hungary trying to save other Jews, he was captured as a gentile. Since, as a gentile, he received better treatment in Auschwitz, he was able to help his fellow brothers and sisters survive in the most challenging of circumstances. He never stopped trying to save his fellow brothers and sisters, and even enabled them to fulfill the commandments they missed so much.

Only one Jew, Reb Yosef Stern from Budapest, was aware of Winneartchik's true identity. He and Winneartchik had been caught at the same time, while trying to save Jews, and they were sent to the concentration camps together. After the war, another riddle was solved. Throughout the war, the Veitzener had a pair of tefillin, which he kept hidden. He risked his life to wear them whenever he could. But puzzlingly, the tefillin were sometimes not in their hiding place. At first, the Veitzener assumed that the Nazis had taken them. But each time the tefillin had disappeared, they would re-appear a few hours later. After the war, it was revealed that Reb Yosef Stern had taken the tefillin for a few hours and given them to the tzaddik Winneartchik to wear.

Reb Moshe Yaakov read the narrative with great interest, but when he read the final paragraph, he was amazed beyond belief. The Veitzener identified Winneartchik as Reb Yechezkel Goldshtuff! How could it be? For so many years, Reb Moshe Yaakov had known this ostensibly simple Jew, and Reb Yechezkel had never mentioned a word about his experiences during the war.

The hand that had lovingly stroked young Moshe Yaakov's cheeks had donned *tefillin* every day, and hidden his actions from the Jewish and non-Jewish inmates, as well as from the Nazi soldiers. The knees of the adopted zeidy that had bounced Moshe Yaakov up and down had run to help Jews in need, and had enabled them to survive physically and spiritually.

As Reb Moshe Yaakov's thoughts brought him back to those years, one verse came to mind:

"*U'mi ke'amcha Yisrael GOY echad ba'aretz* — And who is like Your people, Yisrael, a unique nation [*goy*] on earth?" (*I Divrei Ha-Yamim* 17:21).

Late-Night Stroll

RAV SHNEUR KOTLER, ROSH YESHIVAH OF BETH Medrash Govoha in Lakewood, displayed extraordinary patience with his *talmidim*; he was willing to repeat the same point over and over, not satisfied until the *talmidim's* eyes were aglow with the freshness, excitement, and genuine joy of comprehending the intricacies of Torah.

One *talmid* nostalgically recalled Rav Shneur returning from one of his weekly fund-raising trips and entering the *beis midrash* on a cold winter night. At the time, the boy was a relative newcomer to the yeshivah and was not comfortable with the *shiurim* that were said in Yiddish. Rav Shneur approached him and asked him if he had understood the *shiur*.

When the *talmid* explained that he did not because he could not understand the Yiddish, Rav Shneur took a walk with him and repeated the *shiur* in Hebrew, a language in which the *talmid* was fluent. After two hours, at nearly 3 a.m., Rav Shneur concluded the *shiur*.

The two of them walked back to Rav Shneur's home, completely oblivious to the frigid temperatures outside, comforted by the fire of Torah and the immeasurable warmth, love, and patience that a rebbi displayed for his *talmid*.

The Sweetness of His Soul

We are taught from a very young age to analyze and scrutinize. At times, we carry that attitude into the way we look at other people's behavior. However, Chazal instruct us to judge others favorably. In this regard, no one compared to the Tolna Rebbe, Rav Yochanan Twersky, who was able to perceive the glowing beauty of every Jewish soul; he truly loved every Jew, regardless of observance or ideology.

The Rebbe considered every Jew a close and dear friend. It did not matter if the person was a gadol be'Yisrael or a bareheaded chiloni. In addition, prestige played no role in the manner in which he acted toward others. Whether the fellow ran a small shoe-repair shop or ran the country as the prime minister, the Rebbe loved and truly valued him.

Three vignettes illustrate this point.

EVERY HOSHANA RABBAH, THE REBBE WOULD TAKE THE branches of the *aravah* and cook them in water. The Rebbe held that this water was a *segulah* to keep people safe and bring about *yeshuos*. Many childless couples were blessed with children shortly after receiving a small bottle of this water from the Rebbe, which was always accompanied by his heartfelt prayers on their behalf.

In 1979, the prime minister of the State of Israel, Mr. Menachem Begin, prepared for a historic meeting with the prime minister of Egypt, Anwar Sadat, which eventually produced the Camp David Accords. The goal of the meeting was to make peace between these two countries. There was deep-rooted hatred between the two sides, and some felt that if peace was not brokered, more bloodshed and war were inevitable. Yet some people were pessimistic about the meeting's outcome.

While many hoped and prayed, the Rebbe went one step further. He didn't just see a prime minister, a head of the country; he saw another Jew in need. He took the branches and leaves of the *aravah*, which had fallen off when he had hit them against the ground on Hoshana Rabbah, and wrapped them in an envelope. He enclosed a note saying that when one travels on the road, it is always dangerous. "I know that you are going on a journey," he continued. "Please accept the leaves of the *aravah* as an extra source of protection."

The package was delivered to Begin's home and opened carefully. Upon seeing the leaves and reading the note, the prime minister was overcome with emotion and moved to tears. He never forgot the thoughtful gesture.

One time, the Rebbe traveled to the southern city of Be'er Sheva for Shabbos, a city in which many Jews were far removed from Shabbos observance. He hoped that spending Shabbos there would somehow give them a taste of its *kedushah* and motivate them to become more observant.

On Friday night, 20 to 30 people came to see the Rebbe and bask in his holiness. His beautiful smile and warm demeanor acted as a magnet to bring these people closer to Yiddishkeit. Even the completely non-observant Jews were enamored of him and spent hours on Friday night listening to his pearls of wisdom. Their souls had not been stirred like that in many years.

The next morning, a *Kiddush* was held in his honor. One of the men who had spoken to him the night before decided to make a special dish for the Rebbe, as a way of thanking him for his inspiring words. He did not know that he was not allowed to prepare food on Shabbos. The fellow came to the *Kiddush,* handed the Rebbe the piping-hot kugel, and thanked him for the inspiration. "Rebbe, I think you will enjoy this. I just made it this morning." He had no idea that he had done or said anything wrong. All he knew was that he wanted to thank the elderly rabbi for touching his soul.

The Rebbe was faced with a serious dilemma. On the one hand, he was careful not to put anything into his mouth that had any question of kashrus. Only if he knew for certain that something met the highest standards of kashrus would he consider eating it. This was certainly not the case here. On the other hand, how could he possibly hurt the well-meaning fellow? How could he tell him that the special dish he had prepared was not worthy of being placed on the table? He whispered a silent prayer to Hashem, to help him find a solution to this sticky situation. Immediately, the Al-mighty put the right words into his mouth.

The Rebbe recited *Kiddush* and tasted from the cake that had been placed in front of him. Then he turned to the simple Jew and motioned for him to come closer. "I want you to know that the dish you brought me looks delicious. Would it be all right if I took the whole thing home for myself and my family?"

Instead of possibly causing this fellow irreversible pain, he managed to lift his spirits and make him feel valuable. "What's the question?" the man replied. "It would be my greatest honor and privilege if you were to take it home. I never imagined that you would consider doing that. Thank you so much." The fellow could not contain his smile. He ran home and told his wife that the rabbi loved what he had made and asked to take it home.

Years passed. The fellow felt a spark igniting inside his soul, and he began to learn more and more about his religion. Eventually, he learned about Shabbos, as well. At that point, he realized what the great sage had done for him and how careful he had been not to hurt his feelings.

And that inspired him even more.

It was Chol HaMoed and the Rebbe was returning from davening at the Kosel HaMaaravi, which is something he did every Yom Tov. As he was leaving, he heard the sound of music in the distance. It was not the type of music he would have enjoyed, but he was curious about it.

His escorts informed him that the music was coming from a *simchas beis ha'sho'eivah*. One overzealous fellow added in a cynical tone, "Woe to such a celebration. We can be sure that not a sniff of holiness comes from there."

Indeed, it was a yeshivah for modern young men who were very different from the Rebbe and his followers. The fellow continued to make disparaging remarks about the yeshivah and the young men who learned there. Apparently, he did not realize to whom he was speaking.

The Rebbe wore a pained expression as he said, "How can you talk like that? Who gave you the right to spill the blood of a fellow Jew? These Jews, in their way, are celebrating for the sake of the Yom Tov. Who are you to belittle what they are doing? Just because they don't look like me doesn't mean they're not as good as me."

Deeply disturbed by what he had just heard, the Rebbe asked the fellow who had spread the slander to step away from him. Then, although he was short on time, he instructed his driver,

"Please take me to that *simchas beis ha'sho'eivah*. I want to join their dancing; I want to participate in their joy."

And without any introduction or fanfare, he appeared in the yeshivah building and joined the circle of dancers. The young men could not help but notice the elderly Rebbe. They wondered what had brought this holy man into their building. But his was not merely a token dance. He danced for nearly half an hour, until he had no more strength.

He did what was necessary to remove the stain of slander and disapproval from his heart.

Only after he was certain that the words of negativity he had heard — which had made an impact on his perception of the young men and their yeshivah — were removed from his soul, was he willing to rest.

Ahavas Yisrael at its best.

A Heavenly Kiss

Rav Aharon Kotler, rosh yeshivah of Beth Medrash Govoha in Lakewood, was once zocheh to resolve a shverkeit (difficulty) in a Beur HaGra that had bothered him for more than twenty years. He was so ecstatic that he began singing and dancing.

Later, he explained that he understood why the Al-mighty had opened his eyes to the true understanding of the sacred words of the Vilna Gaon: because even after so many years of not being able to understand the difficult wording, he had never entertained the thought that perhaps the Gra was wrong, and that his question was unanswerable.

Rav Dovid Herschel Meyer, who told over this beautiful vignette, added:

"After twenty years of unflinching emunas chachamim, one is zocheh to receive a kiss from the Melamed Torah le'amo Yisrael [Teacher of Torah to His people, Yisrael]."

RAV SHLOMO BREVDA RECOUNTED THE FOLLOWING incident, which highlights the extent of Rav Aharon's *emunas chachamim*. During a meeting of rabbanim and roshei yeshivah, Rav Aharon, who had just returned from a trip to Eretz Yisrael, spoke enthusiastically and in great detail about the remarkable growth he had encountered there in various aspects of Torah life.

One of those in attendance had the audacity to ask the rosh yeshivah why he did not move to Eretz Yisrael, if he was so excited about all he had seen. The rest of the people in the crowd let out an audible gasp, but instead of pushing aside the question, Rav Aharon said that he would answer as soon as he finished his speech.

The one who had asked the question realized his mistake and approached Rav Aharon and apologized for his chutzpah. Yet Rav Aharon dismissed the apology, explaining that the man had asked a valid question. His response further confirmed the belief and conviction he had in the words of the *chachamim*.

"Rav Chaim Volozhiner, *der tatte fuhn der oilam hayeshivos* [the father of the world of yeshivos], *hut aleh mohl flekt zuggen* [always said], that Torah has been in *galus* the entire time that Klal Yisrael has. In all, there will be ten *galuyos*, where the Torah moves from one *stanzia,* station, to the next. *Un der letzta stanzia fahr Mashiach vet kummen vet zein der galus fuhn America* [And the last exile before Mashiach comes will be the *galus* of America]."

And then, to punctuate his belief in the words of our sages, he concluded, "I have no idea how Torah can grow *oif aza chumriyusdike erd* [on such materialistic ground], *uber oif dem bin ich da* [but it is for that purpose that I am here]!"

Rav Aharon didn't just believe it — he staked his life on it.

If Rav Chaim Volozhiner had said it, then, *"Shechinah medabres mi'toch gerono* — the *Shechinah* was speaking from his throat."* And those words must be heeded.

Because of those words, Rav Aharon's belief in American Jewry changed.

And so did the course of history.

America would become an "achsania shel Torah — *a resting place for Torah," just as Rav Chaim Volozhiner had promised.*

Rav Aharon would make sure of that.

Because he believed in the words of the chachamim — *from Chazal through the Vilna Gaon and his talmid, Rav Chaim* — *through the generations.*

Emunas chachamim in every sense of the word.

A Rebbi Like No Other

RAV DOVID TRENK

DEAREST REB DOVID,

Knowing how much you love stories, I'll begin with a few.

When Rav Gad'l Eisner was appointed the mashgiach of the Yeshivah Chiddushei HaRim in Tel Aviv, a friend of his asked him to define his role. He said, "I still don't know. It depends on what the students need. If they need me to be a mashgiach, then I will be a mashgiach. If they need me to teach a class, then I will teach a class. And if they need me to serve the food in the kitchen, then I will do that. But most important, if the boys need me to be a friend, then I will be their friend."

Every child has different needs, and great teachers are able to accommodate their students. They may not always have the answers. But love for a student overrides all else.

A dormitory counselor was frustrated with the behavior of the boys in his charge, and he decided that he had had enough. When he went to hand in his resignation, the rosh yeshivah asked him what he was planning on doing instead. He responded that his grandfather had been a scribe, and he planned to follow in his footsteps.

The rosh yeshivah complimented him on his choice, but then he told him that there is one difference between the two jobs. A scribe, even if he is writing *Sifrei Torah,* is writing on parchment — dead animal skin. But a teacher writes on the hearts of Jewish children, an imprint that will last forever.

The boy stayed on as a dorm counselor, and went on to become a great rebbi.

No story describes you better, Reb Dovid. You have left your indelible mark on the hearts of thousands. You have given them a reason to believe in themselves, thus writing on countless hearts. Sensing the needs of every *talmid,* you set aside your own *kavod* and give the young man your heart and soul, for nothing is beneath your dignity.

If they needed a teacher, you taught them.

If they needed *mussar*, you chided them.

But most of all, if they needed a friend, you befriended them — and loved them.

And that is something they will never forget.

In Jewish tradition, the number 50 represents an elusive, nearly inaccessible number. Had the Jewish people sunken to the 50th level of impurity in Mitzrayim, they would never have been able to leave Egypt. Conversely, although the Jewish people reached the 49th level of holiness, no one ever achieved the 50th level, the *chamishim shaarei binah.*

While it is remarkable that you have educated *talmidim* for 50 years, even more remarkable is the *manner* in which you educated them. Your 50 years are different from most. You never asked for the best or brightest; you did not feel that was your calling.

Instead, you delved into the depths of the *Yiddishe neshamah*. Where others saw imperfection, you perceived beauty. Where others found weakness, you uncovered strength. Where others noticed only failure, you discovered triumph.

And that is what makes you so beloved in the eyes of so many, but most of all, in the eyes of the *Ribbono Shel Olam*. In you, the *Melamed Torah Le'amo Yisrael* sees a non-judgmental, loving *melamed* — the quintessential rebbi, who has never and will never quit on a *talmid*. Your warm and loving embrace engulfs the child inside us all. Your unfailing efforts and burning desire to see the goodness in others humbles the greatest educators. And every time you refused to give up, we were able to see the beauty you perceived inside us; that's why we treasure the opportunity to be called your *talmidim*.

Gleaning from the guidance of your rebbeim, Rav Kalmanowitz and Rav Shmuel Brudny, you quickly transformed what they invested in you into a peerless warmth, connecting to the next generation and the generation after that. And now, 50 years later, you continue to teach and inspire the *eineklach* of your first *talmidim*.

The *talmidim* of Moreshes Yehoshua are the latest links in a legacy of *talmidim* who owe their lives to you. Today, they look like great success stories. But where would they be without you? Their families, until the end of time, owe you a debt that cannot be repaid.

Aside from the time spent in the classroom, you have influenced *talmidim* in camp, as well. Over the summers of the past half a century in Camp Munk, your ability to connect has reached even the most challenging *neshamos,* who respond to your purity and approachability, forming an eternal bond.

In truth, I came along quite late in the game. It wasn't until I wrote my first book that I had the privilege of meeting you. But immediately, you acquired me as one of your countless admirers and *talmidim.* Your effusive praise can only be taken seriously because it comes from you. No one else can possibly put such genuineness in a compliment. Stemming from the expansiveness of your *neshamah,* you somehow manage to find the right emotion for everyone. A *gaon* in *hergesh,* you have touched our lives more than we ever thought possible.

The Ramak, quoted by Rav Yaakov Meir Shechter, writes that if not for the sin of Adam HaRishon, Shlomo HaMelech would have written *Shir HaShirim* in another manner. Instead of using a parable of a husband and wife to represent our relationship with the Al-mighty, he would have written of the love between a rebbi and a *talmid.* For that is the greatest love that exists.

Reb Dovid, you have proved it.

So on behalf of your *talmidim* of the past 50 years, we say thank you. Thank you for showing the world what a rebbi is meant to be.

Sincerely,
Yechiel Spero, another grateful *talmid*

Believing in Ourselves

Ready to Try

One can glean much inspiration from observing the persever-
ance and commitment of children who are striving to reach
their goals.

*T*HIS STORY IS ONE SUCH EXAMPLE. IT HAPPENED TO A
young man who works incredibly hard in an area that
many find easy to master. His name is Tzvi. He is a bright
boy with much talent. He is a good ballplayer and well liked, but
Tzvi has Asperger's Syndrome. Asperger's is one of over 700 forms
of autism. One of the main ways that this disorder manifests itself
is with communication difficulties. Those affected by Asperger's
often have trouble with social skills and interaction, and generally
do not make eye contact when speaking with other people. Some
develop odd habits: Tzvi, for example, would play with his coins
during class.

Tzvi's rebbi, Rabbi Levine, worked on building the self-esteem
of the boys in his class. To this end, his eighth graders were
assigned a speaking assignment every week. Depending on the
week, they were given a fictitious scenario and had to give a two-
minute *dvar Torah* for that occasion. One week, they made believe
they were speaking at their sister's wedding, and the next week at
their brother's bar mitzvah. They eulogized a great-grandparent

and even spoke at a convention of atheists. After the boys spoke, they would hold a secret vote and choose one winner, who was awarded two slices of pizza. During the course of the year, almost everyone had an opportunity to win. Tzvi, however, never won, as he never tried to speak. One time, he was offered the opportunity, but he turned it down.

Rabbi Levine decided on the perfect culmination for the year. The boys would prepare a five-minute dissertation on the Gemara they were learning. A real *chaburah*. Of course, they were given the support they needed, in the form of the *chavrusa* of their choosing. Some learned with their fathers, while others prepared their topics with older yeshivah *bachurim*.

After each boy had presented his *chaburah,* he typed it up. Two boys in the class were assigned as editors to ensure that each *chaburah* was written correctly and was ready for print.

The program was a wild success.

One day, Rabbi Levine received a phone call from Tzvi's mother. She asked if her son could have a chance to present his *chaburah*. Rabbi Levine was shocked since Tzvi had never spoken before the class, although there was no doubt about his superior intellect. Because he was very familiar with Tzvi's issues, Rabbi Levine was concerned that Tzvi would be unable to deliver his speech. But his mother reassured Rabbi Levine that he had practiced at home and was ready to participate. In fact, not only did he want to speak, but he even asked that his rebbi from the previous year attend, along with the *menahel*. Thrilled that Tzvi was prepared to try, Rabbi Levine arranged for him to give his *chaburah* that Thursday.

By that time, 26 of the 28 boys in the class had already spoken. After recess, Rabbi Levine introduced Tzvi, who stood up and walked toward the *shtender*. But then, as he stood in front of the class, he could not look up and could not say a word.

Standing in the back of the room was Rabbi Levine, the principal, and Tzvi's rebbi from the year before. There was a great deal of tension in the air as Tzvi fumbled with his papers. For over a minute and a half, the room was filled with silence. No one knew what to do. Rabbi Levine held a quick, whispered consultation with the principal, who suggested that Rabbi Levine go to the front of the classroom and help Tzvi along. But when Rabbi Levine approached Tzvi and placed his hand on his shoulder, he jumped and indicated that he did not want any help. Finally, Rabbi Levine quietly offered Tzvi a chance to sit down until after the next boy finished speaking; perhaps he would be more ready then. Tzvi nodded and went back to his seat.

The next and final boy got up to speak. He gave a brilliant explanation on the material they were learning, complete with diagrams and other visual aids. He explained how the Rashba and Meiri both agreed with this explanation. While he was speaking, Rabbi Levine wrote a small note to Tzvi, in which he offered him the chance to speak while sitting down, facing the board instead of facing the class. Rabbi Levine reasoned that Tzvi would feel more safe and confident that way. Tzvi seemed pleased with the idea. As soon as the other boy finished, Rabbi Levine introduced Tzvi once more.

But once again, Tzvi froze. He couldn't say a word. Rabbi Levine looked at him and tears filled his eyes. He wanted nothing more than for Tzvi to be able to break through that invisible barrier that prevented him from speaking. But there was nothing he could do. Rabbi Levine looked around the room and saw that the 27 other boys in the classroom shared his pain. Although they were rowdy and rambunctious kids, some had their eyes closed, some were wiping the tears from their eyes, and some were whispering words of prayer.

Rabbi Levine tried desperately to salvage the moment. He told the boys in the class that sometimes the words of Torah, which are locked in our hearts and souls, are so holy, so sublime, that they never materialize in this world. Instead, they go directly from one's soul to the Heavenly Throne of the Al-mighty. And these, said Rabbi Levine, were the exalted words that they had just "heard" from Tzvi.

Although his explanation sounded really good, Rabbi Levine felt terrible. He dismissed the class for a break while Tzvi hung his head low and sat dejectedly in his chair. Rabbi Levine approached the principal during the break, and they both shed tears. Rabbi Levine said that he was waiting for the moment when, after all the frustration and hesitation, Tzvi would succeed and the class would give him a standing ovation to laud his accomplishments. But it hadn't turned out that way. What had happened was the ultimate failure for a child. And who could know if Tzvi would ever try again?

Rabbi Levine returned to the classroom before recess was over and told Tzvi that he could speak now, in the empty classroom, and he would videotape the speech and send it to his parents. But Tzvi was not interested and just shook his head sadly.

The final half-hour of class went by uneventfully. Rabbi Levine could not concentrate much and neither could the boys. As always, at the 1 o'clock dismissal, the last two people in the room were Rabbi Levine and Tzvi. People with Asperger's often have coordination problems, and Tzvi had a hard time gathering his materials at the end of class. As he stood there in the classroom with this vulnerable young man, Rabbi Levine, who was never at a loss for words, did not know what to say. But as he walked out the door, Tzvi called out, "Rebbi?"

Rabbi Levine turned around. For the first time that day, he saw Tzvi's eyes. For a moment the boy was silent, and then he said the most beautiful thing Rabbi Levine had ever heard. "Would I be able to try again tomorrow?"

Once again, Rabbi Levine's eyes filled with tears. Once again, he couldn't say a word. Finally, he mustered, "Of course, Tzvi, and I'm sure you'll do a great job."

Friday came and Tzvi motioned to his rebbi that he was not ready. When the same thing happened on Sunday, Rabbi Levine assumed that the matter was over and done with. But Monday morning, with no solicitation, Tzvi looked at his rebbi and said two words, "I'm ready."

This time, Rabbi Levine didn't make any introductions. Tzvi just stood up and went to the front of the classroom. To everyone's heartfelt joy and amazement, he delivered a flawless *chaburah*. As soon as Tzvi finished, the entire class erupted in a standing ovation.

Needless to say, Tzvi was quite pleased.

And he won the pizza.

This story teaches us the power of resilience and believing in one's self. We may fail time and time again, but the next time we are faced with a challenge, we must not be afraid to look up to the Ribbono Shel Olam — one more time — and tell Him, "I am ready."

We cannot know if we will succeed, but we must not be afraid to try.

A Carpool Lesson Learned

RIVING CARPOOL IS CERTAINLY NOT THE MOST COVeted of chores. True, it is a great privilege to bring our children to and from school, but it is hard to find inspiration in this mundane and time-consuming activity. Recently, though, I took the time to stop and learn from a carpool experience, one that taught me a powerful lesson in how to view the world around us.

For anyone who has recently driven the Bais Yaakov of Baltimore elementary school carpool, it is hard not to notice a peculiar sight. Bais Yaakov is nestled away in the quiet and woody back roads of Owings Mills, a suburb of Baltimore. Shortly before one arrives at the school on Park Heights Avenue, one enters a long, winding road. There are a number of beautiful homes lining both sides of this road, with long driveways that prevent the homes from being seen in their entirety. But there is one constant.

A short man stands at the entrance of his driveway from the hours of 3:30-4 p.m. and smiles and waves to all the carpool cars that pass him. Yes, every day, this fellow, with a long gray beard, overalls, and a gray ski hat, smiles and waves. He has become part of the scenery.

I don't know if anyone ever bothered to find out his story. Until now.

On Thursday, November 21st, 2013, at 3:35, on my way to pick up my daughters' carpool, he was in his usual spot. Shortly after loading nine little girls into my Suburban, I notified them that on our way home, we were going to stop by the smiling and waving man and take a picture of him.

I drove up the hill out of the Bais Yaakov driveway and within a minute or so, I reached the man's driveway. As he smiled at us, I lowered the window and asked him if I could take a picture of him, and he readily agreed. After taking his picture, I decided — on a whim — to ask him about his unusual practice of standing by his driveway and waving to everyone.

At first, he dismissed it as nothing more than coincidence. "Every day, I come out to get my mail. So when I see the kids passing by, I smile and wave."

I listened to his explanation but questioned whether he was telling the truth. "If you don't mind my saying this, I don't think that you are telling me the whole story. It doesn't take you a half-hour to retrieve your mail, and you don't have to do it at the same time every day."

For the first time that I can remember, the smile disappeared from the fellow's face. He looked at me and bared his soul.

To tell you the truth, this is why I do it: I had a 17-year-old granddaughter, whom I loved with all my heart. Unfortunately, not that long ago she was admitted to the hospital with a bad case of pneumonia, and she didn't make it out alive. I can't begin to describe to you how sad I was when she died. The pain was so real, I felt a gaping void in my heart.

One day, soon after she passed away, I came out to get my mail. I was terribly depressed. As I turned to walk back to my home, I noticed a minivan passing by, and a young child had her nose pressed up against the window. She looked at me, smiled, and waved. It was an amazing feeling to see that smile and that hand waving. I don't know exactly why, but my pain was somewhat lessened.

The next day, it happened again. The little girl's smile took away some of my pain. And so, I started to make it a habit, as I looked forward to the daily wave and smile. One turned to five and five became ten. And ten became hundreds. With each smile and wave, the emptiness in my heart was somehow diminished. The pain was taken away; the void was filled.

That's why I stand here and wave every day.

I thanked the man for sharing his story and wished him well. Shaking my head in disbelief, I marveled at the unimaginable effect of one Bais Yaakov girl's smile.

It also made me think about how we look at people, and how little we know about their lives, their pain, their suffering.

Imagine if we all began looking at each other differently. Imagine if we all began to smile.

How much pain could we take away from others? How many broken hearts could we fix?

The Power of One

RAV RAPHAEL BARUCH TOLEDANO WAS BORN IN Morocco, where he spent many years bringing Jews of all stripes closer to Torah. Toward the end of his life, he emigrated to Eretz Yisrael and settled in Bnei Brak. Rav Raphael Baruch was a Sephardi *gadol* who was well known for his piety, warmth, and brilliance in Torah learning. He knew how to speak the language of the masses.

During one of his visits to a *moshav*, Rav Raphael Baruch met with some of the *moshav*'s communal leaders. Even though most of the *moshav*'s inhabitants were not religious, Rav Raphael Baruch was troubled that the *moshav* had no *mikveh*. The closest *mikveh* was an hour's drive away, and Rav Raphael Baruch knew that if one had to rely on public transportation, making the trip to fulfill the mitzvah could be daunting. He felt that if the *moshav*'s residents knew more about this mitzvah and its significance, they would be inclined to build a *mikveh* in their area. Thus, the first step was to educate the people of the *moshav*.

Knowing that the *moshav*'s population consisted of both Sephardi and Ashkenazi Jews, Rav Raphael Baruch realized that he needed to get an Ashkenazi speaker, as well, so he solicited the services of the famed *maggid*, Rav Yankel Galinsky. Signs were posted all around the *moshav* and announcements were made at public gatherings. Finally, the day arrived.

Rav Raphael Baruch and Rav Yankel came to the shul and waited for the crowd to arrive. But it never did. The event was called for 8:30. By 8:45, only one fellow was seated in the audience in the men's section, with his wife in the women's section. They waited until 9:00 and when no one else arrived, Rav Yankel suggested that they abandon the project for now and reconvene some other time. He insisted that delivering the speeches that night would disgrace the whole idea of promoting *taharas hamishpachah*.

But Rav Raphael Baruch disagreed. "On the contrary," he explained, "if we can make a difference to one couple, then the entire project will have been worth it. If one person was physically ill and needed an ambulance, would we ever say not to make the call because it will save only one person? Of course not. In the same vein, if one couple yearns to be spiritually cured, then we must do everything within our power to accommodate them." With that, he sent Rav Yankel up to deliver his speech. He would not disappoint.

Speaking as if he were facing a crowd of thousands, Rav Yankel delivered a fiery speech about the beauty and importance of maintaining family purity, and how it can affect generations to come. After he concluded his speech, he stepped down from the podium and Rav Raphael Baruch congratulated him on a job well done. Since the man in the audience appeared to be an Ashkenazi Jew, Rav Raphael Baruch determined that Rav Yankel's *derashah* was sufficient.

The two of them then walked over to the man and thanked him for coming. The gentleman, who introduced himself as Noam, appreciated that they had gone through with the event in spite of the embarrassingly low turnout. As they were about to take leave, Noam asked if his wife could come in from the women's section and receive a blessing from both of the rabbanim. Rav Raphael Baruch and Rav Yankel readily agreed, and Noam went to get his wife.

Before coming for their blessing, the couple, who seemed to be in their 60's, spoke to each other for a few moments, occasionally nodding in agreement as they talked. Noam and his wife then approached the rabbanim and thanked them for their words of inspiration. Rav Raphael Baruch and Rav Yankel each bestowed a *berachah* on the couple.

"Before you leave," Noam then spoke up, "I would like to tell you something. My wife and I have decided to do something for your *mikveh* project. You see, we are Holocaust survivors. After the Nazis finished with us, we were unable to have children. We came to Eretz Yisrael to rebuild our lives, but we are alone. We don't have many needs; between both of our earnings, we have enough money to make it. However, we also receive a monthly stipend from the German government. We have never touched it, as we were waiting for the right moment.

"My wife decided that your project is the perfect cause for our money. Hitler and his cohorts brought so much *tumah* and impurity into the world. What better revenge could there be than to build a *mikveh,* increasing the *taharah* and purity they tried so hard to destroy."

Rav Raphael Baruch and Rav Yankel were speechless. The couple donated two-thirds of the entire cost of the *mikveh* to Rav Raphael Baruch. He presented it to the leaders of the *moshav,* who, although irreligious, were extremely moved by the story. They agreed to contribute the last third through the community's fund-raising efforts. Within a year's time, the *moshav* had a functioning *mikveh.*

Today, hundreds of families of the now-religious *moshav* use the *mikveh* on a daily basis.

The revenge is complete.

This story teaches us the power of one couple. Any public speaker prefers to have a large crowd when he speaks. It is good for the adrenaline and energy, and it makes it much easier to deliver the message. But Rav Raphael Baruch and Rav Yankel understood otherwise. They saw the power of one couple and the difference one man and his wife can make.

There is another story that echoes this theme and dovetails nicely with the previous story.

Rav Moshe Shmuel Shapiro was the rosh yeshivah of Yeshivas Be'er Yaakov. Although the yeshivah generally catered to boys from a *Litvish* background, at one point, Binyamin, a very fine boy with a Chassidic upbringing, joined the yeshivah. He had always learned in *Litvish* yeshivos, so he was comfortable with the style of learning and had no problem getting along with the other boys. Still, he was particular about immersing himself in a *mikveh* every day, a custom generally followed by Chassidim.

During those days, the yeshivah was located in a fairly remote area and the *mikveh* was not in use during the week. Until then, there had been no need for it, and heating the water cost money. Thus, in order to go to the *mikveh*, Binyamin had to wake up early every morning and retrieve the key from the *mikveh*'s caretaker. He then walked to the *mikveh* and later returned the key. The entire process took him well over an hour every morning, and the freezing water made the experience challenging and unpleasant. But Binyamin was committed and never missed a day.

When winter arrived, the walk was more difficult and the *mikveh* was unbearably cold, causing Binyamin to cut down the trips to every other day, and then, to Monday and Thursday, and eventually eliminating them altogether.

The caretaker of the *mikveh,* a very *ehrliche* fellow, approached Rav Moshe Shmuel and asked if Binyamin was still in the yeshivah. When Rav Moshe Shmuel confirmed that he was, the caretaker informed him that Binyamin had stopped coming to retrieve the key. Rav Moshe Shmuel approached Binyamin, who shyly admitted that he had stopped going to the *mikveh* because it was too hard for him.

Rav Moshe Shmuel apologized to Binyamin and instructed the caretaker to give a second key to Binyamin, and to heat the water in the *mikveh* every day, to make it comfortable for Binyamin. And he insisted that the yeshivah pay for it. Rav Moshe Shmuel explained that it is the responsibility of the yeshivah to pay for the *bachurim*'s needs — in this case, the need of a Chassidic *bachur* to have a warm *mikveh.*

Many years later, Binyamin is still grateful to his rosh yeshivah for appreciating the needs of one young man.

A Life to Die For

Rav Noach Weinberg, the rosh yeshivah of Aish HaTorah, used to say, "Only after you know what you are willing to die for, can you first begin to live."

Throughout our history, we have always been prepared to die for our religion. From the times of Avraham Avinu, who was thrown into a fiery furnace, we have been willing to sacrifice everything we have for a higher ideal: kiddush Sheim Shamayim. Inquisitors, Crusades, Cossacks, Nazis, and suicide bombers have threatened our commitment to live as Torah Jews, but we have always risen above the fray and lived, truly lived, a Torah life.

We must always keep in mind what is important in our lives. We may love materialism and treasure our money, but if someone would offer to pay us $10 million for one of our children, we would never consider it. Why? Because our love for our children is so much greater than our love for money. The two cannot be compared.

Imagine how excited we would be if someone gave us $10 million. And yet, our children, who are worth so much more, do not generate the same excitement. But if we had perspective, we would learn to appreciate the important things: the Torah and all it has to offer us, our relationship with the Ribbono Shel Olam and with other Yidden, and the blessing of children.

ZEV HAD ALWAYS BEEN A LONER. HE NEVER HAD MANY friends and lacked a spirit and spark for life. Before the Israeli War of Independence, Zev had spent a few months with a group of underground soldiers. However, he never developed a close friendship with any one of them.

At that time, the British imposed strict rules regarding the carrying of a gun. Anyone caught with a weapon was forced to relinquish it and undergo intense questioning. Sometimes, those sessions were debilitating. The British were prepared to use any means at their disposal in order to obtain the information they wanted.

One time, Zev was walking in the street and, in a random search, was caught carrying a gun. Although he insisted that the gun had done no harm, Zev was taken into custody and questioned. After a few hours, the questions became interrogations and force was used. The commanding officer conducting the interview insisted on knowing the names of his colleagues, but Zev refused to divulge their names. He wouldn't even consider it, no matter how severely the interrogators beat him. Zev screamed in agony but refused to implicate anyone else.

In truth, his fellow soldiers were not his closest friends. However, once he was willing to sacrifice for them, he felt an unusual kinship with them, one he had never felt in his life. After days of torture, Zev's leg was so badly injured that it had to be amputated. The pain was excruciating, but he managed to endure and survive.

Eventually, Zev was released from British captivity. He was wounded and scarred, but for the first time in his life, he knew that he was willing to die for something. And because of that, he felt more alive than ever.

Years passed. One day, as he was walking with his wife and children, he met one of the soldiers with whom he had spent those months in the underground. It took some time for the fellow to recognize Zev, but eventually he was able to retrieve the memory of the time they had spent together. When he noticed that Zev was missing a leg, he expressed his sorrow.

Zev responded that he had lost his leg because of this man. This statement caused the man to feel deep remorse. However, before he had a chance to say anything, Zev thanked him.

"You are thanking me?" the soldier asked incredulously. "Why would you thank me for ruining your life?"

Zev smiled. "It was only because of you that I have this." Zev pointed to his wife and children. "I never knew that life was worth living. Only after I was willing to die for something did I realize that life is worth living."

The two friends embraced. The two of them shared a special bond, the bond of those who have gone through the horrors of war and suffering — and emerged on the other side much richer.

> *Rav Noach delivered a talk immediately following the tragedy of September 11, 2001. He mentioned that the most power-ful people in the world are the ones who are willing to die for their cause. On that day, a small group of terrorists had suc-ceeded in taking control of the mightiest country in the world — because they were willing to sacrifice their lives for their convictions.*
>
> *People often wonder what makes the Jewish people so strong. How are we able to survive so much persecution and hostility? Ironically, it is precisely because of the hatred we have had to endure that we are indestructible. Our souls burn strongly because of the innumerable times the world has tried to snuff out our existence.*
>
> *The key to Jewish life is the fact that we are willing to die for what we believe in.*

Pajamas in the Park

SHIMON WAS DEVASTATED. HIS FINANCES WERE A MESS — he owed tens of thousands of dollars to various credit card companies and private moneylenders. Since he wasn't able to cover his minimum payments, he saw no way out of financial ruin. Furthermore, his job, the last of a long line of failed attempts at making a respectable living, was not working out.

How would he face his family? How would he find the will and fortitude to carry on and find another job? How would he be able to face his creditors? With no place to turn, he went to the park to try to find some peace of mind. But after sitting there for two hours, nothing had changed.

Suddenly, a fellow wearing pajamas and shoes sat down next to him on the bench. Shimon gave the man a quick glance and then turned back to stare into oblivion.

The fellow started a conversation. "So, how are you doing?"

"How am I doing?" Shimon replied. "Terrible. My life is in ruins. I have no money and I am drowning in debt. I am about to lose my job and my future looks hopeless. That's how I'm doing."

The man told him not to worry. "I don't know if you know who I am. My name is Warren Buffett, and I am a man of means. I may be able to help you."

Shimon was shocked. Of course, he had heard of Warren Buffett. He was one of the wealthiest men in the world. If anyone would be able to help him, it would be Mr. Buffett.

"You see, I was watching you for the past few hours from my window in the apartment building over there, and I saw how sad you look. So I came down here to help you. Here is what I am going to do. I am going to lend you $2 million today. I want you to use the money well and get back on your feet. One year from today, meet me on this park bench and give me back the money."

Shimon could hardly believe what was happening. Never in a million years had he expected Warren Buffett to appear out of nowhere and lend him money. But he watched as Mr. Buffett took out a pen and signed the check. He had always heard that Mr. Buffett was a bit eccentric, but he gladly accepted the check and thanked him profusely for his generosity.

When Shimon walked away, everything changed. He was a completely new person. The simple knowledge that he had the check in his pocket gave him the self-confidence and encouragement to succeed. He secured a new job and quickly scaled the company ladder into a top position. Every business venture yielded spectacular results. Before long, he began making real money and was paying off one debt after another. By the time the year had ended, Shimon had paid back all of his loans and put away a large amount of money for himself and his family. His wife and children treated him with more respect. Instead of being the neighborhood *nebach'l,* he became one of the more successful and prestigious lay leaders of the community.

On the anniversary of the day his fortune changed, Shimon walked toward the park bench and sat down, as the memories of his past failures rushed through his mind. Like clockwork, Warren Buffett sat down next to him, in his pajamas and shoes. He looked at Shimon and smiled. "So, how are you now?"

"How am I? Spectacular! And it is all because of you. Everything changed the day you gave me that check. With your money backing me, I felt completely different about myself. I carried myself with a new sense of pride; I was no longer ashamed. Consequently, my fortune changed. I found a new job and quickly earned the respect of my peers. I paid off all my debts and put aside a huge chunk of money in savings. And I have you to thank for all of this."

Shimon reached into his pocket and pulled out a crumpled piece of paper. It was the check that Mr. Buffett had given him, which he had never cashed. Just knowing that he had the money to fall back on was enough for Shimon to feel differently about himself. He unfolded the check and handed it to Mr. Buffett, as he once again thanked him for all he had done.

Out of the blue, two men in white uniforms appeared on the scene. Shimon looked up at them, somewhat startled by their presence. "Hello. Can I help you?"

"Yes, you can. We were just wondering if this fellow here is bothering you. This man escapes once a week from the mental hospital up the road. We always have to track him down and find him. He sure is an elusive one." They chuckled at the constant game of cat-and-mouse that they played with the man in the pajamas and shoes.

"You know," one of them explained, "sometimes he even tells people that he is Warren Buffett the millionaire. I hope he didn't give you one of his checks. You know those things aren't worth the paper they're signed on."

The men took "Mr. Buffett" away, and Shimon could not help but smile. After a minute or two, he got off the bench and began walking toward his car. All of a sudden, he stopped. He noticed a small piece of paper, crumpled up, blowing in the wind. If one had bent down to pick it up, he would have seen a check for two million dollars. But Shimon knew it was worth more than that.

Much more.

Each one of us is capable of finding the treasure within. If we would realize that the Al-mighty is backing us every step of the way, we would try harder, go the extra mile, strive for more.

To be sure, Hashem is behind us, encouraging us to do our best. We just have to believe — in Him, and in ourselves.

The Heart of a Soldier

Inspiration is often found in the most unlikely places. In the following narrative, our protagonist finds a priceless lesson in a haven of fun and entertainment. Even there, a person can be inspired; in this case, as he learns about the power of the human spirit.

ELI BORENSTEIN, HEAD COUNSELOR OF CAMP MECHAYA, accompanied his campers on a trip to Busch Gardens Theme Park, in Williamsburg, Virginia. He no longer had the heart or the patience for the rides. Instead, he planned on spending the day looking after his charges and making sure they were safe. The temperature was in the mid-90's, so Eli purchased a soda for himself and sat down on a bench, where he would be available in case anyone needed him.

Standing right near the bench was a beefy security guard enjoying an ice-cream cone. "I know it's a rough job, but someone's got to do it," Eli remarked to the guard, tongue in cheek, as he thought about the guard's uncomplicated and undemanding job. The security guard smiled, and in between licks of his ice cream, assured Eli that he hadn't always had it so easy. "When I did two tours of combat duty in Afghanistan, I paid my dues."

Hearing that the man had spent time in combat, Eli suddenly developed a newfound respect for the hefty guard. Curious about his new friend's experiences, he asked him to share the most memorable moments of his service. The guard didn't have to think for more than a minute. He quickly finished his ice cream and, as if he were now back in soldier mode, related a very inspiring tale:

> This story took place during my second tour of duty. My group was in the middle of a gunfight with Taliban troops. The Taliban fighters had a tremendous advantage over us. They knew the landscape and were familiar with the terrain, aware of the caves and crevices in the mountains, while we had to exercise extreme caution since we were unfamiliar with the surroundings. Many of our men were shot, one by one, until there were only a dozen left. Before long, we realized that we were in the middle of an ambush; somehow, we had fallen right into a trap. The only way to save ourselves was to retreat toward our camp, but we couldn't get out.
>
> One of my best buddies was a guy named Michael. Michael and I had been friends since we were very young, and we had made a pact that if one of us went down, the other would not

leave him on the battlefield. And now, as we were trying to get ourselves out of this mess, a sniper's bullet pierced Michael's chest and he fell down, bleeding profusely. I ran over to him and bent down by his side. But as much as I tried to stop the bleeding by putting my finger in the wound, I was unable to. That was when I grasped that my best buddy was going to die right next to me, on the battlefield in Afghanistan.

Michael begged me to help him. Although I assured him that I would not let him die, I really had no idea how I would save him. The only medical supplies I had were some bandages; what could I possibly do?

The snipers continued to pluck off our men, one after another. With only a few of us remaining, I had no choice but to run toward safety. But my buddy grabbed my other hand. My finger was still plugging the hole in his chest, but the bleeding wouldn't stop. Desperate, I tried harder and pushed deeper into my friend's chest.

And then, I felt something I had never felt before. I felt his heart pumping. As I touched Michael's heart, I sensed how alive he was — and how much he needed my help. At that moment, I promised him that I wouldn't leave him.

And I didn't. I risked my life to save his. I don't know where I got the strength. With snipers' bullets piercing the air around me, I managed to drag his body — while holding my hand in his chest — as I slinked behind a rock for cover and safety.

As he told his story, the security guard relived the experience. When he came to the conclusion, he seemed to travel back to the present day.

Eli looked at the soldier with tremendous admiration. Yet, with a shrug of his shoulders, the soldier smiled and dismissed any notion of heroism. "How can you let a man die, when your finger is on his heart?"

The story is amazing, but the lesson it carries is even more valuable. Often, we find ourselves moved by another person's plight. At first, we feel we must do something to help. But after writing a check, we have a tendency to move on. Perhaps we feel as though we cannot do something significant and because of that, we give up hope.

But if our fingers would touch the hearts of others, we would no longer be able to pay mere lip service. We would have to find a way to help them, change their lives, and alter their future for the better.

Controlling Our Emotions

RABBI HESHY HEILIGBRIM LOVED TO WORK WITH KIDS who had not yet experienced the beauty of Yiddishkeit, and he tried to show them how meaningful a life of Torah is. As part of his job description, on occasion, he would meet with a group of youngsters at a local coffee shop after school. He and the boys would get into discussions about Shabbos observance, the importance of keeping kosher, as well as the challenge of making the Al-mighty part of our daily lives.

However, even when he was with these kids, who were truly thirsting to learn more, he wondered if he was making a difference. Yes, he was inspiring, and yes, they loved interacting with him. But most often, it seemed that they went home and returned to their way of life. And this bothered him.

There was one boy, though, upon whom Heshy had more of an influence. Eric came from a broken home, and he latched onto every word Heshy said. He loved spending time with Heshy and looked up to him as a father figure. Because Eric really had no home to go to, he loved to hang out at the rabbi's house. Heshy's wife Miriam opened her home to everyone, and Eric thought of her as a second mother. In truth, she was more like a first mother; his biological mother was an alcoholic and was rarely home.

The rabbi's family became Eric's adopted family. He loved to play with Heshy's kids and babysit for them. He ran errands for the family and did some of their shopping before Shabbos. This made him feel like he was doing his part in preparing the Shabbos meals he joined. And what meals they were: always so filled with meaning. Eric loved to watch Heshy bless his children every Friday night. Most of all, Eric loved singing with the rabbi, who had a magnificent voice.

Anyone acquainted with Eric was impressed with him. He had a sparkle in his eyes and a drive in his heart. He was the type of kid who was going places. Everyone considered Eric his friend. And certainly, the rabbi and his wife were no different.

One afternoon, in the middle of their coffee club, Heshy decided to take the talks a step further. This time, when he spoke to the boys, he went beyond the theoretical. He brought the discussion down to their level and spoke to the club members with passion about the importance of observing the commandments, and not just adhering to the "peace and love" part of Judaism. Although they usually listened to what Heshy had to say, many of the teenagers did not appreciate this lecture. In their opinion, he was being too forceful with them. They hadn't come for more pressure or more responsibility, and they gave him a hard time and argued with him. The deeper the discussion got, the more argumentative the boys became. Generally, Heshy backed off when any of the teenagers argued with him. Heshy himself did not understand why he did not just let it go this time, too.

After 45 minutes of heated discussion, several boys began to taunt him. A few even mentioned that they would stop attending the coffee club gatherings, while some of the boys just made noise and disturbed the conversation. There was palpable tension in the room; Heshy was extremely upset by what some of the boys had said, and wanted to get out of there before he would lash back in retaliation.

Eric hated to see his mentor mistreated. He knew that Heshy had good intentions, and he couldn't understand why his friends were so stubborn and rude. He immediately ran over to Heshy and asked him if he could speak to him for a second, but Heshy did not want to speak to anyone. He apologized abruptly to Eric and strode toward his car.

Heshy felt terrible, but he was so worked up and embarrassed by the way he had been treated that he could not have a conversation with anyone at that moment. Even Eric, for whom he cared deeply, would have to wait. But Eric did not give up. He ran after Heshy and insisted that he must speak to him, and he promised it would be short. Heshy, for his part, would not relent, and said that it was impossible to speak about anything at all right now.

Heshy went home and discussed the incident with his wife. He was embarrassed by the fact that things had gotten out of hand, but even more upset that he had let it bother him. They were kids, teenagers, who knew no better. And he had let them get under his skin. Yes, for pushing them when they were not yet ready, he should have expected the type of reaction he got. Disappointed in himself, he didn't even remember that Eric wanted to speak to him. And so, he never called him back. He was surprised when Eric did not stop by all week, but he figured that he was studying for his finals.

Over the next week, he called a few of the kids from the group and apologized for being so forceful. They took his apologies in stride and assured him that he would have full attendance the next week at their club. And sure enough, he did. Afterward, he walked over to Eric and apologized for not being able to speak to him the previous week.

As they walked to his car, Heshy asked Eric what his question had been. Eric told him that it didn't matter anymore. But Heshy was not going to make the same mistake twice. He wanted to show that he cared — and he really did. Finally, Eric told him that he had heard that if a person is embarrassed by someone else and doesn't respond, he has the power to bless someone who is seeking any type of salvation.

"A close friend of mine is very sick. When I saw how my friends were embarrassing you and you didn't respond in anger, I was hoping that you would be able to bless my friend that he should recover. But I guess it is too late now. . ."

Heshy felt the tears welling up in his eyes. What a lost opportunity. If only he had had the self-control to stop for a moment and hear someone else out, who knows what kind of a difference he could have made? But now it was too late.

If only...

One Not-So-Measly Ruble

THE NEW *BEIS MIDRASH* OF SADIGUR WAS A MAGNIFICENT edifice, built in vintage-Rizhin tradition. The Rizhiner Chassidim believed that their places of worship should resemble palaces of the king. As such, this building was constructed as a beautiful architectural design, complete with all the ornate trimmings befitting royalty.

At the *chanukas habayis*, one of the main donors asked who had given the first donation for the building. As the crowd grew silent, the Rebbe told his story:

A number of years ago, I decided it was time for a new building. But I wanted to wait until I knew that the first donation was completely genuine, coming directly from someone's heart, with no ulterior motives.

One day, a melamed named Reb Beryl, from a village nearby, came to visit. Living on a paltry salary, he managed to scrape together a few rubles every year to donate to Sadigur's funds. This year, he was struggling financially, and no matter how hard he tried, he wasn't able to save more than one measly ruble. He was distressed that that was all he could come up with.

He usually came for Shabbos. But this time, he decided to come in and out on the same day, so he would not miss teaching his class. He arrived on a Wednesday afternoon and came directly to my house. Although he was hoping to gain immediate entry, he was disappointed when the gabbaim insisted that the Rebbe sees visitors only on Friday afternoon, right before Shabbos.

Reb Beryl was adamant that he could not take off from school, but his pleas fell on deaf ears; they refused to allow him entry. Very determined, he would not give up that easily. He sat on the stoop of my home and remained there for the next 36 hours! Occasionally, he would knock on the door and ask if he could see the Rebbe, but each time, his request was rebuffed.

One time, I was near the door and I answered it. As I welcomed Reb Beryl into my home, I asked him how long he had been waiting there. When I heard that it was 36 hours, I was extremely upset. I apologized and explained that the gabbaim restrict visitors only in order to protect me.

Thankful that he was able to get in, Reb Beryl asked for blessings for his family and his students. In particular, he asked for a berachah for a shidduch for his daughter, and for blessings for health and financial security. As is customary, after receiving the blessings, Reb Beryl put down the money he had brought.

But this time, all Reb Beryl had was one measly ruble.

He was so ashamed that he could not look me in the eye.

But when I saw the silver ruble, I picked it up and looked at it carefully. Then I told Reb Beryl how precious this ruble was in the eyes of the Al-mighty. Indeed, in Heaven they cherish such a beautiful gift.

And then, I returned the ruble to him and gave him a blessing that anyone who will hold this ruble in his hand will find immeasurable success. Beryl quickly made his way toward the edge of town, where he planned on getting a ride back to his village.

However, word spread quickly about the blessing he had received. Everyone wanted to hold the ruble in their hands. Suddenly, a bidding war began; it was only one ruble, but it was worth thousands more. Everyone knew that owning this ruble would deliver success and wealth. Soon enough, Beryl sold the ruble for 10,000 rubles!

Now, Beryl had one more stop before leaving. He returned to my home to thank me for the immediate deliverance. He had spent many years teaching the children of his town, but he was never able to make a living. He had borrowed thousands of rubles, and now he would finally be able to repay those debts. But before he did, for the first time in his life, he was eager and ready to give a tenth of his earnings to charity.

He took out 1,000 rubles and placed them on the table. I picked up the money and held it in my hands. I began to cry as I spoke to Reb Beryl. "Beryl, for a long time, I have dreamt of building a special place where we will be able to daven and learn. But I refused to begin building until I knew for certain that I had received a donation that was 100 percent pure and from the heart.

"The gift you just gave me is the first of its kind. I have never received such a sincere donation in my life. You will have the privilege of giving the first 1,000 rubles toward the building of the beis midrash."

*Even more overwhelmed with gratitude, Reb Beryl
returned to his village to teach his charges.*

"So you see," concluded the Rebbe, "the first 1,000 rubles was not given by any of the wealthy individuals who come to spend time in my court. It was given by a sincere and noble Jew, a well-meaning righteous and pious individual, who gives his life for the *chinuch* of children.

"And that is why this celebration is so special."

The Al-mighty does not care how much we give, but how we give it. If it comes from the depths of our souls and the deepest recesses of our hearts, then it will be precious to Him. It does not matter if it is 10,000 rubles — or one not-so-measly ruble.

Returning to Their Faith

Divine Designs
of Destruction

*A*S AN ARCHITECTURAL STUDENT, HYMAN BROWN spent time learning from the great masters, as he dreamt of becoming the most celebrated building designer in the world. When he was a young student in Hebrew school, Hyman learned about the Al-mighty's Divine creation. And now, he had the opportunity to play G-d. In his designs and blueprints, Hyman visualized himself as a G-d-like figure; these grand building projects allowed him, on some level, to experience the feeling of designing a world. For Hyman, there was no headier feeling.

In 1966, Hyman was recruited by his mentor, a Japanese genius, and offered the opportunity of a lifetime, one that would place him at the forefront of the architectural universe. Hyman was thrilled. This was a dream come true. After months of meetings, Hyman began working on the designs for the World Trade Center, which consisted of seven buildings in Lower Manhattan, of which the most well-known were the Twin Towers.

At the time of completion, the Twin Towers were the tallest buildings in the world, symbolizing America's superiority over the rest of the world. Thousands of employees worked in the Twin Towers. As the epicenter of world finance, many other businesses were influenced by what went on inside those famous skyscrapers.

After the World Trade Center opened in 1973, Hyman was on the fast track of many other mammoth building projects. He was sitting at the top of the world. He took pride in his buildings and could not help but feel that they — and he — were indestructible.

But on September 11th, 2001, the New York City skyline and world security were changed forever. Two planes, flown by Al Qaeda terrorists, crashed into the Twin Towers, sending the United States into a state of chaos. Within an hour's time, the invincible towers came tumbling down in a twisted heap of metal and ash, killing thousands and terrifying millions, leaving them with a newfound sense of vulnerability. The indestructible had been destroyed.

After the initial shock, Sheldon Dorenstein, an aspiring journalist, decided to track down some of the professionals who had been involved in designing and building the towers. Yet one prominent architect remained elusive: Hyman Brown. After some time had passed, Sheldon finally managed to track down Mr. Brown, who was now retired and living in Israel. When he asked if he could meet with him, Hyman acquiesced.

During the interview, Hyman described to him the entire process of his personal journey. He described the feeling of being drafted for the project, and the pride he took in building the towers. After a while, Sheldon asked a penetrating question. "Tell me. How did you feel when you saw the towers come crashing down? As the one who designed these towers, what went through your mind? And how has this experience changed your life?"

Hyman was pensive for a moment. Then he spoke candidly. "When I drew up the blueprints for those towers, I knew that one day they would come down; nothing manmade is eternal. But I thought they would come down only when we decided to take them down. If anything that was built by human beings seemed invincible, it was those towers. But when they came down, I realized how wrong I was. In one split second, I came to the understanding and recognition of how small I am and how powerful G-d is.

"I always loved playing G-d. I thought that I was brilliant, all-powerful, and completely in control. But now, I know that I am nothing. I am a minuscule part of His plan. And just as my creations are subject to His whim, so am I."

Then he added, "I am a Jew. Up until 9/11, my religious affiliation consisted of a yearly donation to the Jewish National Fund, and attending the High Holy Days services twice a year. But since that day, everything has changed. I realize that the only manner in which I can attach myself to the Al-mighty, Who is truly all-powerful, is through the observance of His mitzvos and the learning of His Torah.

"At first, it was hard. I was used to being in control and not having my life dictated by a set of rules. But after learning more and gaining a deeper understanding of the commandments, I am beginning to comprehend the meaning of true greatness."

Indeed, the world changed on 9/11. The destruction of the Twin Towers had an impact on nearly everyone. But the profound change in Hyman Brown's life gives us pause for reflection. How different are we than he? Don't we also believe that we are in charge? Don't we feel that we are in control of our own destiny? Isn't our money the fruit of long hours and hard labor? Certainly many of us believe that it is.

It is incumbent upon us to take note of everything that transpires and learn a lesson from every event. When I was a young child on the way to a cemetery for perhaps the first time, my father told me that it is customary to take a different route home from a funeral than the route one took to get there. When I asked him why, he told me, "Because how can you come back from a funeral the same as you came?"

A Dance in Darkness

*G*IDI KATZ WAS ONE OF THE MOST RESPECTED JET fighter pilots in the Israeli Army. The older pilots listened to his insights, while the younger ones pointed to his stellar track record as a source of inspiration and guidance. He was well known for his sharp mind and lightning-quick instincts. But perhaps the most valuable of his attributes was the manner in which Gidi kept his emotions in check. He always maintained an even keel, knowing that his next mission — whenever it would come to pass — would require focus and balance.

Of all his interests, nothing drew Gidi's attention as much as the study of the Holocaust. He was mesmerized by the stories he read. His Savta Bruriah, a Holocaust survivor, never spoke to him about her experiences. But he knew that she had survived the concentration camps, and it meant a lot to him that he was using his efforts and talents to defend the Jewish people.

One day, Gidi's commanding officer approached him with a tempting offer. The army was offering its top soldiers a chance to travel to Europe, to see the concentration camps and tour the places where famous battles took place. Gidi jumped at the opportunity and immediately packed for the trip.

Even though he was not religious, his mother gave him a small *Sefer Tehillim* before he left. She suggested that he keep it in his pocket in case he would want to say a prayer. Gidi obliged, although he did not view this as much more than an information-gathering trip. Stoic fellow that he was, he didn't expect to break down in tears or to feel the need to pray at any point.

The tour took them to the main concentration camps and the surrounding cities. After touring some of the larger cities, they stopped off in Stutthof. Although not as well known as some of the larger camps, Stutthof was a brutal camp, in which over 85,000 Jews were killed.

As the soldiers walked through the eerily pretty grounds of Stutthof, Gidi took in the experience. He was horrified by the abysmal living conditions and was surprised that so many Jews had lost their lives in this small camp. He had read all about Auschwitz, Treblinka, and Chelmno, but he had never heard of Stutthof. He tried to imagine what life must have been like for the inmates, never knowing if this was their last day on earth.

As he passed the barracks, a building in the distance grabbed his attention. As he approached it, Gidi was shocked to discover that Stutthof housed a gas chamber and crematorium, as well. The tour guide informed them that the camp was originally built as a labor and prisoner-of-war camp, but eventually it became part of the Final Solution; its sole purpose was to expedite the murder and extermination of Jews.

As soon as Gidi stepped into the gas chamber, he felt like he was about to suffocate. He tried to imagine the tens of thousands who had died in this room. But instead of the desire to cry or take revenge, the strangest and most amazing feeling overcame him. Suddenly, he felt like singing and dancing. How could it be? He was always in control of his emotions. That is what made him such a successful fighter pilot. And now, he felt like singing? Struggling to contain his emotions, he stepped outside of the gas chamber.

He reached into his pocket and pulled out the small *Tehillim* his mother had given him. He did not know a lot of songs. In fact, he only knew one, and it was not part of *Tehillim*. The only time he ever went to shul was on Simchas Torah, when they sing "*Sisu ve'simchu be'simchas Torah* — Be joyous and glad with the gladness of the Torah." As he stood outside the gas chamber, he sang that song quietly. He tried not to call attention to himself as he moved his feet along with the tune. He could not figure out where this unusual feeling was coming from. At the same time, he couldn't stop himself from being swept up by it.

While he was softly singing this song, his phone rang. Gidi picked it up; it was his mother. "Imma," he said, "you won't believe what just happened. I am here in Stutthof, and I had the strangest feeling…"

As soon as Gidi mentioned the word Stutthof, his mother interrupted him and instructed him to call his savta. Gidi didn't ask why; he just called his grandmother.

"Savta, it's Gidi."

Savta was thrilled to hear her grandson's voice but was curious as to why he was calling her, as they did not speak on a regular basis. He told his grandmother that he was in Stutthof, but before he could continue, his savta stopped him.

"I know all about Stutthof. I was there with my entire family."

And then there was complete silence on the line. No one spoke.

Finally, after a minute or so, Gidi continued. "I walked around the camp and saw the barracks. Our tour guide described the horrific conditions in which you lived. But when I walked into the gas chambers, the oddest feeling overcame me. I felt like I needed to sing and dance. I know you must think this is bizarre, but I stepped outside of the gas chambers and I began dancing there, right next to the crematorium. My mother gave me a small *Sefer Tehillim* to carry with me. And I danced with it."

Gidi stopped for a moment and listened to the sounds of quiet crying on the other end of the line. He realized how emotional it must have been for his grandmother to hear her grandson describing the concentration camp in which she had been interred. But he had no idea just how astonishing his story was.

"Gidi, I am so happy you are there, and that you are able to see what I lived through. As you know, many *korbanos* were sacrificed there."

And then she shared a fascinating story:

I was only 10 years old when I was taken to Stutthof. I knew that my father, Gideon, for whom you are named, had a job but I didn't know what it was. Later, I found out that he was one of the sonderkommando. As part of the sonderkommando,

*he was forced to remove the dead bodies from the gas chamber
and bring them to the crematorium. One night, after a horrendous day of work, he stepped outside with the others in his
group.*

*When the German officer stepped away for a cigarette
break, my father spoke to the men. "The Nazis have taken
away our sense of humanity. We have been transformed into
animals. But today is Simchas Torah. Even if it is difficult, let
us dance and sing and remember that we are not animals. We
are Yidden, children of the Al-mighty."*

*And as they stood right outside of the gas chambers, next
to the crematorium, my father removed one torn page of a
siddur that he saved in his pocket, and they danced and sang
"Sisu ve'simchu be'simchas Torah."*

Gidi, the one who never let his emotions get the better of him,
felt tears streaming down his cheeks. Somehow, the song his great-grandfather had sung some 60 years before had found its way into
his soul.

Inspired by this heart-stopping occurrence — with its obvious
Hashgachah Pratis — Gidi decided to begin his spiritual journey
and find his way back home.

*As parents, we are careful to do everything within our power
to prepare the path for future generations. We hope that our
davening, Torah learning, sense of integrity, and acts of kindness will somehow leave a mark on our grandchildren and
great-grandchildren.*

*But this story teaches us that if we are able to sing and
dance even in our darkest hour, we will instill in our future
generations the ability to sing and dance through the challenges and vicissitudes of life.*

Making Things Right

*A*FTER HOLLAND SURRENDERED TO THE GERMANS during World War II, its government collaborated with the Nazis and saw to it that 75 percent of the Dutch Jewish population was killed. Mark Van Hoolen, a non-Jew who was born after the war, felt guilty about the actions of his country-men and always felt sympathy for the Jewish people. As an adult, he decided to do what he could to make up for the atrocities of his nation. To that end, he traveled to Israel, hoping that he could somehow make things better.

Upon his arrival, he noted that, as with any country, many areas had room for improvement. However, he wanted to choose some-thing that spoke to his heart. As he was walking down the street in Jerusalem, he passed a center for the handicapped. He walked inside and spoke to the woman behind the desk, who informed him that this was the business office; the complete facility for dis-abled children was 20 minutes away by car. He immediately hailed a cab to the facility.

Even before he entered the building, he was impressed by the surroundings, complete with manicured lawns and well-tended gardens. Growing up in Holland, he had always been drawn to its beautiful flowers and landscapes. Now, these flowers and trees gave him the sense that this was a sign from G-d, and it was here in this place, that he could make a difference.

Mark walked up the steps of the main building. He saw many children in wheelchairs; some were blind and others were physi-cally disabled. He approached the front desk and offered his ser-vices as a volunteer. The woman behind the desk told him to wait in the lobby while she asked her manager if there was a need for volunteer services. Before long, he met with the manager. The fellow was impressed with Mark's sincerity and told him that he could work as an assistant in one of the wards.

He was to help out wherever he was needed. He felt that this was a good start for him; his fellow countrymen had eliminated the ability for healthy Jews to live, so it made sense for him to work with Jews who were handicapped and enable them to live more productive lives.

When Mark walked into the ward to which he was assigned, he saw many children lying in beds. Most of them appeared to be almost completely incapacitated. Over the next few days, Mark slowly became acquainted with the children and their parents. There was one child who caught his eye. The boy was a deaf-mute who was mentally impaired as well. His mother traveled an hour each way every day to visit her child, and she would spend the time holding his hands and speaking to him.

Curious, Mark tried to listen to what she was saying. The Hebrew words she repeated seemed to hold much meaning, but he could not understand why she was repeating them. For what could all this mean to her child? There was no way he heard or understood what she was saying. Additionally, Mark noticed that each day, the mother removed from her bag a small four-cornered garment with strings at the end and placed the garment gently over her child's neck. And then, she made a blessing on the garment, kissed its strings, and placed them next to her son's lips.

After a number of weeks, Mark finally introduced himself to the woman. At that point, he could no longer control his curiosity, and he asked her why she continued to talk to her son even though he was incapable of understanding anything she was saying.

Her response made a strong impression on him. "You are right. There is nothing that I say that his body or brain will understand. He is physically and mentally incapable of comprehending what I am telling him. But his soul can understand. I am whispering to him the words of 'Shema Yisrael' and 'Torah tzivah lanu Moshe.' These are the most basic tenets of Judaism. And I am 1,000 percent certain that his soul understands what I am saying."

Mark was astounded. He could see in her eyes that she believed every word she said. He thanked her for her time and apologized for perhaps overstepping his bounds.

But Mark was not satisfied. He could not stop thinking about what he had just heard. The concept was so simple, yet so profound. There is a body and there is a soul. And even though the body or brain cannot understand, the soul certainly does.

Days turned into weeks, which turned into months, and Mark became consumed with learning more and more about Judaism. Until one day, he decided to make the move — he became a Jew.

About 30 years have passed since that day. Most people who are acquainted with Reb Moshe are not aware of his story. But those in the know realize how far his journey has brought him.

All the way back home.

Chazal tell us that when the Al-mighty offered the Torah to the nations, each of them asked Him what is written inside. And each nation had a problem with some law. For example, the sons of Eisav could not live without killing, while the children of Yishmael could not function without stealing.

Conversely, when the Jewish people received the Torah, the souls of all future converts were present, as well (Shabbos 146a; Devarim 29:14). Apparently, Mark was one of those who screamed from the depths of his soul that he wanted to accept the Torah.

And now he has found his way back home.

Captain Yosef

DURING WORLD WAR I, THE RUSSIAN ARMY ENTERED Romania and instilled fear in its population. Rav Chaim Moshe Mandel, a great *tzaddik* who lived in the city of

Tomshavar, tried to live a normal life despite the volatile situation. But soon, chaos descended on his city, and there was nowhere to run and nowhere to hide. To add to the confusion, every family was required to host Russian soldiers, or risk being thrown out of their homes.

The Friday night after the army arrived, the *tzaddik* stood at the head of his table, surrounded by his family, with his *becher* in his hands. His eyes were closed as he prepared to recite the words of *Kiddush* with concentration. An aura of peace and tranquility descended upon his home. What a contrast it was to the disorder that prevailed right outside.

"*Yom Hashishi. . .*"

Rav Chaim Moshe's voice pierced the air, carrying with it a feeling of confidence and faith.

Suddenly, there was loud banging at the door, as soldiers demanded that they be allowed in immediately. But the *tzaddik* did not stop for a moment. It was as if he did not hear the knocking; as he spoke to the Al-mighty, nothing else existed.

"*Va'yechulu hashamayim ve'haaretz ve'chol tzevaam. . .*"

But the rebbetzin and the rest of the family could not ignore the banging. Rav Chaim Moshe's wife inched closer to the door and whispered a prayer for her family's safety. Then she opened it ever so slightly and peeked outside. The soldiers pushed the door open and shoved her aside. Barking orders at the terrified children, they immediately approached the table.

However, when they saw the angelic-looking man standing before them, everything changed. His serenity and peaceful demeanor placed a cloud of awe upon them. Suddenly, the barbaric soldiers stood before him like young schoolchildren. The transformation was stunning.

Rav Chaim Moshe paid no attention to the commotion, as he was completely immersed in his thoughts and prayer.

"*Va'yechal Elokim ba'yom hashevi'i melachto asher asah. . .*"

It was hard to believe that Rav Chaim Moshe did not see the

soldiers, but nothing in his manner changed. He continued concentrating on every word, enunciating each syllable with *dveikus*.

The captain of the group, a muscular individual who was highly decorated, motioned to his soldiers that they should clear the room and stand outside. Without asking any questions, his entourage left the house and stood guard at the door. The family members did not know what to make of the captain, who waited patiently until the *tzaddik* finished saying *Kiddush*. When it was over, the family sat down and drank a little bit of wine. Rav Chaim Moshe gave the officer a bit to drink, as well. When he finished sipping, the officer suddenly burst into tears.

The family looked on in shock at the officer, who seemed so vulnerable as he cried uncontrollably. Finally, he calmed down enough to explain himself. "When I was a very small boy, perhaps 3 years old, I was snatched away from my parents' home."

He closed his eyes and concentrated, trying to remember an event that had happened so long ago. For he wanted to remember; he wanted to somehow transport himself back to that time.

And then he continued speaking. "They came on a Friday night, in two black cars. In one car, they placed my mother and my father, and they took them away forever. They placed me in the second car." The brawny officer continued to reminisce, as the tears continued to flow.

"I remember what they used to call me. My name was Yosef. And I can see my father standing there just like you were, making *Kiddush*. I remember my mother holding onto me with all her strength, as they tried to take me away from her. As the soldiers dragged away my father, he cried out to me, 'Yossel'la, remember, you are a Jew! Never forget it!'

"But I was so young at the time. For many years I was brainwashed until I forgot where I came from. I forgot to speak in Yiddish the way my parents spoke to me. But now, it all came back to me; when I saw the way you were holding the cup, you looked exactly like my father did when they grabbed him away. Yes, now

I am sure of it. My father was a Jew, my mother was a Jew, and I am a Jew."

The soldiers were waiting outside the house, but the captain was in no rush. He washed his hands with the rest of the family, and he joined them for their Shabbos meal. Rav Chaim Moshe spoke to him during the *seudah,* giving him strength and encouragement. He sang Shabbos songs with him, and explained the foundations of Torah and Yiddishkeit.

And finally, after a lengthy Shabbos meal, the captain thanked the *tzaddik* and his wife for a beautiful experience. Then he placed his cap back on his head, wiped away his tears, and stepped out into the street, feeling at peace with himself.

Captain Yosef had found his way home.

We are privileged to practice Judaism openly and freely, yet there are so many Jewish practices that we take for granted. To an outsider looking in on a Shabbos meal or Kiddush, these rituals can be life transforming.
Let us see to it that they are life changing for us, as well.

Of Soccer and Sickness

GROWING UP IN HAIFA, YORAM LOVED TO PLAY BALL, and his favorite game was soccer. When he was 9 years old, he would spend hours watching the games on television. Afterward, he would run outside and pretend that he was a professional soccer player going in for the game-winning goal. He loved the way the announcers would scream when the players scored, and he loved to imitate the manner in which the players ran around the field in celebration after they scored. He imagined that one day, he would be the one to score the game-winner and he would be the one running around the field in celebration. He envisioned the adoring fans, standing and applauding wildly for him, their hero.

Truth be told, he was by far and away the best player in all the teams in which he played. Although he was young, he dominated the games, even when he competed against boys who were three or four years older than he was. Word spread throughout the youth leagues; everyone wanted to see the future star of Israeli soccer.

By the time the regular season was over, his team was on top of the standings. The play-offs were set to begin, and Yoram imagined himself kicking the game-winning goal and then being hoisted on the shoulders of his teammates as the crowd stood up and applauded wildly for him.

As he was practicing for the big game, however, he began to feel some pain in his knee. He tried to ignore it but as the days passed, the pain became more and more severe. One day, his father, Ilan, noticed that he was grimacing after practice and asked him what was wrong. At first, Yoram didn't want to talk about it and tried to dismiss it as nothing. But since he was generally not the complaining type, his father knew that he should try to get his son to say what was wrong. Finally, after much cajoling, Yoram admitted that he had very severe pain in his knee and he wasn't able to run well at all. While he was merely anxious about not being able to play at his optimum level, his father was concerned about something more serious. He hoped that it was nothing more than a bruise or a pulled muscle, but as the days wore on, the pain persisted even when he was not playing. Ilan decided to take Yoram to a doctor to see what was wrong, and his son had no choice but to agree.

The doctor met with them, and he wisely diverted the discussion to soccer in order to distract Yoram as he examined his knee; he did not find any signs of a sprain or any other reason for Yoram's pain. Just to be cautious, he sent Yoram for X-rays and an MRI, as well as some lab work, and he promised to call as soon as he received the results. Ilan and Yoram left the office with the hope that he would still be able to play in the championship game.

Two days later, Yoram received word that he would not be playing in the game. But that was the least of his troubles. The doctor had discovered a growth, a tumor in his leg. It seemed to have gone undetected for a while, and now it was spreading rapidly. The doctor explained that although he would have preferred to destroy the tumor with chemotherapy and radiation treatments, he felt it necessary to amputate.

Yoram's loving parents tried to break the devastating news in as delicate a manner as possible. But how does one tell a boy that he'll never again be able to run like other boys? How does one tell a boy who dreams of becoming a professional soccer player that he will never play soccer again? After Yoram's parents gently broke the news to him, he began to cry uncontrollably. Although he did not comprehend all of the ramifications, he knew all he needed to know; he was never going to run normally and never going to play soccer again. He would never score the winning goal of the championship game.

The doctor didn't want the cancer to spread any farther than it already had, so he told Yoram's parents to arrange for the surgery to take place within the next week. As they were making plans, a religious friend of the family recommended that Ilan speak to a *chacham*. Although he was hesitant, he decided that he would try it. At this stage, what was there to lose?

And so, Yoram's father brought his son to the *chacham,* and watched carefully as the *chacham* connected with the sick boy. The elderly sage asked Yoram if he still wants to play soccer. The boy cried as he said that he would do anything in the world to be able to play once more. The *chacham* asked him, "Anything?"

Yoram reiterated that he would be willing to do anything if he could still play soccer. The *chacham* then told him that he will guarantee that Yoram's leg will not need to be amputated if Yoram promised to start keeping Shabbos. The *chacham* assured him that he does not need any other blessing, as Shabbos is the source of all blessing. Yoram, with his father's approval, promised that he would never desecrate the Shabbos again. Ilan promised that he and his wife would also keep Shabbos. The *chacham* wished them well, and they left his house hopeful, although somewhat skeptical.

A few days later, they had their first test. Shabbos arrived and as difficult as it was, the family managed to keep the entire Shabbos perfectly; they passed that hurdle successfully. Once they had done their part of the deal, they wondered what would change. The day before the scheduled surgery, Yoram and his parents went to the hospital to take some pre-op tests. The doctor was shocked to discover that the tumor in Yoram's leg had shrunken significantly. The doctor could not understand why this had happened, but he told Yoram's parents that he would postpone the operation for another two weeks. Sure enough, two weeks later, after two more observant Shabbos days, the tests revealed that the tumor was nearly gone. One week later, there was no trace of it at all.

Ecstatic, Ilan and Yoram returned to the *chacham* to tell him what happened. But when they shared the news with him, he was hardly surprised. He told them that he had known it would disappear. The *chacham* then got out of his seat and walked to the back of the room and opened the closet door. He pulled out a bag and handed it to Yoram with a big smile on his face. Yoram looked inside; the bag contained a brand-new soccer ball.

The *chacham* explained, "The day you came to my house, I saw the determination on your face and I sent someone to buy you a soccer ball. I knew you would have the strength to keep to your promise. And I knew that your tumor would disappear."

> *Yoram continues to play soccer. But now, when he plays, he does so with a kippah on his head and tzitzis strings bouncing at his side.*
>
> *And about his dreams of winning the championship game? He's already done so.*

Nothing Like a Brother

There will come a time when we will be asked the question: "What did you do to bring your brother closer to the Al-mighty?" And history may one day point to the quiet revolution of Acheinu, the kiruv movement of Dirshu, as an instrumental factor in the ultimate fulfillment of the pasuk in Malachi (3:24), "Ve'heishiv leiv avos al banim ve'leiv banim al avosam — And he [Eliyahu] will turn back [to Hashem] the hearts of the fathers with [their] sons and the hearts of sons with their fathers."

Instead of merely touching the peripheral souls of our ignorant brethren, Acheinu embraces each and every one and further connects them to their roots. Whether it is through its revolutionary mentoring programs or its sensational Batei Chizuk — after-school Torah programming centers — Acheinu stands at the cutting edge of Torah outreach. Through its staff of dedicated professionals and volunteers, Acheinu has developed a three-step program that includes mentoring, enrollment, and follow-up.

Acheinu begins its work when a child is in eighth grade. Although the child may have attended an elementary day school in which he learned Torah, now he has reached a crossroads; he is searching and exploring his options for high school, where his spiritual future will be determined. In the first stage, Acheinu mentors develop a close, brotherly relationship with their charges, as well as with their families.

Now that the initial relationship has developed, it is time for the second component: the targeted enrollment. This crucial step will not only change the life of a child, but will almost certainly impact the entire family in a very profound way.

The third and perhaps most important level of Acheinu's work is the hemshech stage: follow-up. At this critical stage, although the child is already attending a yeshivah high school, it is of utmost importance that his mentor keeps up the connection: to encourage him and his family in this new undertaking, and smooth any rough spots.

*D*AVID AND NURIT, WHO LIVED IN THE CITY OF RAMLE, enrolled their son Eliran in the local Chinuch Atzmai school, because they were told by one of the local activists that the school had a good secular-studies department and was free of violence.

When Eliran was in eighth grade, Acheinu sent a charismatic young man by the name of Michoel Berlin to give a weekly talk to the eighth grade. Immediately, the boys took a liking to their mentor and wanted to get to know him better. Eliran, in particular, enjoyed being in Michoel's company. Within no time at all, the two became close friends. In keeping with the philosophy of Acheinu, Michoel got to know Eliran's parents, as well.

Later in the school year, when the topic of Eliran's future came up, Michoel spent hours speaking to his parents about how attending a yeshivah high school would change and improve their son's life. Although the young man was truly excited about this thrilling new venture, David, Eliran's father, was vehemently opposed to the idea.

Attempting to avoid internal family strife at all costs, Michoel was determined to do everything within his power to convince David, instead of having Eliran go against his father's wishes. To this end, he spent hours addressing the boy's father's concerns. Among his many worries, David was concerned that if his son went to a yeshivah instead of a high school that offered a good secular education, it would be difficult for him to earn a respectable living.

Months passed. Finally, just at the time that Eliran graduated eighth grade, Michoel succeeded in convincing David to enroll Eliran in yeshivah for a trial period.

Michoel now faced the daunting task of convincing a yeshivah that this young man, who possessed a minimum knowledge of Torah, was ready and prepared to attend yeshivah and endure the rigors of its daily program. When the yeshivah administrators gave Eliran a *bechinah,* they were less than impressed with the young man's ability to learn. They were also hesitant because he came from a completely irreligious home. Who knew what type of baggage he would bring along with him? The *hanhalah* members thus expressed hesitation about accepting Eliran into the yeshivah. It was only due to Michoel's exceptional track record that they were willing to admit him. Eliran, for his part, was very excited about the prospect of attending a yeshivah.

However, he spent the two-month summer vacation in Ramle, which proved detrimental to his spiritual health. He attached himself to a group of friends who did not share his positive feelings about yeshivah. They ridiculed his decision and mocked him for the course he had chosen. They urged him to attend a secular high school, one that would be devastating to his spirituality and his growth as a *ben Torah.*

Regrettably, Eliran's friends wielded a tremendous influence over him, and after much persuasion, Eliran changed his mind. Instead of attending the yeshivah, he decided to go to the secular high school his friends attended.

Eliran expected his mentor to be angry, frustrated, and disappointed, after all the time and energy he had invested to convince Eliran's father. Yet, when Eliran informed Michoel of his decision and apologized, the mentor's reaction shocked his younger friend. Instead of appearing outraged, he reacted in a cool, calm, and collected manner. He told Eliran that although he did not agree with his decision, he still respected him.

The next day, Michoel invited him out for pizza, and he continued to get together with Eliran. Although it was not easy for Michoel to travel from his hometown of Bnei Brak to Ramle, what won't one do for a brother? The two would spend time talking, and Michoel was never judgmental. Eliran saw how much Michoel cared for him, and he made the most of the deep friendship that had blossomed between the two of them.

Less than a week before the secular school was scheduled to begin, Michoel met one more time with his younger friend, and he made one last-ditch attempt. "Eliran, you know that yeshivah begins four days before your high school opens its doors. Why not try out the yeshivah for four days and see how it goes? What do you have to lose? If, after four days, you decide that you don't like it, you can begin your high school without having lost a day of the school year."

After all the time the two had spent together, Eliran knew that he could trust his older friend, and he did not want to disappoint him even more. He agreed to try it, on one condition. If he was even a bit unhappy after four days, Michoel would agree to let him go to his high school, and he would never say a word about the issue again.

Realizing that Eliran's spiritual life was at stake, Michoel agreed.

Unfortunately, things did not go as smoothly as they had hoped. Going to yeshivah was a major adjustment for Eliran, one that brought much heartache and tears. But regardless of the problem, Michoel was always there for his younger brother.

Therefore, even when the four days passed, Eliran decided to stay on, despite the challenges he faced. And even when he continued to encounter frustration in his new setting, Michoel continued to hold his hand and help him along.

> It would be easy to say that everyone lived "happily ever
> after." But Acheinu knows that in real life, problems arise.
> Yet, regardless of what the problems may be, Michoel and the
> Acheinu family will be there to hear the call of, "Hashomer
> achi anochi — Am I my brother's keeper?" (Bereishis 4:9).
> And they will answer with a resounding "Yes!"

Return to Who You Are

ENDEL WIEDER WAS BORN IN HUNGARY. HE WAS blessed with a brilliant mind and an outgoing personality. By the time he was 7 years old, he had outgrown his town's *melamed* and was ready to move on to a larger center of learning, where he would be more challenged. His journey carried him throughout Hungary, and he came in contact with some of the greatest Torah minds of the generation. But within a few months' time, he was always ready to move on to the next town, and then to the next. At a certain point, he became a *talmid* of the She'eiris Menachem, the Rebbe of Vishva, who was the son of the Ahavas Yisrael of Vizhnitz.

Mendel had a difficult time keeping his brilliance under wraps. He constantly felt the need to show how smart he was; because of this less-than-admirable trait, many of his peers disliked him. Yet their attitude toward him did not cause him to do some soul-searching and become more humble.

When Mendel turned 13, he awed the crowds with his intricate and complex discourses on any and all subject matters of Torah. This further boosted his ego. Although the rabbanim and Chassidic masters he encountered encouraged him to work on himself and acquire the trait of humility, he dismissed their admonishments.

Mendel's father, who was a rav, died at a young age, and Mendel hoped to take over his post, so he could support his widowed mother and orphaned siblings. However, because he was still so young, the community members refused to hire him. He was left without a job, and his family members were left without a source of livelihood. What a shame it was to sit on the sidelines while his family was starving.

Eventually, Mendel became frustrated with the situation; his adherence to his religion began to wane, until one day he decided that he was going to leave it all. He walked into a church and met with some of the priests, who were very impressed by his personality and charisma. They recognized his brilliance and were thrilled that a Jew was ready to give up his aspirations of becoming a rabbi, and instead use his talents for the Church. What a unique opportunity for the Church to present a learned Jew, who was willing and eager to lecture about the inconsistencies and fallacies of Judaism.

Mendel was thrilled with his new position. His desire to impress large groups of people was finally realized. No longer facing the obstacles he had encountered when applying to become a rav, Mendel used his talents to rile the crowds and stir up hatred against his former religion. The mobs loved him and he loved the attention. With each speech, word spread throughout the region, and Mendel became a sensation.

Anti-Semitism was raging in Eastern Europe, and Mendel used his golden tongue to further incite the non-Jews against his brethren. Rising up the hierarchy of the Church, Mendel became a cardinal. His fellow cardinals knew that he was a Jew — he was known as Cardinal Mendel — and some of them disliked him for it. But he was too powerful for anyone to do anything about it. When World War II broke out, at first Mendel continued to play the role of the Jew-hater. However, as Hitler conquered one country after another, causing the Jews so much suffering, Mendel began to feel sympathy for his brothers and sisters. Witnessing the atrocities, he wanted to do something but he felt powerless to stop the insanity.

And then, one night, Mendel had a dream that changed his life. His Rebbe, the Rebbe of Vishva, appeared to him and told him, "Mendel, until now you were under the spell of the *yetzer hara*. Since I was still in your world, my power was limited. But now that I have ascended to Heaven, I am warning you that you must return to your roots. Otherwise, your fate will be a terrible one."

At that point, the cardinal woke up. He had not been aware

that his Rebbe had passed away. In order to check the veracity of the dream, he investigated to see if his Rebbe was still alive. He found out that the Germans had come to the wealthy people of the city, and demanded that they reveal where they had hidden their precious possessions. The Nazis had placed additional pressure on the people, by forcing the Rebbe to come and watch the proceedings. The Rebbe had not been able to witness such cruelty; his heart had given out and he had died. Right after his passing, he had come to his student and warned him to repent.

But Mendel ignored the warning and remained in his position. The Rebbe reappeared the next night, and then the next. At that point, Mendel realized that the dream must be true. He packed a few necessities, along with a golden cross that was studded with diamonds, and disappeared in the middle of the night.

He had hoped that he would be able to use the valuable cross as a bribe, if necessary. But the Skulener Rebbe, Rav Eliezer Zisha Portugal, instructed him to discard it because it had been used for idol worship, and it was forbidden to derive any benefit from it. Mendel did as he was told and threw the cross into the river. Now he was penniless.

Mendel's return to the Jewish fold was not warmly received. Although he had never hurt any Jews directly, he was indirectly responsible for the suffering and untold heartache of hundreds. Anyone who recognized him made sure not to interact with him. Although this was very difficult for Mendel, he knew he deserved any punishment he received.

Soon, the Nazis took over Hungary and sent the majority of Hungarian Jewry to the gas chambers in Auschwitz. Although Mendel kept a low profile, as a Jew, he was also sent to Auschwitz, where he experienced its horrors, but somehow managed to avoid the fate of the gas chambers.

After the war, he made his way to Eretz Yisrael where he remained, for the most part, in seclusion. He cried bitterly and fasted for the terrible sins he had committed. Even there, enough people knew his story to make sure that he did not live a comfortable, relaxing, and worry-free life.

As we know, no Jew, no matter how far removed, is beyond repentance. Although Mendel had committed many evils, he spent decades immersed in remorse and regret. And there was one noteworthy Jew who did not keep his distance: the Skulener Rebbe. Mendel felt comfortable speaking to him and confessed to the horrible sins he committed during his tenure as a priest and then a cardinal. The Rebbe told him that he must not despair and that no Jew is beyond hope.

One day, the Rebbe asked Mendel an obvious question: "How is it that you strayed so far, yet you did not change your name in the Church?"

The *baal teshuvah* began to sob. And then a small smile formed on his lips. "Rebbe, my name is Mendel 'Wieder,' which means 'again' in Yiddish. As far as I had strayed, something deep inside of me told me that I would come back again. Just like my name: Mendel Wieder, Mendel Again…

"I never stopped hearing that voice: 'Come back again, Mendel…Return…' "

Mendel Wieder is buried in the cemetery in Tzfas, next to his brothers and sisters. It says on his tombstone that anyone who passes his grave should say a *perek* of *Tehillim* for his *neshamah*.

> *Every Jew has a voice inside of him, encouraging him to grow and become all that he can be. Unfortunately, we get sidetracked and stray off the path. And then, after we have been away for so long, we want to come back. We must listen to that inner voice, which beckons us to find that path once more.*
>
> *Because we know that when we are ready to return, He will be there waiting for us.*

Changing of the Guard

NEAR THE HOUSE OF RAV YOCHANAN TWERSKY, THE Tolna Rebbe, there was a reservoir with a small gatehouse. Shlomo the watchman sat at the gatehouse day and night, never veering from his post. The leathered and worn skin on the hunchback told a story, but nobody knew what that story was. The children of the neighborhood, as children will often do, teased him and tried to get him to leave his post, but Shlomo remained at his spot at all times. He kept to himself and never smiled. For the most part, he was all but forgotten to the community.

But there was one person who thought of him constantly.

The Rebbe.

If it was cold outside, he worried about him. And on the night of the Pesach Seder, when Jewish people sit around the tables with their families, he thought of him. He would approach him at these times and warmly invite him to his home. He'd promise that no one would steal the reservoir if Shlomo wasn't watching. But Shlomo the watchman would not smile and would not accept the invitation.

He remained at his post during snowstorms and during Pesach Sedarim. Purim, Chanukah, and Shavuos. Bar mitzvahs and weddings.

On Rosh Hashanah, the intense atmosphere inside the Rebbe's *beis midrash* revealed the seriousness of the day. Sounds of crying could be heard as the people in the shul prayed for their lives. The highlight of the davening was always when the Rebbe walked up to the *bimah* and blew the shofar. On this day, the *tzibbur* waited for the Rebbe to begin, but for some reason he just stood and waited. After a short while, he called over his *gabbai* and whispered in his ear, "Go call Shlomo the watchman, and tell him I am waiting for him to come so I can begin blowing the shofar."

The *gabbai* quickly made his way to the gatehouse by the reservoir and knocked on the window. "The Rebbe is waiting for you to come before he blows the shofar. He asked that you come right now."

As soon as Shlomo heard the word shofar, his face turned white. He turned away from the *gabbai* and closed the window. The *gabbai* tried his best to get him to agree to come, but there was nothing to talk about. Left with no choice, he went back and informed the Rebbe that Shlomo had no intention of coming. But the Rebbe was not prepared to give up. He apologized to everyone for the delay and immediately went down to the reservoir to speak to Shlomo himself. The *tzibbur* understood that if the Rebbe decided that he had to go, they must not ask questions but just wait patiently.

When he got to the reservoir, the Rebbe spoke to Shlomo. A short while later, the two walked into the *beis midrash,* hand in hand. The Rebbe found a *tallis* and handed it to the elderly watchman. Realizing that all eyes were on him, Shlomo quickly wrapped himself in the *tallis* as the Rebbe cried out the opening words of the paragraph recited before the blowing of the shofar: "*Lamenatzei'ach livnei Korach mizmor.*"

A few minutes later, after reciting the Psalm seven times, a hushed silence overcame the crowd. The *makri* called out the sounds of *tekiah, shevarim, teruah,* and the piercing sound of the shofar reverberated through the shul. Accompanying the cries of the shofar were the heartrending sobs that came from beneath Shlomo's *tallis.* As the sounds of the shofar continued, the sobs grew louder and louder, and his body was seized by trembling.

Everyone standing in his vicinity was overwhelmed with emotion. It was the most sincere display of repentance they had ever witnessed: a remarkable transformation from a tough and emotionless watchman to a vulnerable and visibly moved individual.

No one dared approach him after davening; the congregants did not want to intrude on his moments of privacy. However, during the *Aseres Yemei Teshuvah,* the Rebbe cleared his schedule and went to visit Shlomo. "Tell me what happened," he requested. "What was it that melted your heart like that?"

Shlomo closed his eyes and transported himself to a time long ago and a world long-forgotten.

I grew up in the city of Charnowitz, Romania. I was very young at the outbreak of the war, yet I remember the day that the soldiers stormed into the synagogue and demanded from my father, who held all the keys to the aron kodesh and the shul, that he give them over. But my father refused. The Nazis beat him mercilessly but my father would not tell them where the keys were, even as he began to bleed profusely. He knew that if they were to open the aron kodesh, they would desecrate the Sifrei Torah.

The soldiers grew impatient with him, and one of them pulled out his revolver and pointed it at my father. He warned him that he better hand over the keys, but my father refused. I was standing right next to my father, when suddenly, shots rang through the air; the soldier shot my father and he fell to the ground.

I bent down next to my father and tried to stop the bleeding but I couldn't do anything. My father made me promise him that I would be a good frum Jew — that I would eat matzah every Pesach, and listen to the sound of the shofar on Rosh Hashanah.

I was holding his head in my arms when he closed his eyes and died. I was left completely alone in the world.

When Shlomo finished telling the Rebbe his heartbreaking story, he continued to speak.

"Since that time, I have gone through many challenges. At one point during the war, I was taken to Siberia, but I survived the horrors of the Holocaust; I have scars and wounds on my body to show what I suffered.

"After the war, I wanted to break off from my past and forget the suffering and pain that follows me everywhere. And that is why I did not want to associate with anyone in the community.

"But when you invited me to come for the blowing of the shofar, I felt this was my one chance. And when I heard the sound of the shofar, I remembered my father's last words. I had always tried to block them out; I did not want to remember that terrible event. But everything came back to me in one moment, and I heard my father's voice. I became completely overwhelmed and could not stop crying. I knew that my father was looking down at me and that finally, for the first time since that horrible day, my father was happy with me.

"He was happy that I remembered the promise I had made."

Our life story may not be as dramatic as the life story of Shlomo the watchman. But the message is there for all of us. Our parents went through much sacrifice to instill in us the timeless traditions of old. At times, we wander off into a life that is not necessarily void of these ideals, but not replete with them either.

However, when the Yamim Noraim arrive and we hear the sound of the shofar, it touches the deepest recesses of our souls. We suddenly feel connected to our father — not only our earthly father, but our Heavenly Father, as well.

Keepers of the Faith

A Vision for Millions

RAV OVADIA YOSEF

*T*HE WORLD HAS LOST A JEWEL.

Never in recent history have so many Jews felt the piercing loss of a Torah giant. By many estimates, over 800,000 Jews came to mourn the death of their precious Rabbeinu Ovadia.

He was a *gadol hador*. Yet for so many, he was much more than that. He was their leader, their *chacham*, their father, and grandfather.

Young Ovadia's unusual intelligence and *hasmadah* in his learning captured the attention of the rosh yeshivah and the other members of the administration of Yeshivat Porat Yosef, where he was a student. Perhaps that was why Rav Ezra Attiya, the rosh yeshivah, was so surprised when Ovadia did not show up to class for a number of days. Worried that the boy was ill, Rav Ezra paid a visit to Ovadia's home. As Rav Ezra approached the rundown home, he noticed that even in this poor neighborhood of Yerushalayim, this house seemed particularly shabby.

Rav Ezra knocked on the door and waited. The boy's father came to the door, embarrassed that the rosh yeshivah had come all the way to their home. He asked the rav why he had come, and Rav Ezra explained his concern.

The boy's father responded in a somewhat distraught manner. "What should I do? I need help in my small grocery store, carrying the merchandise and loading it onto the shelves."

Rav Ezra listened patiently but explained that nothing in the world is more important than Torah. As the conversation continued, each man maintained his position. Rav Ezra finally decided to leave, and he thanked the man for his time. As he walked out of the house, he saw his *talmid* standing in the corner of the room, looking heartbroken that Rav Ezra had not convinced his father to send him back to yeshivah.

The next morning, Ovadia's father entered his store, donned his apron, and then noticed someone standing in the corner. It was Rav Ezra, his son's rebbi, wearing a work apron.

"What are you doing here?" he asked Rav Ezra. "And why are you wearing an apron like one of my workers?"

Rav Ezra replied that he had informed Ovadia that he had found someone who was willing to work without pay: the rebbi himself.

"You said you needed someone to help," he explained to the boy's father. "It is preferable that I be the one to help you in the store, while your son is allowed to continue learning, undisturbed. Nothing is more important than your son's learning!"

His point was made. The father agreed to allow his son to continue learning, on the condition that Rav Ezra remove the apron.

And Ovadia continued to excel in yeshivah, setting the foundation for a life of Torah learning.

"Yom le'yom yabi'a omer — Day following day utters speech" (*Tehillim* 19:3). As the Malbim explains, each day brings to light more and more of the wisdom of the Creator.

Among the thousands of holy books found in Chacham Ovadia's library, there is an old, worn-out, tiny *sefer,* titled *Reishis Chochmah.* Leafing through the pages, one can find a young boy's writings, thoughts he jotted down on the subject matter.

In the front flap of the volume, we find an inscription:

This book was given to me as a present from the great Rav Shlomo Abu, who, when I was a young child, tested me on the Mishnayot of Masechtot Shabbat, Pesachim, Makkot, and Succah, as well as on the Gemara of Masechet Bava Metzia, Perek Shnayim Ochzin, Eilu Metziot, HaMafkid, and HaZahav — be'al peh.

Ve'anochi, hadal, ha'iroti ka'asher hisigah yadi — And I, poor of mind, added some thoughts that came to me.

We find in these words, in all probability, the first original Torah thoughts of Chacham Ovadia.

If his quill could speak, his parchment could talk, and the worn-out benches he sat upon could share the tale, they would regale us with stories of a poverty-stricken young man, huddling beneath torn blankets and relishing the unparalleled sweetness of Torah, while his children slept together to stay warm and protect themselves from the cold and rainy Yerushalayim nights.

"Ve'laylah le'laylah yechaveh daas — And night following night declares knowledge" (*Tehillim* 19:3).

Yes, they would tell stories …

Of a nearly peerless life of erudition, brilliance, and diligence.

Of a towering giant, whose humility and unbridled desire for truth united all walks of Jews.

Of a man who plumbed the depths of Torah, yet never hesitated to share words of humor, encouragement, and comfort to the simplest folk, who smiled at the mere sight of their beloved and revered *chacham.* In fact, it was not uncommon for people to come and ask for his blessing and leave a *petek* stating, *"Please pray for the well-being of Rabbeinu Ovadia Yosef ben Georgia sheya'arich yamim al mamlachto biv'riut ve'osher* — who should live for many years upon his kingdom with health and good fortune." He was their *melech*, and Sephardic Jewry prayed for the well-being of their king.

Lost souls turned to him in their darkest times, hoping that he could and would find the answers to all their personal and halachic problems.

In 1947, in war-ravaged Yerushalayim, a question was posed to the 26-year-old *chacham*. The British soldiers issued a strict curfew warning. Anyone found outside after dark would be shot, no questions asked. With Purim approaching, people wondered if it would be better for the *tzibbur* to hear the *Megillah* reading after *plag haminchah* on Taanis Esther, while it was still daylight, or if it would be preferable to read the *Megillah* after dark, privately, but safely in one's home. Rav Ovadia's published response, written in his *sefer Yabi'a Omer*, includes 150 *mareh mekomos*!

The first word of the *Aseres HaDibros* is אָנֹכִי. The Gemara (*Shabbos* 105a) writes that the word *Anochi* stands for אֲנָא נַפְשִׁי כְּתָבִית יְהָבִית , which means: "I [The Al-mighty] placed My soul into writing and gave it." In other words, the Al-mighty was *me'tzamtzeim* (constricted) Himself into the words of the Torah, so that we would be able to relate to and interact with Him through our learning of Torah. He gave us the Torah so that we can better understand Him and His ways.

In a similar vein, in order to connect to the multitudes, Chacham Ovadia placed his entire *neshamah* into his scholarly works, which include *Yabi'a Omer, Yechaveh Daas,* and *Chazon Ovadia.* Even the most learned Torah sages were humbled at the brilliance and encyclopedic scope of his *sefarim*.

Rav Tzvi Pesach Frank, the rav of Yerushalayim, held Chacham Ovadia in the highest regard, offering his *he'aros* on the first volume of *Yabi'a Omer,* along with his *haskamah*. In 1956, Rav Shlomo Zalman Auerbach wrote, "I have yet to see a *sefer chashuv ka'zeh* mi'mechabrei zemaneinu — such an important sefer from authors of our time." The Tchebiner Rav, Rav Dov Berish Weidenfeld, showered Chacham Ovadia's sefarim with praise. When Chacham Ovadia was only 35 years old, Rav Weidenfeld declared that he was "baki be'chol chadrei haTorah — an expert in all areas of the Torah."

And yet, his approachability and warmth concealed that greatness. Much like the dark sunglasses he wore to protect the vision he nearly lost, Chacham Ovadia guarded himself from all prestige and honor. The Kad HaKemach (Rosh Hashanah 2) teaches, "Ein melech be'lo am — There is no king without a people." Chacham Ovadia, the king of Sephardic Jewry, held in awe by the greatest Ashkenazic poskim of the past 70 years, viewed himself as nothing more than a necessary figurehead, a leader to turn to, a monarch to unite all Sephardim — even those who had yet to taste the sweetness of Torah. But in his anivus, he felt he had little merit of his own.

When Rav Ovadia finished writing the second volume of Chazon Ovadia on Maseches Shabbos, his son, Rav Avraham Yosef, the rav of Cholon, entered his father's office and asked for a copy. His father handed him the volume. Rav Avraham then asked his father for a second volume for his son. When Chacham Ovadia asked him why, his son exclaimed that all the grandchildren should merit "to be yonek [to glean from] Abba's sefarim."

At this point, Chacham Ovadia began to cry. "My son, the Gemara (Bava Metzia 85a) reveals that Rav Yosef fasted forty days to ensure that he would be successful in his learning, as it says (Yeshayah 59:21): 'lo yamushu mipicha — My words will not be withdrawn from your mouth.' Afterward, he fasted another forty fasts to ensure that his children would also be successful in their studies, as it says: 'u'mipi zaracha — nor from the mouth of your offspring.' And finally, he fasted another hundred fasts to ensure that his grandchildren would also succeed in their Torah learning, thus fulfilling the words: 'u'mipi zera zaracha — nor from the mouth of your offspring's offspring.' "

At this point, Rav Ovadia began to cry uncontrollably. "With what *zechuyot* will I merit that the learning of Torah shall not be forgotten from the hearts and souls of my grandchildren?"

Fear not, Chacham Ovadia. *Asita shelichutcha* — You have fulfilled your mission. As you ascended to *Shamayim*, your earthly royal garb was replaced with its heavenly counterpart, bejeweled with the precious gems and pearls of Torah.

Your Torah will ensure that your deepest wish comes true: that your children and grandchildren will perceive the beauty of the Torah, until the end of time. The *Chazon Ovadia*, your ultimate vision, will come to fruition.

For your children and your grandchildren.

All 800,000 of them.

Yehei zichro baruch.

The Giant of Novaradok

RAV YAAKOV GALINSKY

*I*T IS HARD TO FORGET THE FIRST TIME I SAW RAV YAAKOV Yitzchak Galinsky, the well-known *maggid*. I was 17 years old and learning in Telshe Yeshivah in Cleveland. Noting his diminutive appearance — he was not much taller than five feet — I could hardly imagine that his words would make an impression on me. Yet from the time he entered the *beis midrash*, a buzz filled the room. After *Maariv*, we gathered in the back *shiur* room where the *shmuessen* were often delivered, and then, standing before a *shtender*, with his hands holding onto its edges, Rav Yankel began rocking the *shtender* back and forth. I don't remember everything he said that night, but one phrase has remained.

Rav Yankel quoted the Gemara in *Eruvin* (54a), where Shmuel advised Rav Yehudah: "*Shenina chatof ve'echol chatof ve'ishti de'alma de'azlinan minei kehilula dami* — Sharp one, grab and eat; grab and drink, for the world that we are departing is like a wedding." Rashi explains that Shmuel was encouraging Rav Yehudah to enjoy this world since life goes by quickly, just like a wedding, which is over so fast. But what type of enjoyment are we talking about?

Rav Yankel said that when he was learning in Yeshivas Novaradok in Bialystok, he once heard a young man repeating this phrase over and over. "*Shenina chatof ve'echol chatof ve'ishti. Chatof, chatof, chatof, chatof. . . .*" Sitting in the *beis midrash*, immersed in a *mussar sefer*, that young man admonished himself again and again to use every moment of his life properly, to grab every moment he possibly could.

When Rav Yankel repeated this story, he sang the haunting melody over and over, and with his heavy *Litvish* accent, he cried out repeatedly, "*Chateif, chateif, chateif, chateif. . .*"

That young man in the *beis midrash* in Bialystok became the Steipler Gaon.

But as the following stories show, Rav Yankel was describing his own life, as well. Although short in stature, he was a tower of spirit. Emulating the *maggidim* of yesteryear, he inspired thousands to become better Jews. As he camouflaged his penetrating *mussar* in stories and humor, the world became his audience, and his infectious smile brought *simchah* and joy to Klal Yisrael.

One underlying theme accompanied his every thought: *Chatof, chatof. . .* And this theme runs through the stories that the Giant from Novaradok would recount.

Once, while spending some time in Yerushalayim, Rav Yankel asked for directions to the home of the Tchebiner Rav, Rav Dov Berish Weidenfeld, in Shaarei Chesed. Even though everyone in Shaarei Chesed knew precisely where the rav lived, Rav Yankel, who was from Bnei Brak, was unfamiliar with the neighborhood of the *gadol*. After he was directed to the rav's home, he waited inside for a private audience. Soon enough, he was escorted into the rav's office.

Rav Yankel asked the rav if he recognized him. "It's me — Yankel!" The rav looked carefully at the stranger and informed him that he knew many people named Yankel, but he did not recognize him.

"I'm Yankele *der kurtzer*, the short one."

The rav still had no idea who his visitor was. Left with no alternative, Rav Yankel closed his eyes and began to sing, "*Kol Hashem yachil midbar, yachil Hashem midbar kadeish. . .*"

The rav listened to the song, and then suddenly, he fainted! His household members quickly revived him and sat him in his chair. When he came to, he looked around and spotted Yankel in the corner of his room, and called out, "Yankele! Rav Yankele Galinsky!"

Years earlier, during the war, the two had spent meaningful time together. Although they had not seen each other for many years, the *niggun*, that very special and memorable song, had jolted the rav and jarred his memory, and he and Rav Galinsky began to reminisce about the time they had been together in a labor camp in Siberia.

Then Rav Galinsky, in his inimitable style, told the story of the *niggun* to all those who were assembled in the rav's home. "When we were in Siberia, we were far away from the physical and emotional warmth of our homes. It was so cold there that the icy winds cut through our skin like a knife. But even worse, our hearts and souls were in danger of turning cold. We needed a good, *varme davenen,* warm davening. But how could we go about finding inspirational prayers in Siberia?

"One Friday morning, the rav suggested that we gather a *minyan* for *Kabbalas Shabbos. A minyan?* I wondered. *From where?*

"There were no *siddurim;* there wasn't even an empty room in which we could daven. There were no willing people. There was nothing! How did the rav expect to assemble a *minyan*? But nothing would stand in his way.

"Although the men were beyond exhaustion from the harsh conditions and backbreaking labor, the rav begged and cried to them to join us for *Kabbalas Shabbos,* in a place outside — yes, outside — between two of the barracks.

"And so, in the subzero temperature, with frozen limbs and chapped faces, we made our way outside the barracks as the sun began to set. The bit of warmth it had provided was now gone as we set out to daven *Kabbalas Shabbos.*

"The rav began *Lechu Neranenah.* The men repeated the words after him as he completed the first chapter, and then went on to the next ones. With each passing word, one could sense our hearts warming and our souls flickering.

"As we prayed the words in the third chapter, '*Anan va'arafel sevivav* — Cloud and dense darkness will surround him,' the darkness of our lives gave us pause for reflection. Would we ever escape the dark cloud of the Russian authorities?

"But we prayed further, with more conviction, and with more tears. Eventually, we broke out into a *niggun* — the *niggun* I just sang. We sang the song over and over, as the emotion and energy continued to build. And then, all of a sudden, someone fainted! He was completely frozen and had succumbed to the elements. We quickly ran to him and revived him. Then, we helped him back to the 'warm' barracks, and just like that, our *minyan* was disbanded.

"The other eight men seemed relieved that the prayers had concluded, but I was devastated. I ran over to the rav, searching for *chizuk*, for an uplifting word. After all, we weren't even able to complete one *Kabbalas Shabbos* together. What possible inspiration could there be from our failed venture?

"Even so, the rav's eyes burned with fire. He was anything but depressed. And he continued to sing that *niggun*, as he joined it to a verse from the sixth chapter of *Kabbalas Shabbos*: 'Kol Hashem yachil midbar; yachil Hashem midbar kadeish — The Voice of Hashem convulses the wilderness; Hashem convulses the wilderness of Kadeish.' The rav looked into my eyes and explained, 'The term *yachil midbar* means that the wilderness trembles from the Voice of Hashem. But there is another meaning, as well. *Yachil midbar* can also mean that the wilderness yearns. The *midbar* of Siberia has yearned for 5,700 years to hear the *Kol Hashem*. And we, with our 20 minutes of an unfinished *Kabbalas Shabbos*, satisfied the frozen Siberian wilderness' yearning to hear it. And now, that *midbar* has been transformed into a *midbar kadeish*, a holy wilderness. Why? Because it has heard the *Kol Hashem*!' "

Just like Rav Weidenfeld, Rav Yankel saw an opportunity to teach, and lessons to be learned, in every moment of every day. The circumstances did not matter. Where others viewed mundane activities, Rav Yankel saw *mussar*. Humorous anecdotes became timeless teachings. Every nuance, every second, was an opportunity to become better, closer to the Al-mighty. He taught us to truly appreciate the small things in life.

Chatof, chatof. . .

Another anecdote comes to mind, which also occurred in the prison called Siberia, but one that bespeaks loneliness.

Rav Chaim Binyamin Brodt, Rav Yaakov's father-in-law, was hauled away by the Russian authorities, as he was unable to defend himself against the trumped-up claims of the government. Rav Chaim Binyamin was forced to spend a long period of time imprisoned in Siberia, away from any hint of Yiddishkeit.

For an agonizingly long period of time, Rav Chaim Binyamin was forbidden any form of contact with other prisoners. Not that it would have made any difference; no other prisoner would admit to being Jewish in those days, because doing so would award him endless abuse and mistreatment.

After his years of imprisonment were over, Rav Chaim Binyamin's family was overjoyed to see him, and his *talmidim* and those whom he had inspired for so many years felt as if they were given a gift: the ability to see their mentor again.

Soon after Rav Chaim Binyamin's release, his family members and *talmidim* noticed that he would disappear for long periods of time. One day, they followed him after he finished davening. They discovered that, in fact, he went nowhere; he stayed in his own shul and merely drifted from one *minyan* to the next. He wasn't learning, just sitting in the shul. Finally, his son-in-law, Rav Yaakov, asked him why he had begun this strange practice.

Rav Chaim Binyamin pulled out a piece of paper from his pocket and held it high in the air. "Rav Yankel, do you know what this is? This is a *cheshbon* that I kept in prison, when I was alone."

Rav Yankel looked at the paper and was shocked to see that his father-in-law had kept a *cheshbon* of how may *amens* he had missed during those years in Siberia.

"And now I have a chance to make it all up. So I sit in shul and cherish the opportunity that I have to answer every additional *amen* that I can. . ."

For many, *amen* is nothing more than a split second of spirituality. But the Giant from Novaradok, through the lesson learned from his father-in-law, taught us otherwise. *Amen* is eternal.

Chatof, chatof. . .

And one more story that took place in Siberia. This story, as well, was later used by Rav Yankel to lift spirits and bring smiles, and to convey important lessons with passion, spirit, and strength.

In 1941, Yankel Galinsky arrived in Siberia with a group of 100 *bachurim* from Novaradok. Although they were far from their families and their yeshivos, they felt a sense of comfort that they had each other. In addition, they had brought along their *tefillin*, several *sefarim,* and some other articles of *kedushah*, such as a *Megillas Esther* and a shofar.

They arrived on the Sunday of *Parashas Mattos-Masei*. But within a few hours, the Russian soldiers confiscated all religious articles and constructed a huge bonfire. The *bachurim* watched in horror as their only tangible link to the *Ribbono Shel Olam* was destroyed before their eyes. Although they were a resilient group, they were terribly despondent. For that reason, small spontaneous groups formed for the sole purpose of lending *chizuk* to one another. The men were aware of the impending danger if they were caught sharing "religious propaganda," so the messages of encouragement could take only 90 seconds or less. During this short session, one of the young men kept a close watch outside the door, prepared to warn his friends if a guard would come by.

Of all the words of *chizuk* spoken at that time, one thought remained etched in young Yankel Galinsky's mind. It was offered by a fellow named Hertzel Drogitziner. He quoted the *pesukim* (*Yeshayah* 40:27,28), "*Lamah somar Yaakov u'sedaber Yisrael, nisterah darki mei'Hashem u'mei'Elokai mishpati yaavor. Ha'lo yadata im lo sha-mata Elokei olam Hashem, Borei ketzos ha'aretz, lo yi'af ve'lo yiga, ein cheiker lisvunaso* — Why do you say, O Yaakov, and declare, O Yisrael, 'My way is hidden from Hashem, and my cause has passed by my G-d'? Did you not know? Did you not hear? Hashem is the eternal G-d, the Creator of the ends of the earth; He does not weary, He does not tire; there is no calculating His understanding."

Hertzel Drogitziner explained that when someone is suffering, there are two components to the pain he endures. The first is the intensity of the pain itself. But the second, and perhaps more challenging aspect of his suffering, is the fact that it can go on indefinitely. Not knowing when it will be over is the most difficult part of any trial.

But the *Ribbono Shel Olam* has promised us that although He is *Elokei olam Hashem,* the eternal G-d, Who is without limits, nonetheless, He is *Borei ketzos ha'aretz,* He created limits within His world, and there will be a *keitz,* an end, to all the suffering. There will come a time soon, when *"Mi she'amar le'olam dai, yomar dai le'tzarosai* — He Who said to the world, 'Enough,' will say, 'Enough,' to my troubles" (Rashi: *Bereishis* 43:14).

The *bachurim* felt invigorated. They knew that the Al-mighty *"chishav es hakeitz* — calculated the end of bondage," as it says in the *Haggadah,* and the end of their *tzarah,* too, would come.

But until then, they grabbed every opportunity for growth, as they spent time strengthening one another.

The clock is ticking, and time is passing us by. Another spiritual giant has left this world. But if we listen closely, we will hear the eternal cry of the Giant of Novaradok:

"Chatof, chatof, chatof, chatof. . ."

A Paradigm of Atzilus

RAV AIZIK AUSBAND

*A*TZILUS. NOBILITY.

It describes one who is distinguished, revered, dignified, as it says, "*Ve'el atzilei Bnei Yisrael lo shalach yado* — Against the great men of the Bnei Yisrael, He did not stretch out His hand" (*Shemos* 24:11).

It would be foolish for someone like me to attempt to write a *hesped* on our great rebbi and rosh yeshivah, Rav Aizik Ausband. He was much greater than any of us can fathom. I merely wish to share how we, as *talmidim*, viewed him; to us, he was the paradigm of *atzilus*, reflecting the radiance of the *Shechinah*.

My childhood image of Rav Aizik was formed when I was an impressionable eighth-grade boy, during my first Elul *zman* in Telshe Yeshiva. I had heard that Rav Aizik stood an entire Yom Kippur, from *Kol Nidrei* through *Ne'ilah*. How could it possibly be? Yet, with eyes full of wonder, I was privileged to stand but a few feet from him. Not only did Rav Aizik never sit down, he never even leaned on his *shtender*. In fact, he barely moved at all. He stood facing the wall for nearly the entire day. After *Ne'ilah* concluded, when Rav Aizik finally turned around, we caught a glimpse of his face — framed by his long, flowing, majestic beard — completely aglow. It was as though Rav Aizik was a guest, an ethereal visitor from another time and place, who had graced us — to be with us, to protect us.

Using the same *shoresh* as *atzilus*, the *pasuk* says, "*Ve'atzalti min ha'ruach asher alecha ve'samti aleihem* — And I will increase some of the spirit that is upon you and place it upon them" (*Bamidbar*

11:17). *Chazal* tell us that Moshe was the conduit through which the seventy *zekeinim* would glean inspiration for their vision and understanding of *nevuah*. As Rashi explains, Moshe was like a candle used to light others; even though the candle gives others light, its own flame remains undiminished. We basked in Rav Aizik's *taharah* and *kedushah* that never diminished, even as he helped each of us shine on our own.

Yet, Rav Aizik stood inconspicuously. He wanted no part of the world of *kavod* and glory, and he distanced himself from any such talk. Rav Aizik wanted nothing more than to be a complete *oveid Hashem*. His Gemara provided him with all the *kavod* he needed.

Rav Aizik treasured every second of *limud haTorah*. When speaking in learning with his *talmidim*, he listened to every word, never interrupting. Only when the *talmid* was finished would Rav Aizik begin to explain once more, with measured words.

It was from this discreet corner of *tzniyus, kedushah, derhoibenkeit,* and *hasmadah* that the *Ribbono Shel Olam* plucked our rebbi, as an *eved ne'eman* who had completed his mission: "*Asher hechezakticha mi'ketzos ha'aretz u'mei'atzileha kerasicha va'omar lecha avdi atah becharticha ve'lo me'asticha* — You whom I shall grasp from the ends of the earth and shall summon from among all its noblemen and to whom I shall say, 'You are My servant' — I have chosen you and not rejected you" (*Yeshayah* 41:9).

Rav Aizik's warm smile allowed us a glimpse into his tenderness. Even his *mussar* was gentle. One Shabbos, in which Rav Aizik ate with the *bachurim* in the yeshivah's dining room, he noticed a group of younger *bachurim* making sandwiches at the Shabbos *seudah*. Rav Aizik wished to communicate the inappropriateness of such behavior. His response was understated, yet effective. He smiled at them and raised his fork and knife. Through his aristocratic demeanor, his subtle message was received. Rav Aizik never yelled, never even raised his voice. Indeed, it would be unbefitting of *atzilus*.

Rav Aizik had witnessed *atzilus*. He learned it from his rebbi and father-in-law, the Telzer Rav, Rav Avraham Yitzchak Bloch.

When the Nazis beat the Telzer Rav upon the head with hammer blows and taunted him, "Where is your G-d, *Herr Rabbiner?*" the Telzer Rav replied, "He is not only *my* G-d; He is *your* G-d. And the world will yet see this."

In a world where some men turned into animals, others became angels.

Angels of *atzilus*.

With the *petirah* of Rav Aizik, the era of Telzer European roshei yeshivah has come to a close.

Oy, how terribly lonely we are. The great *gedolim* of yesteryear have left us orphaned and alone.

Utterly alone.

Rebbetzin Chaya Ausband is known as "Morah" to her thousands of Yavne Seminary students. During the last few years of his life, Rav Aizik's health began to deteriorate. It was especially during those years that Rebbetzin Ausband displayed unswerving dedication to her husband, demonstrating to her students the essence of an *eishes chayil*.

One time, when she noticed a button dangling from a jacket of one of the *bachurim* who visited their home, she asked him to bring the jacket by so that she could sew on the button. When the boy hesitated, she insisted, "My father taught me that the *tafkid* of the rebbetzin in yeshivah is to be *meshameish* the *bachurim*, to help their learning in any way she can," she said. "Please, it is my *zechus.* . ." As she sewed on the button, she asked the *bachur* to spend some time davening together with Rav Aizik, an honor he would always treasure.

After Rav Aizik had slipped into the twilight of his life, a group of *talmidim* would come over to his home for an *oneg* on Leil Shabbos and sing for him. Through most of the *oneg*, Rav Aizik remained unresponsive, except when they sang the song, which is based on the words in *Tehillim* (93:4): "*Mikolos mayim rabim adirim mishberei yam adir bamarom Hashem* — More than the mighty waters, mightier than the waves of the sea, You are mighty on high, Hashem." At that time, Rav Aizik's eyes brimmed with tears. His *neshamah* sensed that they were singing his song, the song of his life, the melody of his exalted *neshamah*.

More than the roars of the mighty waters. . .

Mightier than the waves of the sea, a soft soulful melody rises. "*Adir bamarom Hashem.*"

The singular song of *atzilus*.

Yehei zichro baruch.

The Mashbir

RAV YOSEF TENDLER

"**V**E'YOSEF. . .HU HAMASHBIR LE'CHOL AM HA'ARETZ* — And Yosef. . .he was the provider to all the people of the land" (*Bereishis* 42:6).

When Yosef HaTzaddik became the viceroy of Mitzrayim, he filled many roles. But above all else, he was the *mashbir*, the provider. In times of hunger and starvation, it was Yosef who had the necessary vision and means to sustain the people.

Rav Yosef Tendler was the *mashbir*. He provided for the *bachurim* of Mechinas Ner Yisroel for nearly half a century.

Imparting wisdom, offering guidance, giving advice, supplying *mussar*.

For young men who were starving for *ruchniyus*, confidence, and *hadrachah*, Rav Tendler, their menahel, was the *mashbir* for the "*am ha'aretz.*"

Ignorance comes in many forms, but the greatest ignoramus is one who is not even aware that he is lacking knowledge. As Rav Tendler told one naïve teenage *bachur*, "When I was younger, one thing drove me: I didn't want to become an *oisvarf*, an outcast."

Growing. Learning. Rav Yosef was the master of the short *seder*; countless *bachurim*, sometimes 30 a week, had the privilege to learn with him. They delved into the hallowed words of Rav Shlomo Wolbe in *Alei Shur*, as well as other works, such as *Matnas Chaim*, as Rav Yosef provided each boy with his specific needs. He would often quote from Rav Hirsch, as well as from contemporary *gedolim*. He learned from everyone, for he wanted to become a complete person and to make his students into complete people.

It takes a man of absolute truth to develop *emesdike mentchen*. And that was Rav Tendler's method of *chinuch*; he spoke the truth and steered his *talmidim* in the direction where they could see it for themselves.

The word מַשְׁבִּיר contains the same letters as the word שְׁבָרִים, *broken pieces*. For that is the calling of the *mashbir*: to lift up those broken pieces and piece them together by providing them with sustenance.

My relationship with Rav Tendler revolved around our yearly discussions regarding the boys in my eighth-grade *shiur*. There were always a few boys for whom I would campaign to gain admittance into the yeshivah. Sometimes, after I had spoken with Rav Simcha Cook, the sgan menahel, he would direct me to Rav Tendler. Often, Rav Tendler would convince me that it would be best for the boy to go elsewhere. He did not want the boy to fail.

But a few years ago, a boy in my *shiur* — let's call him Bentzion Steiner — told me that he wanted to go to Ner Yisroel for one unusual reason: because Rav Tendler was like his zeidy.

I was surprised. But upon hearing the following story from Bentzion's father, I gained new insight into Rav Tendler's personality.

Mr. Yonasan Steiner related that when he first came to Ner Yisroel as a *bachur*, he did not yet comprehend what is expected of a *ben Torah*. Soon, though, under Rav Tendler's influence, he would learn. However, once, while in 12th grade, Yonasan and a group of friends went somewhere they should not have. Rav Tendler heard about it and spoke to each boy privately.

Except one.

For the next few days, he would shoot penetrating looks in Yonasan's direction, but never chastised him. Yonasan felt sorry for his action and vowed to himself that he would never do it again. The disappointment he had caused was the worst punishment of all.

Eventually, Yonasan became a *chassan*. At his *chasunah*, moments before he was ready to begin a new chapter in his life, he asked Rav Tendler why he had never said anything to him, why he had not given him *mussar*.

Once more, Rav Tendler looked at him carefully. But this time, he smiled. "It all worked out. Didn't it?" Yonasan sensed that when he and his friends had misbehaved in 12th grade, Rav Tendler felt that the other boys needed a *mussar shmuess*, but for him, another method was called for. Rav Tendler always provided what the *bachurim* needed. Sometimes it was warmth and understanding, and at other times, it was *mussar* and discipline. But it all stemmed from the love he had for each and every *talmid*.

A few years later, Yonasan lost his father, and Rav Tendler became the primary role-model in his life. Every time the family needed guidance, it was Rav Tendler to whom they turned. And he was there for them each step of the way. For every *simchah* and every tragedy.

And this is why Yonasan's son, Bentzion, wanted to attend Ner Yisroel.

He wanted *hadrachah* from his zeidy.

On another occasion, a boy had to be removed from the dormitory. Yet, Rav Tendler was worried that the boy may go off the *derech* if he threw him out of the yeshivah. So Rav Tendler made room in his small apartment for the boy to move in with him. He would become part of the family.

Rav Yosef Tendler built men.

Molded *bnei Torah*.

Instilled confidence.

He saw in others what they could not yet see in themselves.

For that is what a *mashbir* does. He foresees the future and prepares what the people will need.

Sensing the need to provide *chalav Yisrael* milk for the Baltimore community and surrounding cities, he took the initiative to found Pride of the Farm, a *chalav Yisrael* milk company.

Together with his remarkable rebbetzin, he sustained generations of *talmidim,* the future of Klal Yisrael.

But now, the *mashbir* is gone.

His *talmidim* and the yeshivah are utterly bereft.

But he instilled in all those whose lives he touched the wherewithal to forge ahead, to be *mekadeish Sheim Shamayim.*

To sustain themselves, and to sustain others.

To become *mashbirim.* . .

Yehei zichro baruch. . .

The Father of Torah Chinuch in America

RAV NOCHUM ZEV DESSLER

*T*HE MAJESTY.

The *malchus*.

It was Kelm.

And it was Rav Nochum Zev Dessler.

Rav Nochum Zev personified the place from whence he came.

Nowadays, the need for Jewish day schools seems obvious; how can a community survive without one? But it was not so obvious to American Jewry of the early 1940's. In fact, it seemed ludicrous. Nevertheless, as the menahel of Hebrew Academy of Cleveland from 1944 until his *petirah* in 2011, Rav Dessler worked hard to recruit students for the fledgling school. He weathered the mockery and scorn of the parents who told him that Jewish education was a thing of the past. And today, Torah Jewry in America has Rav Nochum Velvel Dessler to thank. Because without him, it is hard to imagine what the Torah landscape of America would look like.

Raised in the lap of *malchus*, the majesty of Kelm guided his every move. How fitting that he stemmed from David HaMelech. The glory of *malchus Beis Yehudah* was carried on by one whose life was dedicated to Torah education and *Yiddishe kinderlach*.

"Ve'es Yehudah shalach lefanav el Yosef lehoros lefanav Goshnah — He sent Yehudah ahead of him to Yosef, to prepare ahead of him in Goshen" (*Bereishis* 46:28).

Rashi comments that Yaakov sent Yehudah to set up and establish a *beis talmud*, a school where the children would learn and be protected from the negative influence of Egyptian culture.

Thousands of years later, a descendant of Yehudah would do the same.

For American Torah Jewry needed someone talented and driven.

And Rav Dessler heeded the call.

Although I am not qualified to properly describe what Rav Dessler meant to the city of Cleveland and to Torah *chinuch* in America, I am privileged to have a unique perspective. I attended the Hebrew Academy of Cleveland from pre-kindergarten with Morah Rochel Munk, until after Rabbi Yitzchak Scheinerman's class in seventh grade, when I left to attend Telshe Yeshiva.

My parents and in-laws are all Hebrew Academy alumni.

My wife's grandmother was Rav Dessler's personal secretary for many years, and her husband, Rav Moshe Lefkovitz, worked together with Rav Dessler for nearly 40 years as the executive director of the Hebrew Academy.

One can safely say that the Hebrew Academy runs through my family's veins.

The Academy, as it was called, was the only Jewish day school in Cleveland. It was built under the guidance of the Telzer roshei yeshivah, Rav Elya Meir Bloch and Rav Mottel Katz, whose striking portraits hang in the hallway of the Yavne building attached to the boys' school.

In addition to the portraits in the lobby, there is also a plaque for my paternal grandfather, Mr. Herbert (Chaim Isaac) Spero. Over 70 years ago, he was one of those who provided Rav Dessler with unfailing support and sent my Uncle Shmulie to the school as one of its first students.

By the time I attended, Rav Dessler's office was in the new

Yavne building. He spent most of his time in that building, while Rabbi Yosef Meisels was the assistant principal of the boys' section. If there was a discipline problem, the students were sent to Rabbi Meisels. However, one time, I was sent to Rav Dessler's office. I do not recall why. But I do remember the long walk from my classroom to Rav Dessler's office. I had never been sent there before, and I didn't know what to expect. Needless to say, I was pretty scared.

Although this incident happened 35 years ago, I remember it like it was yesterday. Rav Dessler called me over. I walked around his desk and he held onto my hands. He asked me what I did wrong and I told him. He then looked at me and told me something I will never forget: "Yechiel, I knew both of your grandfathers. And I know that they would not approve of such behavior." And then he lifted his hand and gave me a soft, loving *gletteleh* (stroke) across my cheek.

"Don't let it happen again. *Ess past nisht* — It is not befitting. You don't want to disappoint them."

I told this poignant story at my *sheva berachos* and, once again, when I had the special privilege of interviewing Rav Dessler for the book I wrote about Rav Mordechai Gifter. In truth, I did not know what to expect when I visited him for that interview. I was told that he was not well; I hoped to get 10 minutes. He gave me an hour. With a strong and reassuring demeanor, he presented himself as the prince I remembered from my school days. Sharp. Decisive. Determined. He took me on a journey through Kelm and Telshe, and he shared with me his incredible escape across Japan. Finally, he dazzled me with stories about the early days of the Hebrew Academy.

His children kept asking him if he wanted to stop, as they, too, were amazed at how long our conversation lasted. But he never wavered.

Rav Dessler did not try to duplicate the world of Kelm. He understood too much about American culture to think that it could become another Kelm. But he wanted us to know that it existed. And by looking at him, we were able to see it.

Honesty. Integrity. Dignity.

Handed down through his grandfather, Rav Reuven Dov Dessler.

Through his father, the brilliant mashgiach, Rav Eliyahu Eliezer Dessler.

And continuing through Rav Nochum Zev, another prince, another link in the *malchus Beis David*, the majesty of Kelm.

It inspired everything Rav Dessler did and accomplished. As Rav Moshe Shapiro said at his *levayah* in Eretz Yisrael, "*Er is geven der letzte fun der mechunachim in Kelm. . . Rav Nochum Velvel, der velt is geven asach sheiner mit eich* — He was the last of those who had been educated in Kelm. . . Rav Nochum Velvel, the world was a lot more beautiful with you around!"

I remember when there was an influx of Russian immigrants in school in the mid-70's, and several of these boys joined my class. Although some hesitated to admit these children who were not-yet *shomrei Shabbos,* Rav Dessler only worried about *neshamos.* And saving them.

For the cry of Yehudah pierced his soul. "*Eich e'eleh el avi ve'hanaar einenu iti* — For how can I go up to my father if the youth is not with me?" (*Bereishis* 44:34). Interpreting this *pasuk* homiletically, the great *baalei mussar* extrapolate that every Jewish child must receive his due, a Jewish education. For how can we face our father, the Al-mighty, if the youth are not with us, and not being cared for spiritually?

Rav Dessler ensured that no child was turned away.

No child was left behind.

Rav Dessler valued people and forged relationships, lifelong relationships, with them. He earned their respect, but never compromised on the standards of Torah to which he had grown accustomed. Hundreds walked through Rav Dessler's home after his death to be *menachem avel*. Some were great roshei yeshivah; others put on a yarmulke before they walked in.

Yet, there was one common link between them.

They all loved and respected Rav Dessler.

Because he gave value and honor to all of them.

Mr. Irving Stone brought Jewish philanthropy to new levels, and Rav Dessler guided him to help the Academy in innovative ways. He forged relationships with the Federation that helped set the bar for generosity in giving by a federation.

He was an educator's educator, a *mechanech's mechanech*.

He was the one to whom so many principals and administrators turned to for advice.

Drawing on his wisdom, experience, and integrity, he taught them and guided them how to build and how to grow. What to do and how to do it.

Rav Shlomo Wolbe writes about the dichotomy of *chinuch*: the *zeriah*, the planting, and the *binyan*, the building.

Rav Dessler excelled at both. He was *zorei'a*, he planted the seedlings for thousands of Jewish children, and then he was *boneh*, he built for them — and inside of them — skyscrapers of Torah and its wisdom.

Rebbetzin Miriam Dessler was the devoted preschool principal for many decades. But it is her role as an *eishes chayil* for which she will be remembered most. She stood by her husband's side, providing loyal support for nearly 70 years.

Rav Nochum Velvel Dessler is gone. But through the thousands of children and families whose lives he touched, Kelm lives on.

Yehei zichro baruch.

An Adam Nichbad

REB MOSHE REICHMANN

*T*HE WORLD HAS LOST AN *ADAM NICHBAD,* A "*MECHU-badekeh mentch,*" a rarity in today's world, which is almost completely devoid of such a commodity.

Although Reb Moshe Reichmann was perhaps the greatest philanthropist in recent times, he was not merely a philanthropic benefactor; his money never defined who he was.

By nature, Reb Moshe was not a conversationalist. His side of the conversation was succinct, and his words were well chosen. Perhaps that is why the world listened to what he had to say. Torah giants of yesteryear considered Reb Moshe a trusted friend and dear confidant; he was beloved by Rav Shach, as well as a *yedid nefesh* of Rav Berel Povarsky, among others. They treasured the friendship and reliance an *adam nichbad* provided. They marveled at this Zevulun — who learned enough to be a Yissachar — but who was willing to embrace his role of *parnas hador,* benefactor of the generation.

The Gemara in *Shabbos* (12b) warns against learning on Shabbos by the light of a candle. However, according to one opinion, Rabbi Yishmael did learn by the light of a candle on Shabbos and accidentally tilted the candle. Rav Chaim Shmulevitz (*Sichos Mussar*: 5732, *Maamar* 7) explains that the Gemara did not expect Rabbi Yishmael ben Elisha's *tzidkus* and *yiras Shamayim* to have prevented him from stumbling in this area. Rather, it was because he was an *adam nichbad*, a respectable person — someone's whose natural demeanor would not allow him to do such an act, even during the week. There are certain actions that an *adam nichbad* simply doesn't do.

Born to parents who sensed an *achrayus* to save Klal Yisrael in their darkest moments, Reb Moshe reminded the world what Jewish aristocracy — being an *adam nichbad* — was all about. Dragged through a raging inferno of anti-Semitism, treated like vermin, the Jewish people struggled to recall our *tafkid,* to be the *am hanivchar.* Chosen. Unique. *Derhoiben.*

Emerging from life as a fugitive, Reb Moshe helped a nation restore its glory, reminding us that whether one is in a *beis midrash* bent over a Gemara, or conducting a high-profile business deal in a high-rise office building in Manhattan, a Yid is a *ben melech.* His actions taught that adhering to our time-honored principles will only increase respect and admiration.

Reb Moshe gave and taught others how to give. When he gave, he was *mechabeid* the recipients of his donations. "*Eizehu mechubad? Ha'mechabeid es habriyos* — Who is honored? One who honors others" (*Avos* 4:1). He didn't need his name draped on walls. Instead, he insisted on *yenem's kavod.* Unwilling to compromise on anything that may threaten this honor, Reb Moshe made it fashionable to be a *baal tzedakah.* Supporting Torah became *mechubadek* once again. Thanks in large part to him, *kvod haTorah*, the honor and glory of Torah, was restored.

Someone who was present at a meeting where billions of dollars were being negotiated marveled that when Reb Moshe's mother called, he interrupted his meeting to take the phone call: "Yes, Mamma. Four cucumbers, two onions. . ." Noticing the shock on the other person's face, Reb Moshe remarked, "When my mother calls me, the whole world stops."

An *adam nichbad* trains himself to do the right thing, regardless of his surroundings. Nothing other than unshakeable *yashrus* dictates his every move. Indeed, Reb Moshe's status as a global icon never minimized his closeness to his family. An exemplary father and husband, Reb Moshe placed his family first.

It was not common to see Reb Moshe on the streets of Toronto. Generally, he did not attend banquets, weddings, or funerals. But when a 35-year-old man died suddenly, Reb Moshe came to the *levayah*. Although no one seemed to remember a connection between Reb Moshe and the *niftar,* he approached the young *almanah*, whispered something in her ear, and then stood there stoically until the funeral's conclusion. Later, it was revealed that that the young man had borrowed a quarter of a million dollars from Reb Moshe, who attended the funeral to let the frightened young widow know that the loan was forgiven. For when he gave, it was not merely *"nesinas haprutah,"* it was *"nesinas hanefesh"* (*Chochmas Chaim*). He gave over not only his money, but his *neshamah* to each recipient.

Years ago, a wealthy businessman entered into a business partnership with Reb Moshe. As they discussed the profits of their first transaction, Reb Moshe sat down and pulled out a small piece of paper. On it, he jotted down names of *mosdos* and accompanying dollar amounts, and then articulated each commitment in his thick European accent, for his partner to hear: "*Bais Yankev, seventy-tree toisand dollars. Yesodei HaToirah, one hundred and fifty toisand dollars. . .*" If Reb Moshe said it, it was done.

Now, that tiny scrap of paper still sits in the fellow businessman's desk drawer. It serves as a memento and reminder of how one must first tithe his earnings and only after take for one's self. Now an older gentleman, this man credits Reb Moshe for the charity fund he's established; he is comforted to know that through this fund, he will continue to give *tzedakah*, long after his own passing.

Reb Moshe was a giver. He didn't wait to be asked. Sensing and knowing what needed to be done, he approached others and offered to give, grateful to be the one to have the *zechus* and means with which to help others. As the sole benefactor of the first Lakewood Kollel established outside the city of Lakewood, Reb Moshe accepted the responsibility; he felt honored to be the one to elevate the learning of Torah in his city, thus setting an example for others.

He conducted himself scrupulously in business and earned a reputation as one with whom a handshake was as binding as a legal document; it was obvious that he put his trust in Hashem, not in his business acumen. Once, a young man who was close to him asked whether it was true that he carried the *Sefer Emunah U'Bitachon* from the Chazon Ish in his briefcase. He hesitated, and then he humbly acquiesced, "It is an easy and light *sefer* to carry."

In 1992, Olympia and York, the Reichmann financial empire, suffered a crushing blow, losing billions of dollars. The Gemara in *Sanhedrin* (20b) reveals that Shlomo HaMelech originally ruled over the *elyonim*, the upper spheres, but his monarchy diminished until the day came when: "*lo malach ella al maklo* — he only ruled over his staff." Rav Chaim Shmulevitz (*Sichos Mussar*: 5731, *Maamar* 13) explains that Shlomo remained a *melech,* if only on his staff. His royalty was not determined by exterior factors; an inner *nichbadus* continued to shine. Reb Moshe's inner regality always remained intact.

While speaking with his close *chaver,* Reb Chaim Greineman —

with whom he often conversed in *"velteshe zachen*, worldly matters" — Reb Moshe once cited two tactical errors he had made that caused his financial downturn. Rav Chaim responded, "Reb Moshe, in the same manner you always credited your success to the *Aibeshter*, you must attribute your failure to His, and only His, doing." Reb Moshe accepted the gentle *mussar* and retold it to others.

When Reb Moshe was approached with a request, he turned ever so slightly — so that he could truly listen. He gave the person his full attention, and then responded. One of the *mosdos* he supported sought guidance on whether to purchase a new building. After the question was asked, Reb Moshe's response consisted of two words: "*Koif, koif* — Buy, buy." There was no need for additional discussion. He was refreshingly efficient, decisive yet humble, and the embodiment of "*Emor me'at va'aseih harbeih* — Say little and do much" (*Avos* 1:15).

Anyone who has ever visited the city of Toronto will attest that the city carries with it a certain class. Make no mistake; Reb Moshe Reichmann is part of the reason behind it. But it wasn't class. It was *nichbadus* — his *nichbadus*. His mere presence elevated his family, his city, and the entire Klal Yisrael.

The Gemara (*Berachos* 58b) tells us that Rav Chana bar Chanilai always kept his hand in his pocket because he knew that a poor person may solicit funds from him, and he did not want the fellow to suffer any indignity while waiting for the donation. Hence, his hand was in his pocket, and he was always prepared to give.

Reb Moshe Reichmann changed the world by keeping his hands in his pockets.

Yehei zichro baruch.

Glossary

Acharon (pl. *Acharonim*) — latter day Torah luminary who lived after the 1400's

achrayus — responsibility

adam — person

adam chashuv — important person

adam nichbad — a respectable person

Aggadah —homiletical, non-halachic teaching of the Sages

Aibeshter — (Yiddish) lit., the One Above; G-d

al kiddush Hashem — done for the sanctification of G-d

aleph-beis — Hebrew alphabet

almanah — widow

anivus — humbleness or humility

aravah — willow twig; one of the Four Species taken on Succos

Aron — (in Mishkan) Holy Ark that housed the Tablets (*Luchos*)

aron kodesh — (in shul) ark into which Torah Scrolls are placed

Aseres Yemei Teshuvah — the Ten Days of Repentance between Rosh Hashanah and Yom Kippur

askan (pl. *askanim*) — community activist

askanus — community activism

assur — forbidden by halachah

atzilus — nobility

aveil (pl. *aveilim*) — mourner

aveirah (pl. *aveiros*) — sin

avodah — work; service (prayer)

avodas Hashem — service of Hashem

Avos — the Patriarchs; Forefathers

baal mechazeik — one who encourages and inspires others

baal mussar — one who toils in the study of ethical conduct

baal teshuvah — one who is returning to his faith

baal tzeddakah — one who is generous to charity

bachur (pl. *bachurim*) — young man; an unmarried young man, used to denote a student in a yeshivah

be'al peh — orally; from memory

becher — a cup or goblet, esp. one used to make *Kiddush*

bechinah (pl. *bechinos*) — test

beis midrash (pl. *batei midrash*) — house of learning or prayer

ben melech — prince

ben Torah — literally "a son of Torah," usually referring to someone who is learned in Torah

bentch — (Yiddish) recite Grace after Meals

berachah (pl. *berachos*) — blessing

bimah — table or platform in the synagogue from which the Torah Scroll is read

bitachon — faith

blatt — folio page

bnei aliyah — people pursuing exalted spiritual levels

bris — circumcision

chaburah (pl. *chaburos*) – 1. a group (usually a group that learns together). 2. lecture or discourse delivered to a group

chacham (pl. *chachamim*) wise man

chalav Yisrael — milk that has been supervised by a Jew from the time of milking

chazer — pig

chassan — bridegroom

chassidei umos ha'olam — righteous gentiles

Chassidishe maaseh — Chassidic tale

chasunah — wedding

chaver (pl. *chaveirim*) — devout Jew; friend

chavrusos — study partners

chayal (pl. *chayalim*) — soldier; esp. a soldier in the Israeli Army

cheder (pl. *chadarim*) — school, usually an elementary school, esp. for Jewish studies

chesed — kindness; acts of beneficence; charitable giving

chesed Hashem — the kindness of G-d

cheshbon — an accounting

chiddush (pl. *chuddushim*) —Talmudic or halachic novella

chiddushei Torah — novel explanations of Torah subjects

chillul Hashem — desecration of Hashem's Name

chiloni (pl. *chilonim*) — secular Jew

chinuch — Jewish education; Torah education (of minors)

chizuk — encouragement

Chumash — Five Books of Moses

chuppah — wedding canopy

daf — lit., page; one folio of the Gemara

Daf Yomi — daily study of one folio of the Gemara

darshan — to lecture, esp. on a Torah topic

dayan (pl. *dayanim*) — halachic decisor or judge

derashah (pl. *dershos*) — sermon or Torah discourse

derech — the way or manner

derhoibenkeit — (Yiddish) state of being uplifted

derhoiben — (Yiddish) uplifted

din — (Jewish) law

dvar Torah (pl. *divrei Torah*) — a lesson from the Torah; a Torah thought

dveikus — bonding

ehrlich, ehrliche — (Yiddish) upright; honest

Eichah — Book of *Lamentations*

eineklach — grandchildren

eishes chayil — 1. woman of valor. 2. verses from *Proverbs* recited before the Friday night Sabbath meal

eltere Yid — (Yiddish) older Jew

emesdike — (Yiddish) truthful

emunah — faith

emunas chachamim — belief in the advice of Torah scholars

frum — (Yiddish) observant

gaon — revered Torah scholar

gabbai (pl. *gabbaim*) — synagogue sexton; attendant of a Chassidic Rebbe

gadol (pl. *gedolim*) — great Torah personality

gadol be'Yisrael (pl. *gedolei Yisrael*) — outstanding Torah scholar

gadol hador (pl. *gedolei hador*) — the primary Torah and spiritual leader of the generation

galus (pl. *galuyos*) — the Jewish exile; (cap.) the Diaspora

gam zu le'tovah — "even this is for the good "

gartel — (Yiddish) belt worn to distinguish between the upper and lower parts of the body

gezeirah — an edict

goy — non-Jew

gut yahr — (Yiddish) a good year

gutte — (Yiddish) good

gzar din — judicial verdict

he'aras Panim — a reference to Divine grace

hadlakah — candle-lighting; making a bonfire on Lag Ba'omer

hadrachah — guidance

Haggadah – liturgy recited at the Pesach *Seder*

HaKadosh Baruch Hu — lit., The Holy One (i.e., G-d), Blessed Is He; G-d

Hallel — lit., praise; a a thanksgiving prayer comprised of selected Psalms, recited on Rosh Chodesh and most festivals

hanhagah — behavior

hanhalah — guiding elders, usually used in reference to the administrators of a Torah institution

hartzige — (Yiddish) heartfelt; heartwarming

Hashem — G-d

Hashgachah, Hashgachah Pratis — Divine intervention

haskamah — agreement; written approbation for a Torah work

hasmadah — diligence in learning

havtachah — promise

he'arah (pl. *he'aros*) — comment

heilege — (Yiddish) holy

hemshech — continuation

hergesh — emotion

Ivrit — Hebrew

Kabbalas Shabbos — the traditional prayer recited at the beginning of the Sabbath service on Friday evening

Kaddish — prayer said in memory of the dead

kadosh (pl. *kedoshim*) — holy, martyrs

kallah — bride

kavannah — positive attitude or intensity in prayer

kavod — honor

kedushah — holiness

kehillah — congregation

kesavim — writings

kever — a grave

kevius — permanence

Kiddush — the prayer said over wine, before the Friday evening or Saturday Sabbath day meal

kiddush Hashem — sanctification of G-d's holy Name

kiddush Sheim Shamayim — to sanctify the holy Heavenly Name kinderlach — (Yiddish) children

kippah — yarmulke, skullcap

kiruv — word used to define the "bringing Jews closer" to their heritage

kittel — long white garment worn by men during the Yom Kippur prayer services and at the Passover seder, and, in Ashkenazic tradition, by the groom during the wedding ceremony

kiyum — ability to last; permanence

klal —the community

Kol Nidrei — opening prayer recited at the onset of Yom Kippur

korban (pl. korbanos) — sacrificial offering

krechtz — (Yiddish) complain; groan

Kvod haTorah — the honor of the Torah

lashon hara — lit., evil language; gossip

le'chaim — 1. party celebrating an engagement. 2. toast over a drink of wine or whiskey

levayah — a funeral

limud haTorah — the learning or teaching of the Torah

Litvish — lit., "Lithuanian"; adjective describing non-chassidic Jews of Eastern European extraction

Maariv — the evening prayer service

machzor (pl. machzorim) — holiday prayer book

maggid (pl. maggidim) — speaker or lecturer who uses stories to teach moral lessons

makri — the one who announces the shofar blasts and determines their validity

Malach HaMaves — the Angel of Death

malchus — kingship; royalty

malchus Beis David — the royal House of David

malchus Beis Yehudah — the royal House of Judah

marbitz Torah (pl. marbitzei Torah) — one who disseminates Torah

mareh mekomos — sources

masechta (pl. masechtos) — tractate of Talmud

masmid (pl. masmidim) — exceptionally diligent student

matzeivah — headstone

mechabeid — giving shonor

mechanech (pl. mechanchim) — male educator

mechaneches (pl. mechanchos) — female educator

mechazeik — to strengthen, often spiritually

mechubadek —respectful, respectable

mechutan — one's child's father-in-law; a relative through marriage

Megillah — a scroll (or story); usually refers to the Book of Esther, which is traditionally read on Purim

mekadeish Sheim Shamayim — to sanctify the Name of Heaven

melamed (pl. melamdim) — 1. a teacher, esp. of young children. 2. one who teaches; a male teacher

Melamed Torah Le'amo Yisrael — "who teaches Torah to his nation, Israel"

melech — king

menachem aveil — to comfort a mourner; to pay a condolence call

menorah — candelabrum used to hold the Chanukah lights

mentch (pl. mentchen) — (Yiddish) all-around good person

meshadeich — to make a marriage match with

meshameish — n. attendant. v. to serve

mesirus nefesh — self-sacrifice

mezuzah — a parchment that is affixed to one's door post on which has been written the complete "Hear O Israel, the L-rd our G-d, the L-rd is One" prayer

midbar — desert; wilderness

Middas HaDin — attribute of strict justice

mikveh (pl. mikvaos) — ritual bath

Minchah — the afternoon prayer service

minhag (pl. minhagim) — custom

minyan (pl. minyanim) — quorum of ten men necessary for conducting a prayer service; the group assembled for communal prayer service

Mishnah — teachings of the Tannaim that form the basis of the Talmud

Mishnayos — the six volumes of the Oral Law

mishpachah — family

misnaged (pl. misnagdim) — opponent, esp. one opposed to the Chassidic movement

morai ve'rabbosai — "my teachers and my rabbis," a respectful form of address to a group

mosad (pl. modsos) — institution

moshav — settlement

mussar — rebuke

mussar shmuess — lecture on self-refinement

nachas — joy; pleasure

nebach — (Yiddish) n. pitiful, ineffectual,

and timid person. *adj.* poor; unfortunate. *interjection* how unfortunate!

nebach'l — (Yiddish) one who is pitiful and ineffectual

nechamah — comfort

Neilah — concluding prayer service of Yom Kippur

neshamah (pl. *neshamos*) — soul

nevuah — prophecy

nichbadus — respectability, regality of bearing

niftar — *n.* person who passes away. *v.* passing away

niggun (pl. *niggunim*) — a tune

nisayon (pl. *nisyonos*) — a test, esp. a spiritual test

Oheiv Yisrael — one who loves Jews; one who supports Jewry

Olam Ha'Emes — the World of Truth; *Olam Haba*

Olam Haba — the World to Come

oneg — joy

oneg Shabbos — lit., joy of Sabbath; a gathering to celebrate the Sabbath

oveid Hashem — a servant of G-d

oy — (Yiddish) *interjection* what a pity!

pashuta — simple

pasken — answer practical questions in halachah

pasuk (pl. *pesukim*) — verse in the Tanach or liturgy

perek (pl. *perakim*) — chapter

petek — a slip of paper, esp. one with supplications placed at a holy site

petirah — the passing away of

pidyon haben — redemption of the (firstborn) son: the ceremony of the redemption of the firstborn son

pidyon shevuyim — ransoming imprisoned Jews

plag haminchah — midpoint of the time permitted to recite the afternoon prayer service

poseik (pl. *poskim*) — halachic authority

prat — individual; exception

psak (pl. *psakim*) — a halachic decision

regel — lit;, foot; one of the three Pilgrimage Festivals

Ribbono Shel Olam — Master of the Universe; G-d

roshei teivos — initial letters, often forming an acronym; abbreviation

ruchniyus — spirituality; spiritual growth

seder (pl. *sedarim*) — 1. study period. 2. (u.c.) Pesach-night ritual during which the Haggadah is recited.

Sefer HaChaim — Book of Life

Sefer Torah (pl. *Sifrei Torah*) — a Torah Scroll, written on parchment

sefer (pl. *sefarim*) — book, specifically a book on a holy or learned topic

segulah — spiritual remedy

seudah — a festive meal, esp. one served on the Sabbath or a holiday

Shacharis — morning prayer service

shalom aleichem — traditional greeting; "peace be unto you"

shalosh seudos — the third Sabbath meal

Shamayim — Heaven

she'eilas chalom — kabbalistic inquiry in which a Heavenly answer is received in a dream

Shechinah — Divine Presence; the spirit of the Omnipresent manifested on earth

shechitah — ritual slaughter; the ritual manner in which an animal is slaughtered

sheifele — (Yiddish) little lamb; a term of endearment

sheirut — semi-public taxi service in Israel

sheliach mitzvah — someone on his way to perform a mitzvah

Shemoneh Esrei — lit., 18; the prayer, originally eighteen blessings but now nineteen, that forms the central core of each weekday prayer service

sheva berachos — lit., seven blessings; 1. the seven blessings recited at a wedding. 2. festive meals, celebrated during the week after a wedding, at which the seven blessings are recited

shevarim —the tripartite shofar blast

shidduch — a match, usually referring to a marriage

shiur (pl. *shiurim*) — a Torah lecture

shivah — lit., seven; the seven-day mourning period immediately following the death of a close relative

shmeichel — (Yiddish) a smile

shmuess (pl. *shmuessen*) — (Yiddish) lecture on Torah topics; Torah discourse

shomer Shabbos (pl. *shomrei Shabbos*) — those who observe the Sabbath

shomrei Torah u'mitzvos — those who observe the Torah commandments

shoresh — root

shtender — lectern

shtiebel — (Yiddish) lit., room; a small synagogue, often situated in a house; small
synagogue, used mainly by Chassidim

Shulchan Aruch — Code of Jewish Law

shver — father-in-law

siddur (pl. siddurim) — prayer book

siman (pl. simanim) — 1. symbol. 2. foods
traditionally eaten on Rosh Hashanah
because of their symbolic implications.
3. chapter in a legal code

simchah — joy

Simchas Beis HaSho'eivah — gathering held
on the intermediary days of the Succos
holiday, which includes music, dance,
and refreshments, commemorating the
Water Libation Ceremony performed in
the Holy Temple in Jerusalem

simchas hachaim — joie de vivre; joy of life

siyata d'Shmaya — Heavenly assistance

siyum (pl. siyumim) — a celebration of completion of a Torah subject

siyum haShas — the celebration of the completion of the study of the Oral Law

sugya — topic

taanis — fast day

tafkid — job; calling

taharah — purification; ritual cleansing of the
dead

taharas hamishpachah — the laws of family
purity

tallis — four-cornered prayer shawl with
tzitzis, worn during morning prayers

talmid (pl. talmidim) — male student

talmidah (pl. talmidos) — female student

talmid chacham (pl. talmidei chachamim) —
lit., the student of a wise person; a Torah
scholar

Techiyas HaMeisim — Revivification of the
Dead

tefillah (pl. tefillos) — Jewish prayer

tefillin — phylacteries

tefillin shel yad — phylacteries worn on the
arm

Tehillim — Psalms

tekiah — the sound of the longest shofar blast

teruah — the sounds of the staccato shofar
blast

teshuvah — answer; repentance

ti'ere — (Yiddish) dear

Tikkun Chatzos — prayer mourning the
destruction of the Holy Temple, recited at
midnight

tiyul — a hike or trip, esp. one taken for pleasure

Torahdik — very pious; Torah-like

tumah — moral degeneration; spiritual impurity; defilement

tzaddik (pl. tzaddikim) — righteous male person

tzarah (pl. tzaros) — difficult, painful situation

tzeddakah — charity

tzibbur — congregation

tzidkus — righteousness

tzitzis — fringed garment worn by Jewish
men and boys; fringes at the corners of
a tallis

tzniyus — modesty

vatranus — the act of giving in

Viduy — confession recited on Yom Kippur
and before death

yahrtzeit — anniversary of a person's death

yashrus — uprightness

yechidei segulah — exceptional individuals

yedid nefesh — "beloved of the soul"

yehi zichro baruch — may his memory be for
a blessing

yenem — (Yiddish) others

yeshuah (pl. yeshuos) — salvation

yetzer hara — the Evil Inclination

Yiddishe — Jewish

yingel — (Yiddish) young boy

yiras Shamayim — the fear of Heaven

yissurim shel ahavah — suffering from
Heaven

yonek — nursling

yungerman — (Yiddish) young married man,
usually referring to one studying in a
yeshivah or kollel

zechus (pl. zechuyos) — privilege; merit

zekeinim — elders

Ziv HaShechinah — the glow of the Shechinah;
the radiance of the Shechinah

zman — semester; time

zocheh — to merit